Professional Communication and Network Interaction

Heidi McKee and James Porter theorize the use of social media tools in business settings using a fresh, practitioner-oriented research approach that will appeal to business communication scholars, teachers, students and business practitioners alike. With the growing use of social media among both businesses as well as the general public to facilitate communication, this book provides a toolkit by which educators and practitioners can think about how to use those digital tools ethically and productively.

—Dirk Remley, Kent State University

Digital technologies and social media have changed the processes, products, and interactions of professional communication, reshaping how, when, with whom, and where business professionals communicate. This book examines these changes by asking: How does rhetorical theory need to adapt and develop to address the changing practices of professional communication? Drawing from classical and contemporary rhetorical theory and from in-depth interviews with business professionals, the authors present a case-based approach for exploring the changing landscape of professional communication. The book develops a rhetorical theory based on networked interaction and rhetorical ethics: seeing professional communication as involving new kinds of networked interactions that require an integrated view of rhetoric and ethics. The book applies this frame to a variety of communication cases involving, for example, employee missteps on social media, corporate-consumer interactions, and the developing use of artificial intelligence agents (AI bots) to handle online communication.

Heidi A. McKee is an Associate Professor in the Department of English at Miami University, USA. She also serves as the Roger and Joyce L. Howe Professor of Written Communication and the Director of the Howe Writing Initiative in the Farmer School of Business at Miami.

James E. Porter is a Professor of Rhetoric and Professional Communication in the Armstrong Institute for Interactive Media Studies and the Department of English at Miami University, USA.

Routledge Studies in Rhetoric and Communication

For a full list of titles in this series, please visit www.routledge.com.

Professional Communication and Network Interaction
A Rhetorical and Ethical Approach

Heidi A. McKee and James E. Porter

Routledge
Taylor & Francis Group

LONDON AND NEW YORK

First published 2017 by Routledge

2 Park Square, Milton Park, Abingdon, Oxfordshire OX14 4RN
52 Vanderbilt Avenue, New York, NY 10017

Routledge is an imprint of the Taylor & Francis Group, an informa business

First issued in paperback 2019

Library of Congress Cataloging-in-Publication Data
CIP data has been applied for.

ISBN: 978-1-138-71521-9 (hbk)
ISBN: 978-0-367-88839-8 (pbk)

Typeset in Sabon
by codeMantra

To
Charles Dunn McKee and James M. Porter,
excellent professional communicators from whom
we learned much

Contents

List of Figures and Tables

Figures

Tables

Acknowledgments

We acknowledge and thank the 21 professionals who consented to interview with us for this project (listed in Table 1.1). We appreciate each person's willingness to share their time and expertise and to explore in thoughtful and engaged ways the impact of digital technologies on professional communication. Although we were not able to draw explicitly from every interview, experiences and insights from each and every professional significantly shaped the research presented in this book.

We thank our colleagues and students at Miami University in the Farmer School of Business, in the Armstrong Institute for Interactive Media Studies, in the Department of English, in the Professional Writing major, and in the Rhetoric and Composition graduate program for the many conversations about rhetoric, technology, media, and professional communication that helped our thinking on this project.

We gratefully acknowledge the support of our home institution, Miami University, which awarded both of us Academic Research Appointments during the Spring 2016 semester to work on this book.

We also thank Roger and Joyce Howe for their support of writing and writing research at Miami University and for endowing two writing centers on campus, including the Howe Writing Initiative in the Farmer School of Business.

We thank the editors and editorial team at Routledge Press, especially Senior Editor Felisa Salvago Keyes, Editorial Assistant Christina Kowalski, and Project Manager Assunta Petrone.

We thank the three anonymous reviewers for Routledge Press, whose comments, suggestions, questions, and thoughtful challenges helped us rethink and revise portions of the book.

We thank our family members—especially Sean, Thomas, Kathleen, Jaime, Nick, and Nina (Heidi's mother)—for their patient understanding and support while we worked on this project.

***

Portions of Chapter 3 appeared in the following article published in *Business & Professional Communication Quarterly* (Sage Press): Porter, James E. (2017). Professional communication as phatic: From classical *eunoia* to personal AI. *Business & Professional Communication Quarterly.* © James E. Porter.

Figure 3.1 is a reproduction of a diagram appearing on p. 381 in the following journal article from *Bell System Technical Journal* (Alcatel-Lucent). Shannon, Claude. (1948). A mathematical theory of communication. *Bell System Technical Journal, 27,* p. 381. Permission courtesy of Nokia © 1948 Nokia Corporation. All Rights Reserved.

1 Introduction

Professional Communication in the Digital Age

We begin with a claim that we take as a given: Professional communication has changed dramatically in the digital age.

This is neither a new nor a controversial claim. Scholarly research, the popular press, and social media postings are replete with discussions and examples of how digital technologies have impacted all aspects of contemporary human society. From self-driving cars to automated warehouses to online shopping and virtual reality travel, digital technologies have and are transforming the processes and practices in many fields, including professional communication.[1]

In all realms of professional communication, the claim that the digital technologies we use to communicate have radically altered *how* we communicate is not new, with these "technologies" referring to the combination of hardware (the physical interfaces of laptop, smartphone, mobile device, car dashboard, etc.) and software (the applications and programs shaping communications), and the deep infrastructure of networked connectivity (the internet and the World Wide Web and the laws and regulations shaping those systems). It is that combination of hardware, software, and infrastructure—and the particular human designs, applications, and uses of it—that has led to what the philosopher Luciano Floridi (2014) identified as a revolutionary new digital age that is not only changing *how* we communicate but is also changing *us*. Floridi (2014) saw the digital age as "the fourth revolution" in this history of humankind, a revolution that is not only changing our communication interactions but is also reshaping our fundamental sense of self, our culture, and our very "human reality."[2]

Digital communications are truly global. As of 2016, over 3.5 billion people worldwide access the internet (most through the Web and attendant applications). The percentage of the population with access to and use of the internet is very high in some countries (e.g., Japan 91%, United States 88%, France 86%, Russia 71%, Brazil 66%), moderate in others (e.g., Turkey 58%, China 52%, Mexico 45%, Kenya 45%), and low or just emerging in others, often because of widespread poverty, still-developing infrastructure, government censorship, and/or war (e.g., India 34%, Uganda 19%, Iraq 13%, Sierra Leone 2%, Somalia 1%) (Internet Live Stats, 2016).

For those with access, the rise of mobile and smart, connected devices has led to a digital ubiquity—connected 24/7 at work, at home, and when travelling. In this omnipresent digital network, the boundaries between home and work, personal and professional, and private and public are becoming increasingly blurred. Our professional communications are also becoming more and more multimodal with the increased ease with which audio, video, and textual elements can be merged. We video chat and conference with each other from all over the world; company leaders need to learn not just the art of the letter and email but also of the corporate video (as so many have done to announce product releases or to apologize for corporate misdeeds).

Our computers themselves now talk to us in ways that are increasingly human-like. The rise of artificial intelligent agents in all fields, including professional communication, is remarkable, and we are in the midst of an interface revolution where computers no longer need to look or interact like computers, an issue we discuss in Chapter 7. More frequently than many people realize, our communications are occurring not just with fellow humans but also with AI agents who aim to "learn" from us and who also, as part of their programming, gather, search, and data mine our communications, delivering to individuals and corporations petabytes (and maybe even at this point zettabytes) of data. Nearly everything we say and do online is—with and without our permission—being collected, aggregated, de-aggregated and analyzed by computer and human agents. We are immersed in digital technologies that shape how, when, where, why, and with whom we communicate.

So, yes, professional communication is definitely changing, and in this book, we want to examine the claim, raising what we think are two important follow-up questions. Given that digital technologies are changing communication, then:

1 Exactly how is professional communication changing? And what difference do those changes make in terms of not only how we create, design, publish, distribute, and encounter professional communication but also how we interact in professional settings?

2 How does our thinking about communication—our fundamental rhetoric theory for professional communication—need to change to keep up with the dramatic changes in communication technologies? What frameworks will help individuals and organizations effectively analyze and produce professional communications in the digital age?

In regard to the second question, for many people, professional communication thinking, especially business communication thinking, is still guided by older rhetoric theories and ideologies from the age of print and broadcast media, or even, perhaps, from an older version of the digital realm (e.g., a Web 1.0, linear transmission model). One of our key arguments is that we need to update our fundamental framework for thinking about professional communication. Drawing from our research, which includes interviews with business professionals from a wide variety of organizations working in and with a wide variety of technologies, we build and articulate here a rhetorical/ethical network frame for analyzing and producing professional communications.

In this introductory chapter, we start by providing a few brief examples, drawn from corporate use of social media, to illustrate how communication in the digital age has changed, and reflect on what difference that makes. In the second part of the chapter, we outline the framework and describe the methodology we use to conduct this inquiry, providing an overview for the chapters that follow.

Professional Communication Practices: Some Corporate Social Media Examples

On April 19, 2013, the Ford Motor Company posted a tweet on its corporate Twitter site (@ford), praising the first responders in the Boston Marathon bombing that killed three persons and maimed 264 others. The tweet read:

> To the first responders of Boston: THANK YOU. You are true American heroes. Sincerely, Ford Motor Company

The text of this tweet was layered into the foreground of a photograph of a new black Ford car and a new black Ford truck, both upgraded and detailed as police vehicles.

The public response to this tweet on Twitter was immediate and harshly critical—not so much because Ford praised the responders, which people found admirable, as because of the photograph, which showed Ford using the tragedy as a sales opportunity. The presence of what was clearly an advertisement, a billboard-like image, crossed a line in the public's eye from appropriate to inappropriate.

The tweet was considered tasteless and inappropriate, but one marketing analyst, Augie Ray (2013), saw Ford's mistake as more than a simple lapse, but actually an ethics issue: "Not everyone will agree, but I feel that Ford's use of brand imagery not only reduced the sincerity of the message but demonstrated questionable ethics." Ray went on to note that the problem could have been avoided if Ford had simply used the text without the photograph. The text itself Ray viewed as an appropriate sign of corporate support and appreciation for first responders.

The negative publicity generated by this tweet prompted Ford to get "serious" (Laskowski, 2013) about social media. Ford hired what they called a Global Digital and Multimedia Communication Manager, whose assignment was to build Ford's social media presence in ways that would promote the company. Just a few months later, an October 2013 *Boston University Today* feature article praised Ford for being a corporate leader in the use of social media, noting that its Twitter site had 206,000 followers (versus General Motors, with only 91,000 followers) (Laskowski, 2013).

Hiring a "digital and multimedia communication manager" is one sign of corporate recognition that a different approach is called for, and that the old model for public relations and communication management has changed. An Oracle (2012) white paper advises businesses to create a "social contact center," that is, a distinct organizational structure for managing social media interaction and for, as we discuss in Chapter 6, making an ethics paradigm shift to corporate listening that doesn't simply include data-gathering from customers (the old model) but also affords opportunities to create value for customers in ways specific to their interests, priorities, and needs.

Corporations who have a presence on social media are expected to say something about bad news, natural disasters, tragedies, or celebrity deaths, but there is, for example, an art to crafting the social media condolence (d.Trio, 2016). The Ford tweet (and many others like it) have become examples of what not to do with corporate social media. But this clumsy approach to social media is by no means a rare event.

In June 2013, clothing retailer Kenneth Cole posted a tweet that seemed to be using the protests in Cairo happening at that time as an occasion to promote a spring clothing line. The tweet read:

> Millions are in uproar in #Cairo. Rumor is they heard our new spring collection is now available online at http://bitly/KCairo-KC.

The Cairo "uproar" was a complex political and social upheaval that, unfortunately, included violence in which 16 people were killed and over 200 injured, hardly the occasion for a sales pitch, much less a joke.

Kenneth Cole had to hire a crisis management firm to deal with the flak created by this tweet, but what came out later was that the tweet was intentional (Nudd, 2013). The executive who authorized the tweet saw it as an opportunity to garner attention. He was unrepentant about posting the tweet, because, as he said:

> Billions of people read my inappropriate, self-promoting tweet, I got a lot of harsh responses, and we hired a crisis-management firm. [...] But our stock went up that day, our e-commerce business was better, the business at every one of our stores improved, and I picked up 3,000 new followers on Twitter. So on what criteria is this a gaffe? [Laughs] Within hours, I tweeted an explanation, which had to be vetted by lawyers. I'm not even sure I used the words I'm sorry—because I wasn't sorry.
>
> (Nudd, 2013, laugh notation part of original)

This executive pursued the strategy that many companies and individuals take with social media: "There is no such thing as bad publicity."[3] "Billions" of people read the tweet, Kenneth Cole stock went up that day, the executive picked up 300 new followers. Success, one might think, at least by one set of measures.

The executive's response raises a question that we must seriously consider: In the age of social media, is it strategically smart to be outrageous and to deliberately violate standards and norms, even offend people, in order to garner attention? Is that where we ought to go with social media? Should we see "being a jerk on Twitter" (Nudd, 2013) as simply good business, maybe even as being a digital genius?

Here is an example showing how business strategy overlaps with issues of rhetoric, communication, and ethics. From the standpoint of communication ethics, you could object to the Kenneth Cole tweet because it treats people as objects to be used for one's own self-promotion. Making a joke based on a tragic event, using people's misfortunes to sell clothing, would strike many, if not most, as lacking empathy, ethics, integrity, and basic human decency. *Tone deaf* is the term often used to describe this kind of communication: a posting that fails to demonstrate sufficient awareness of and respect for people's identities, feelings, or situations. So from the standpoint of business ethics and public relations, the strategy is questionable.

But even from a strictly bottom-line profit standpoint—the claim the executive makes—the strategy may also miss the mark: The executive measured success in terms of short-term metrics. What more substantive marketing research shows is that customers (as distinctly different perhaps from shareholders) want companies to have integrity, to tell the truth, to be good citizens, to practice social responsibility, to label products accurately and clearly, to treat employees well, to put customers ahead of profit, and to engage in ethical practices (Rooney, 2011; Ray, 2012b). Trust is a key quality, the basis for the relationship between a business and its customers. The company brand or image is key to establishing and maintaining that trust—a point we will return to in our discussion of phatic communication and *ethos* in Chapter 3. If you "drive traffic but harm trust" (Ray, 2012b), you are ultimately doing damage to your brand and your business ethos. Trust matters, and it matters a great deal (Edelman, 2015; Etlinger, 2015b). "Bad metrics lead to bad strategies. More than that, bad metrics can lead to unethical behaviors" (Ray, 2013).

The Kenneth Cole executive is simply wrong. In putting "buzz before brand" (Tossona, 2015), he has confused metrics with value, favoring short-term measures of attention (likes, hits, monthly sales) over long-term measures of success. The preponderance of social media marketing research seems to indicate that this is *not* the way to use social media. So what *are* some ways to use social media?

Executives in Kellogg's Global Corporate Affairs team, including the Senior Vice President for Global Corporate Affairs (Kris Charles), the Director of Brand Public Relations for the U.S. (Brandy Ruff), and the Senior Director of Consumer Engagement (Rick Wion), discussed in an interview with us how their company, which has operations in over 30 countries and sells products in 160, needs to be always aware of emerging news and cultural events in each of its markets so as to strategically join conversations when and where it is appropriate to do so. Unlike the spring uprising tweet from Kenneth Cole, where the company was just trying to insert their brand into a public conversation with no right to speak, Kellogg approaches their public conversation work much more carefully and, we would say, ethically.

As Brandy Ruff explained, when looking at traditional and social media and choosing what conversation to join, Kellogg first asks, "What right we have in the conversation? Is it a conversation we want to be involved in? Is it a conversation we have a true voice, purpose for?" As Kris Charles noted, Kellogg looks to join conversations "where we would have a right, relevance, and credibility on that topic because of our leadership in that area." Rather than trying to wedge their way into every trending conversation, Kellogg focuses on key areas, such as breakfast, food sustainability, world hunger, and workplace diversity (the first topic given the founding and still primary focus of the company and the latter topics given Kellogg's commitment to corporate responsibility). Kellogg has received awards and widespread recognition in multiple countries for their philanthropic work to ease world hunger and to build sustainable food supply systems. Committing to being an active player with a credible, relevant voice in public conversations is part of Kellogg's corporate and philanthropic mission.

Clearly, the technologies of social media have altered expectations for company participation in public discussions and, further, the technology of social media has altered standards by creating a venue in which "consumers have higher expectations of what a corporate brand is and does—for them and for their neighbors and communities" (Rooney, 2011). In other words, corporate behavior is not as invisible as it used to be: If a corporation screws up, people will know about it—and the virality and spreadability of social media communication will make sure that everybody knows about it and talks about it and spreads the word to others. In a sense, social media has raised the bar on corporate participation in public conversations. How a company responds to those open forums is key, as our next brief example shows.

On December 19, 2011, during the holiday season, a FedEx delivery driver came up to a house with a package (containing a computer monitor, as it turned out) and threw the package over a fence onto the porch. The person receiving the package, who happened to be home, made a video of the event that he posted on YouTube, under the title "FedEx Guy Throwing My Computer Monitor." The video very quickly went viral, receiving 800,000 views in the first week alone (Belsie, 2011) and generating a twitterstorm of controversy and criticism. Once the video went viral with millions of views, broadcast network news agencies picked up the story as well. Suffice to say, FedEx faced a major public relations crisis.

Two days after the video was posted, the company responded to the crisis, strategically posting its own YouTube video (FedEx, 2011), a video of Matthew Thornton, III, the Senior Vice President, speaking to the public. Thornton offered a public apology, and noted that the driver in the video "is not working with customers." FedEx also posted a written apology on its blog, and engaged in a Twitter campaign addressing the video and apologizing for the event, saying in one tweet, "We saw the video and quite frankly were shocked."

Instead of ignoring the video and hoping the bad PR would simply go away, FedEx, in classic bad news messaging style, took responsibility for the driver's actions, apologized for them, and then engaged the public in conversation about the video. But in so doing, FedEx leveraged social media extensively and effectively to change the frame for the conversation, and to turn attention away from the bad behavior of the driver who threw the package toward the more productive question of how FedEx was going to address the problem in its policies and training. The public comments in response to the blog apology were overwhelmingly positive or neutral—and only 18% were negative (Collier, 2012). The FedEx case is now a standard example used in PR of how to deploy social media to handle bad PR (Howell Marketing, 2011). Don't try to hide, don't try to control; rather, engage and converse.

These examples illustrate, in just one area of professional communication, how digital technologies, especially social media, have changed the relationship between corporate communication practices and the consumer public (and, by extension, the relationship for individual business professionals and the broader public as well). The social web links the consumer and the corporation in an interactive network, and this provides a new kind of opportunity for interaction, one where consumers are co-creators of content.

Further, businesses must strategically and actively *plan* for this form of engagement: They must learn how to "design for interactivity" and "collaborative production" (Wittke & Hanekop, 2011) so as to create multi-directional dialectic engagements across and between actors that encourage the co-creation of meaning (Lauring, 2011; Wolff, 2013). In all sorts of ways, the social web not only changes how business communicates with the public, it changes the very nature of business itself.

At the same time, the Ford Motor case (and related cases) show us that old habits and practices die hard. Ford used its tweet inappropriately as an ad billboard or flyer, when the context for the communication required a different kind of response, a sincere condolence. Ford failed to understand how their posting would be viewed in light of a tragic public event, and they underestimated the virality of Twitter. The FedEx employee thought that there was no harm in throwing the delivery box because at most maybe one person would notice. In that respect, he failed to appreciate how surveillance now happens: Smartphone camera technology conspires with a video-based social media platform (You-Tube) to expose and publicize his carelessness. Social media platforms such as YouTube helps make what formerly would have been invisible bad behavior not only visible and capturable as evidence but widely public. When Justine Sacco, whom we discuss in Chapter 5, sent out a racist tweet, she thought that she was tweeting to a few friends only to discover hours later that her audience had grown to thousands of people, including her employer.

In every one of these cases, the person or company involved was behaving according to the norms of an older understanding of how communication works—but was tripped up by the new technology, because they failed to consider how that technology has dramatically changed not simply *where* communication happens but *how and how fast*. It is not that these people don't know about the technologies (no doubt they do), or know how to use them (probably they do). The issue is that their actions betrayed a gap between what they cognitively knew and how they practically acted and communicated.

And maybe this is true for all of us. Even though we may live in the age of social media and networked communication, and use the networks daily, our writing and communication habits, practices, and concepts have not yet quite caught up. And maybe that gap is not unusual. Maybe people's communication practices *always* operate in lag time: Maybe we are always communicating according to the norms and models of older technologies. As each generation learns in a particular era of technology, technology changes our contexts of use change and we have to catch up. As literacy scholars have noted, we carry the literacy practices of a known domain (home, for example) with us into new domains (such as school) (see Heath, 1983 for one of the first, extensive studies of this learning phenomena). And as learning transfer theorists have noted, there is *positive transfer* that "occurs when learning in one context improves performance in some other context" and *negative transfer* that occurs "when learning in one context impacts negatively on performance in another" (Perkins & Salomon, 1992, pp. 3–4).

Communicators working with new digital technologies may also get confused and fall into negative transfer because, in fact, the new technologies carry in them many of the features of older forms of communication: Twitter and Instagram can sometimes look and act like personal, face-to-face, word-of-mouth communication—and that can result in unpleasant surprises when we fail to remember that they are not private or intimate channels (as frequently happens): For example, when a personal note you thought you were sharing with a small group of friends gets publicized and retweeted to thousands of people. Or when personal photographs you posted on your Facebook page in college are used by a potential employer to decide not to hire you. Or when a "joke" you thought you were sharing with a few colleagues creates a PR disaster for your company and ends up getting you fired. You might be fooled into thinking you are communicating in a private, personal, secure world—but that is very much not the world of social media or of any digital communication technologies given the reach of the Web and, too, the ubiquity of data storage and collection. Very little online is private, personal, or secure. And when something bad happens, when you make a mistake, say something dumb or hurtful, or post the wrong thing in the wrong place, it happens fast and spreads virally and, as is often the case on the Web, it never goes away.

The Features of Professional Communication in the Digital Age

The brief examples above are, obviously, just a sampling of the ways in which digital technologies are impacting professional communication. But even with these few examples we can begin to assemble a list of features of professional communication in a digital age.

Dyadic and Interactive

More so than ever, professional communication is dyadic and interactive. With the ubiquity of networked technologies, people literally have at their fingertips the means to not just read but also to share, remix, and reframe and repurpose content. They have the ability to reach wide audiences, and they can do so quickly. For corporations, this means, among other things, that the message can be challenged, criticized, refuted, mocked, and parodied—and that happens within the same communication space and can, potentially, be distributed just as widely as the corporate message.

Companies often struggle with the dyadic nature of social media, wondering what to do with negative feedback online. Shara Clark, a social media consultant whom we interviewed, explained how "Lots of companies want to take those complaints down; they don't want people to see the angry consumer stuff. But social media is about this two-way conversation and being authentic and opening those barriers. So taking it down is the exact opposite of what social media is meant for" (Interview, September 21, 2015).

Certainly, this two-way, dyadic feature can cause problems for those who either don't know how or who forget how to use it, but, when the dyadic nature of social media is properly understood and effectively deployed, it can also provide an opportunity for improved communication, as we show in a corporate case presented in Chapter 6.

Viral and Spreadable

One key difference between older communication technologies and the new social media model pertains to what is called "spreadability" (Jenkins, Ford, & Green, 2013) or "virality" (Nahon & Hemsley, 2013): that is, speed and reach. How broadly and quickly is the communication dispersed? Thanks to the "radical connectivity" (Morgan, 2013), postings online can "go viral" quickly.

The viral metaphor is, of course, a negative one: Bad news, embarrassing events, and salacious gossip, especially, travel widely—and fast, like a contagious disease. And the more people who see it and tag it and repost it, the more people it is transmitted to. In other words, because of the way networks operate, there is an exponential growth rate, not simply a steady, proportional one. The other negative aspect of virality is the ease with which misinformation and fake news can be distributed, as seen, in 2016, in the U.S. Presidential election and Facebook's failed algorithms for catching fake news. Professional communicators need to be aware of how "the darknet" (Delamarter, 2016) can pose a threat, upsetting social media communications and potentially destroying corporate brand.

But the virality and spreadability of online communications also create many positive opportunities for individuals and corporations. Companies can use virality and spreadabililty to more widely promote and share their philanthropy, as Kellogg Company does, using social media to showcase its Breakfasts for Better Days program that exceeded its goal in 2016 of providing 1 billion breakfasts to hungry children in countries around the globe. Using the hashtag #3billionbetterdays, Kellogg not only shares stories about its work for hunger relief but also shares information about ways people and corporations can help. Individuals, too, can leverage the power of virality and spreadability to more immediately learn about and reach out to help others. Crowdfunding sites like GoFundMe campaigns help people spread their message, their needs, and their goals, and help others learn about and contribute to worthy endeavors.

Everyday citizens with no media experience can rise to national prominence, even if just for a few days, as spokespersons for public service messages, as happened to Kayli and Ricky Shoff (2016), who shared on social media the remotely captured video of one of their twin two-year-olds saving the other who was trapped under a fallen bureau. The Shoffs decided to post their video in order to raise awareness of the need for furniture safety. The video posted to YouTube received 15 million views in the first week of posting and was picked up by news agencies around the globe—and the news stories often included information about the importance of pursuing furniture safety practices. There's no telling how many children's lives around the world will be saved because, upon viewing that video and hearing the story, some caregivers will install furniture anchors.

So virality and spreadability, as with so many features of communication technologies, bring both beneficial and problematic impacts depending on the context.

Public and Archived

Communications in a digital age, especially social media communications, are public. This can help shine a light on individual and corporate transgressions. At an individual and collective level, for example, consumers are able to report on product defects or poor customer service, receiving—from responsive companies at least—apologies or offers of returns or wide-scale product recalls. In the old days of print or even Web 1.0, if you had a problem with a company, you'd write or call and your communication would be logged and filed by the company for no one else to see. But now communications can be made publicly and are archived publicly.

But *public* may be the wrong word because so many of our communications are not occurring in the public sphere but rather in corporate-owned spaces where, in exchange for our usage of the service, we give Facebook and Twitter and the like world-wide license to use our materials. In our interactions online, we also consent to terms of service and privacy policies that allow organizations of all types, including law enforcement, to collect and archive a great deal of data on us. In the workplace, employee surveillance and the archiving of the actions recorded is happening globally through digital technologies designed to monitor Web usage, keyboard clicks, globally-positioned movements, etc. Whether they work onground or online, when workers leave work for the day, they certainly don't leave the company—the archived digital records of their screens, their searches, and their video presences continue on in company files.

Amid this shift to click agree to terms of service and user agreements (for third-party platforms that most people don't read) or to sign employment contracts (that people must sign if they want a job) is a profound shift in privacy and what is considered private and not-private (e.g., Kerr, Steeves, & Lucock, 2009; Nissenbaum, 2009). As Floridi (2014) put it, "Never before in the history of humanity have so many people monitored, recorded, and reported so many details about themselves to such a large audience" (p. 62). Numerous theorists have commented on the erosion of the boundary between private and public, as digital technologies like smartphones and video apps like Instagram and YouTube give us the capacity to instantly publish and widely distribute private moments (the selfie).

And attitudes toward privacy are changing as well, as we see in the U.S., where there are generational differences between notions and standards of privacy (Raine & Duggan, 2016). At the same time that digital technologies and their networks of use blur the boundaries of public and private (in different ways for difference cultures; see Bennett & Raab, 2006; Dwyer, 2015; Krotoszynski, 2016), they also blur the boundaries of employee and not-employee. Companies can be impacted by employee actions outside the workplace in ways both more long-lingering and more immediate.

Any professional communicator must consider both the archival and public nature of digital communications.

Fast and Mobile

Digital technologies are also changing the speed, mobility, and timeliness of communications. One of the senior executives we interviewed—Henry Truslow IV, President and CEO of Sunbury Mills—reflected on how business-to-business communication has changed over the past 30 or more years. As he noted, early on in his career they started with the telex which was slow and cumbersome: "It took a week for us to send a telex because we had a queue at the mill, there was only one drum and one person who operated it." From the high-tech telex, they moved to fax machines, and then in the early 1990s they shifted to email, which is still one of their primary communication channels (as it is for many companies). But Sunbury Mill executives also frequently use text messaging for 1-to-1 messages and web conferencing for sales meetings, and they are moving more and more communications to cloud computing and, as we discuss in Chapter 7, many other companies are moving to physical and virtual bot communications. These technology changes have dramatically impacted the immediacy and pace of communication interaction.

Among the professionals we interviewed for this project (see Table 1.1), all but one was old enough to remember a world without the World Wide Web and mobile technologies. When we ask asked them to reflect in general on what has changed with digital technologies, each one mentioned the impact of speed and how that's changed work communications and practices. They noted both the advantages and the pressures of the expectation for immediate response. They also reflected on how some digital communication technologies are already too slow and cumbersome. For example, for active projects involving the immediate need for interaction and response, email was seen as slow and static compared to mobile text applications and video chat. Tamar and Peter Lask, co-owners of the small business and clothing boutique Juniper, described how when communicating with employees they "use email for policy statements and longer stuff like that," but that most of their digital communications with employees occur via texting because "you can get information to people quickly." Also, especially for their mostly young adult employees, email is a "hassle" that they see "as sit-down-and-go-through-your-emails. It takes more time, whereas a text is instantaneous."

Table 1.1 Professionals interviewed

Name	Position and Company[1] (company focus)
Steve Caldwell	Founder & CEO, Strap (mobile data)
Kris Charles	Senior Vice President, Global Corporate Affairs, Kellogg Company (food manufacturing)
Shara Clark	Owner, Shara Clark Communications; Instructor, Strategic Communication, Miami University; Past President, Public Relations Society, Cincinnati, OH Chapter
Jill Dunne	Marketing and Communications Director, Cincinnati Art Museum
Susan Etlinger	Industry Analyst, Altimeter Group (industry consulting)
Malcolm Faulds	Head of Global Marketing, dunnhumby (marketing)
Anthony Gargiulo, Jr.	VP Human Resources, World's Finest Chocolate (manufacturing/sales)
Paul Hunter	Visiting Executive Professor of Marketing, Farmer School of Business, Miami University; Former Head of Operations, dunnhumby
Tarek Kamil	Founder & CEO, Cerkl (personalized/automated communications)
Peter Lask and Tamar Lask	Co-Owners, Juniper (clothing boutique, 3 locations)
Austin Mace	Founder & CEO, SubVRsive (virtual reality)
Dennis Mortensen	Founder & CEO, x.ai (artificial intelligence)
Rob Poetsch	Director, Public Affairs and Engagement, Taco Bell (restaurant chain)
Brandy Ruff	Director, Brand Public Relations, Kellogg Company (food manufacturing)
Jaime Schaeffer	Owner, Yellowbird Social Media (communications)
Stephen Seiple	Solution Specialist Azure, Microsoft (technology)
Brian Smith	COO, ThinkVine (marketing)
Henry Truslow IV	President and CEO, Sunbury Textile Mills (manufacturing)
Rick Wion	Senior Director of Consumer Engagement, Kellogg Company (food manufacturing)
Anonymous[2]	Director of Ethics (multinational manufacturing)

[1] Position held at time of interview.
[2] Interviewees could consent to share or not share their names, as per informed consent agreement.

A theme related to speed and timeliness for the professionals we interviewed was mobility: It was important to be able to communicate with clients and with colleagues while moving, while driving to work, while flying to a conference, during a meeting. The mobility and increasing interoperability of communication systems, especially with the advent of interdevice communications, enables professional communications to occur in changing locations, times and ways. Some of this is not all good, as some interviewees discussed the eroding line between homelife and worklife and the pressure to be always in communication with their workplace. But the mobility and changing pace of communications also enabled people to communicate with much more freedom, including working entirely virtually.

Enabling Virtual Presence

It used to be if you couldn't physically get to work you missed the meeting. Then conference call technology was developed, which is helpful but still awkward, especially for larger meetings or when you don't know the people with whom you're communicating as well. The ability of digital technologies and the increased bandwidth of networked communications also enables an increase in virtual presence through audio-visual technologies, including, increasingly, virtual reality. Onground, physically in-person meetings and business travel are not entirely obsolete, but they have certainly been reduced because web-based voice and videoconferencing platforms and applications make physical presence less necessary.

In providing an online, virtual space for collaborative work activity, digital technologies change the nature of teamwork and collaboration. In fact, even professionals working at the same location, perhaps housed in the same building or office space, will use the virtual tools instead of face-to-face meeting—because it can be faster and more efficient, and because it allows for multi-tasking across different projects. Platforms such as Basecamp, Slack, Yammer, and others change teamwork space—and, thus, the dynamic of teamwork—insofar as the space is entirely virtual and communications about the project, as well as documents related to the project, occupy the same space. As Paul Hunter explained of dunnhumby's use of Yammer, "What it does, for people who are on Yammer and post, you have followings and it brings personalities out, and it makes the larger world quite small. And I think it benefits the company overall. We connect people much faster. We trade ideas and inform individuals of things that you had no idea that was going on before. It's all out there in the open" (Interview, September 10, 2015).

The characteristics of dyadic and interactive, viral and spreadable, public and archived, fast and mobile, and enabling of virtual presence weave through, in various ways, all networks of digital communications and are characteristics that any framework for the analysis and production of professional communication in a digital age must consider.

A Rhetoric for Professional Communication

We are approaching the question of professional communication in the digital age primarily from the point of view of rhetoric, a discipline and art that is 2,400 years old, with its origins—its Western origins at least—in 5th century BCE Athens, Greece. We certainly do value and carry forward insights from the classical rhetoric of ancient Athens and from classical Roman rhetoric, but Aristotle and Cicero are not the only rhetoricians on the block. Their rhetoric is not our rhetoric. The rhetoric framework we offer as suited for digital communication sees rhetoric from a different frame: as intertwined with ethics, as phatic, as multimodal, as global and intercultural, as performative action, and as networked.

Rhetoric as Intertwined with Ethics

We do not define rhetoric primarily as persuasion (getting people to do what you want them to do), but rather we adapt Quintilian's notion of rhetoric as "the good man speaking well"—or, we would amend, more inclusively, the good person speaking well. But even that is not inclusive enough. It's also *the good corporation (or organization or group) speaking well*—and now, too, *the good machine speaking well*. Despite the popular construct of rhetoric as pejorative, rhetoric means ethical communication. The motivating force behind any symbolic action is, or should be, a good, and so when rhetoric takes up the question of purpose—why am I speaking or writing, or posting this video, or launching this marketing campaign? Or coding this algorithmic communication agent?—it is interlaced with considerations of ethics. *Cui bono?* For whose good, and for what benefit, are we communicating?

Viewing rhetoric as intertwined with ethics runs into a centuries old disciplinary division between rhetoric and ethics (as we discuss in Chapter 2). We see this division still alive and operating in professional communication literature, which generally does not ignore ethics, but treats ethical concerns separately, as apart from (and usually prior to) concerns related to communication. Textbooks often treat questions of ethics in the token "ethics chapter" and rarely elsewhere. We see this split evident in business communication journals as well: *The Journal of Business Communication* (for instance) deals with communication (writing, speech), and the *Journal of Business Ethics* deals with ethics (actions, behaviors), but each journal seems reluctant to trespass into the other's domain.

The split between rhetoric and ethics is evident in much of the research published in business communication journals. While this research is certainly relevant to rhetoric and to ethics, and vice versa, it is striking how seldom business communication research even mentions the words *rhetoric* and *ethics* explicitly. Take, for example, a 2013 article in the *Journal of Business Communication* titled "Effects of Directness in Bad-News E-Mails and Voice Mails" (Jansen & Janssen, 2013). This article is thoroughly about rhetoric and ethics and audience, but the article never once mentions those words. Similarly, a 2011 *Journal of Business Communication* article titled "Intercultural Organizational

Communication: The Social Organizing of Interaction in International Encounters" (Lauring, 2011) never uses the terms *rhetoric*, *audience*, or *ethics* either (except in the titles of two citations). Even a 2011 *Journal of Business Communication* article on "Corporate Social Responsibility" (Waller & Conaway, 2011) never uses the term *ethics*. To us, that lapse is striking and troubling. In Chapter 2, we develop the argument for why rhetoric and ethics need to be considered as overlapping, intertwined concerns, and why that matters to professional communication.

Rhetoric as Phatic

Related to reconnecting rhetoric and ethics is seeing communication as phatic. Phatic refers to the purpose of building communication channels, keeping them open, and establishing ongoing and fruitful relationships. A phatic model posits that the purpose of communication is not simply informing or persuading. Rather, the ultimate end goal of discursive action is to build goodwill, trust, cooperation, partnership, and harmony—that is why we are communicating in the first place. We communicate to develop a relationship, a dialogic and mutually beneficial relationship, between rhetor and audience. We develop this aspect of our rhetorical theory in Chapter 3.

Rhetoric as Multimodal

Rhetoric as an art pertains not only to writing and speaking. Rhetoric provides a lens for analyzing and producing any and all symbolic action, or interaction, a frame that enlarges the scope of rhetoric to include performance, action, dress, behavior, visual and cinematic image, slide design, embodied activity, social media postings, YouTube videos, Instagram postings, Trello chat sessions, etc., all the variety of multimodal elements that often work together to comprise rhetorical action.

But it's not just aural and visual and even physical delivery to which rhetoric attends, it's also the software programs, algorithms, and interfaces that shape digital communications. The design of digital interfaces and infrastructure matters, shaping people's understandings and actions (Selfe & Selfe, 1994; Johnson, 1998; Potts, 2014). As we discuss in Chapter 4, objects are agents with rhetorical effects. Interfaces and infrastructures that may work for one culture—Xiaoice in China—don't work so well for people in another culture—Tay in the United States.

Rhetoric as Global and Multicultural

Digital communications on the internet are global in the respect that they spread widely, crossing national boundaries—which means that they potentially encounter difference to a greater extent, meaning difference in terms of identity as well as culture. Much of traditional rhetoric theory—for instance, Aristotle's theory for 4th-century BCE Athens, or George Campbell's theory (1776/2004) for 18th century England and Scotland, or Strunk and White's (1959/1995) 20th-century style guidelines for US college students—assumed a monocultural model: That is, it assumed that rhetors and their audiences were all members of the same culture, the same class, the same gender (male, typically), and shared the same general cultural values, customs, habits, and expectations (if not always the same religious or political views). In other words, the prevailing assumption was that there was a "general audience" that you were communicating with, and that general audience was very similar to you.

One of the key contributions of late 20th-century rhetoric theory was to emphasize the importance of cultural difference and identity difference: Difference, not similarity, is in fact the basis of most public communication situations we are likely to find ourselves in. Rather than starting with the assumption that people are largely the same, rhetoric needs to begin with the opposite assumption: People (and machines) are different; they have different identities; and understanding, acknowledging, and respecting those differences are key to effective interactive communication. Acts of rhetoric reside in "contact zones" (Pratt, 1991) between differing cultures. All effective acts of rhetoric are, in a sense, *mestiza rhetorics* (Anzaldúa, 1987) to the extent that they mix or blend cultural difference, creating a third space that allows for communication across difference. Understanding the importance of differences as related to race, ethnicity, class, gender, age, sexual orientation, ability, religion, customs, practice, language, religion, as well as, for professional communicators, organizational culture is key to professional communication in the digital age.

For example: There can be profound cultural differences about how to interpret silence in a communication situation. In some cultures—like Chinese culture, for instance—silence is valued as a sign of respect: not silence in the sense of apathy or disengagement, but engaged, attentive silence showing respect for other. Conversely, glib or empty talk, the "small talk" that is often used as an icebreaking strategy in US business meetings, is distrusted by other cultures. In Chinese culture, silence is seen as "a positive tool for building relationships" (Lyon, 2004, p. 137) and as signaling that the listener wishes to place emphasis on actions rather than words and avoid using meaningless language as tool for manipulation. This kind of cultural difference in attitude can have profound implications for digital interactions.

Cultural difference cannot be equated with nationality. Even within a given national boundary, there can be a diversity of cultures. And across national boundaries, as people of various cultural backgrounds interact, they adapt to the new communities that they are forming, particularly on social media—and those new communities can develop their own values, conventions, ethical standards, and rhetorical principles. So we need a flexible view of culture, or as R. Peter Hunsinger puts it, we need to focus less on *culture* (as a fixed, stable entity) and more on the *intercultural*, the various ways that cultural habits, practices, values come into play—and sometimes lead to conflict or confusion in communication (2006, p. 42). We discuss the significance of global and intercultural rhetoric in more detail in Chapter 3.

Rhetoric as Performative Action

As an art, rhetoric is concerned both with *making* an object (a communication message such as a report, a video, a business presentation, or a tweet) and with *doing* something, such as having an effect (e.g., creating value for some audience, building a relationship with someone, exposing corporate bad behavior). In short, any rhetorical act is both a *saying* and a *doing*; it is both expression and action.

For most of its history, rhetoric has focused mainly on making and delivering—making an effective speech, writing an effective report, delivering a made product. But rhetoric is also an action: Rhetorical actions also *do* something (Austin, 1962). And, related to this, rhetorical actions are embodied; they belong to somebody (or bodies) or, in the case of artificial intelligence, something (or somethings). Even when a written text or posting comes across our screens as disembodied, there is a body there behind it—or sometimes in it, as postings are often conveyed with visual embodied representations. An important aspect of our rhetoric is seeing professional communication not simply as expression or representation but also as action; seeing communication as embodied, not disembodied (Butler, 1997, 2010; Cassin, 2009); and recovering an expanded and remediated notion of rhetorical delivery (Porter, 2009; Morey, 2016). Seeing communication as performative action is also part of repairing rhetoric's relationship with ethics.

Rhetoric as Networked

We need to think of rhetorical activity as networked. When discussing digital technologies people often hear "network" and think of the internet and the World Wide Web. But all communications—not just digital—are networked. The executive who wrote the Kenneth Cole tweet exists in overlapping, interconnected onground and online networks, both local and global, comprised of human and non-human actors interacting and reacting across time and space. To build our rhetoric network theory that we borrow from actor-network theory, as developed by Bruno Latour and others, and from ecological theory, as developed by rhetoric and composition scholars. We talk about this theory in more detail next, and in Chapter 4.

Our Methodology: Applying Theory *to* Practice and Building and Adapting Theory *from* Practice

Our methodology for this project is based on the critical interchange between (1) rhetoric and communication theory and (2) professional practice as evident in stories, experiences, and cases—as provided both by others' published research and experiential accounts but also as developed through our own person-based qualitative research, from our interviews with 21 business professionals (see Table 1.1). Thus, our approach meshes theory with practice. Rhetoric theory is the frame we use to understand and analyze practice; practice informs, challenges, critiques, and modifies our rhetoric theory.

Our rhetoric theory is constructed both from classical and contemporary rhetoric. Classical rhetoricians, particularly Isocrates and Quintilian, provide a philosophy of rhetoric that integrates (rather than divides) rhetoric and ethics—and that is key to our overall approach. As we mentioned above, the crux of our position can be summed up in Quintilian's definition of rhetoric as "A good man [or person or corporation or machine, we would add] speaking [or writing, we would add] well" (*Institutio,* 12.1.1). There Quintilian insists that in order to achieve effective rhetoric, the rhetor must, first, be a virtuous person—or else they will not have the rhetorical credibility (*ethos*) to compel an audience. The good speaker must be guided, first, by knowledge and expertise, but also by her public position and her duties and obligation to the *polis*. The rhetor is speaking in favor of *the good*; the aim of rhetorical action is, ultimately, the good of the audience, the good of state, the good of the *polis*, some mutual good that serves as the ultimate aim of any speech, or piece of writing, or social media interaction. Classical rhetoric returns us to a notion that rhetoric should serve the social good. This aspect of our theory informs the entire book, but the argument is articulated most explicitly in Chapter 2.

In Chapter 3, we continue to build rhetoric theory for professional communication by examining an underappreciated purpose for professional communication: the *phatic purpose*. Phatic (from the Greek word *phanai*, to speak) refers to the rhetorical function of creating effective communication channels, keeping them open, and establishing ongoing, productive relationships. The core of the phatic function is the formation of an ethical relationship between rhetor and audience, and that relationship is very much based on ethos, the persuasive appeal having to do with the character and credibility of the rhetor. Chapter 3 identifies the sources of phatic theory in linguistics and rhetoric, making the case for seeing the phatic function as a primary purpose for human communication interaction, not a secondary or meaningless one; considers the cultural role of the phatic function, particularly in regards to global, multicultural interactions; and considers several types of professional communication contexts in which the phatic plays a special role.

Relationships are key to networks, and contemporary rhetoric theory, particularly digital rhetoric theory, provides us with a developed view of how *network interaction* changes the nature of professional communication. In Chapter 4 we develop a rhetoric network theory. Our approach owes much to actor-network theory, or ANT, as developed and described by Bruno Latour (2005). Using an ANT framework, we are not studying only writers or texts as isolated objects, or genres, or even the writer in the act of composing. A network frame looks at the larger rhetorical social scene: at the collections and interactions of various communicators and communications. Our rhetoric network theory focuses in particular on ethical interactions and relationships within networks.

Our work on network theory also draws on the valuable scholarship of digital rhetoric theorists working within the field of rhetoric/composition as well as communication and media theorists, many of whom are working across and between several different disciplines: Yochai Benkler (2006); Collin Brooke (2009); Douglas Eyman (2015); Jane Bennett (2010); Henry Jenkins, Sam Ford, and Joshua Green (2013); and Karine Nahon and Jeff Hemsley (2013). Our notion of network is also informed by work on the ecology of writing by scholars in the field of rhetoric/composition. Rather than focusing on individual objects (text, writer, audience), an ecological framework sees communication as occurring in a rich activity system that includes multivarious agents and objects. However, in contrast to the activity systems metaphor, an ecology metaphor emphasizes that the system is alive and dynamic, strives for harmony and balance (even in the presence of conflict and stress), and abuts and intersects with other ecologies (see, for example, Nardi & O'Day, 1999; Spinuzzi, 2008; Edbauer, 2005; Fleckenstein, Spinuzzi, Rickly, & Papper, 2008). We find this theory highly relevant and applicable to a network view of social media communication. Though we stick with the term *network* as our primary keyword, the ecological perspective on network interaction is highly germane to our thinking throughout this work.

To apply theory *to* practice and to build and adapt theory *from* practice, we conducted an IRB-approved qualitative study based on in-depth interviews with 21 business professionals holding a variety of positions. Table 1.1 provides a list of the professionals we interviewed.

The professionals we interviewed all worked in the United States for U.S. companies or non-profit organizations or for multinational corporations with significant operations in the U.S. However, a number of the people we interviewed worked in international, global divisions and communicated both internally and externally across geographic borders, and all interviewees frequently discussed communicating across cultural borders (individual, organizational, regional, etc., particularly given the diversity of many of the industries in which they worked). In our discussion of the cases we build from some of these interviews, we aim to develop the rhetorical situatedness of the case while also drawing out implications applicable and helpful for those working in other contexts.

Although we draw on interviews and cases in all of our chapters, Chapters 5, 6, and 7 are where we examine specific issues through more detailed case analysis. Chapter 5 addresses some key questions about business communication through the lens of networked, phatic, and ethical rhetorics: When and where are people *employees* and when are they *individuals* who have rights of privacy and expression beyond their work lives? When faced with employee use of social media how much should a company try to make employees conform to expectations, and how much should a company aim instead to change itself and its own corporate culture?

In Chapter 5 we present three cases of employee usage of social media and corporate response: (1) The well-publicized case of Justine Sacco, her ill-conceived tweet, her firing for that tweet, and how the company interpreted her role as a communicator. (2) A case drawn from our interview with Henry Truslow IV, the President and CEO of Sunbury Mills, who found himself faced with an employee blogging derogatory statements about a named company executive in a public blog. And (3) a case of a U.S. candy making company, World's Finest Chocolate, that is making the transition into social media, including changing how it interacts with former employees. Our analysis includes insights shared with us by the Director of Ethics for a multinational manufacturing company.

From employee use of social media and questions of public and private ethics, we move to corporate use of social media. In Chapter 6 we present a case analysis of one company, Taco Bell, drawing from our interview with Rob Poetsch, the Director of Public Affairs and Engagement, to examine the changing dynamic of company-customer relations. While recognizing the dangers of data mining, we also examine the potential of an ethic of listening for building more reciprocal and mutually beneficial relations. We ask, can a company really be a *friend*? Our answer is, it depends, but for Taco Bell's 20-something millennial audience, Taco Bell certainly seems to be perceived as a friend whom they are eager to engage with on social. The ways in which Taco Bell has re-organized the company so that consumer voices are shared *and acted upon* through the company showcase the potential for more integrated interaction in communication networks.

From corporate-customer interactions, we turn to examine human and non-human interactions. In Chapter 7 we look at two interconnected transformations in digital communications: the rise of human-like agents (e.g., Siri, Cortana) and efforts to create more and more intelligent communicating machines. We begin by considering the changing interface, and raising such questions as what does it mean for professional communication that we're now talking to our computers? How does that change not only what we do and how we do it but also the relationships and interactions we build (or don't build)? Can and should companies and business professionals hand over communications to bots?

The latter question we explore first by looking at the short and tragic life of Microsoft's Tay, who in the space of less than 24 hours turned into a Hitler-loving genocidal racist, sexist, and homophobe. Tay failed so spectacularly because she was thrown into the deep end of the social media pool without the background knowledge or ethical capacity she needed to swim at that end. But can a machine ever learn enough to talk in more open-ended conversations with humans? That's the question that leads us to consider Amy Ingram. Amy Ingram (and her brother Andrew) are the creation of Dennis Mortensen, the founder and CEO of x.ai. In his interview with us and in numerous venues, Mortensen described in detail how he and his team spent (and are still spending) years teaching and training Amy to do one task and one task only—schedule meetings. But unlike Siri who talks to you and anyone else who is around your phone, Amy talks to other people via email *on your behalf*, a machine talking to human for humans. The implications of this for professional communication in a digital age are fascinating and profound.

In Chapter 8 we consider changes needed in a number of areas. We return to examining the question of *Cui bono?* in relation to rhetoric theory and the ethos of technological agents. We consider the ways in which communication practices need to continue to change, within changing networks of regulations and laws. And we discuss how organizations, including universities, need to adapt structures and curricula for digital communications.

Conclusion

Digital technologies are now part of the networks of professional communication—and that changes everything. Digital technologies have changed the processes, products, and interactions of professional communication, shaping how, when, with whom, and where business professionals communicate. Professional communication today happens in diverse, digitally mediated ecologies where information circulates and recirculates in data-rich, multimodal social networks involving both human and, increasingly, non-human communicators.

We do not think it is an exaggeration to say that we are in the midst of a professional communication paradigm shift. Our fundamental approach to doing, teaching, thinking about professional communication—our fundamental framework for understanding and performing professional communication—needs to change accordingly. We need to update our old theories and develop new rhetoric theories attuned to the impact of digital, socially mediated, and networked technologies to help professional communicators (and those who educate them) succeed in the digital age.

Notes

1 What do we mean by *professional communication*? In the generic sense *professional communication* refers to any form of workplace-based communication—oral, written, digital, multimodal—including both internal communications (among members within an organization) and external communications (with business partners, clients, customers, the public at large). *Professional communication* also refers to a professional area of expertise—a field of practice as well as research and scholarship. Professional communicators are specialists in workplace communication, who hold positions in a variety of areas. The term *professional communication* is sometimes seen as synonymous with or as an umbrella term for: business communication or business writing; professional writing; and technical and scientific communication/writing. We aim for this book to be useful to a wide array of people who intersect with *professional communication* either as professionals who communicate, as professional communicators, or as educators of professional communication.

2 Floridi (2014) defined the four revolutions in terms of four particular scientific discoveries by European scientists: (1) the heliocentric revolution shaped by the work of Copernicus; (2) the evolutionary revolution based on the work of Charles Darwin; (3) the neuroscientific revolution from the work of Sigmund Freud; and (4) the information revolution marked by the work of Alan Turing. According to Floridi, what Turing did was "displace us from our privileged and unique position in the realm of logical reasoning, information processing, and smart behavior. We are no longer the undisputed masters of the infosphere" (p. 93), as we discuss in Chapter 7 when we analyze artificial intelligence and professional communication.

3 This phrase has been attributed both to P.T. Barnum, the 19th-century circus showman who founded the Barnum & Bailey Circus, and to Oscar Wilde, who famously said, "The only thing worse than being talked about is not being talked about" (from *The Picture of Dorian Gray*, 1890). More recently, Donald Trump noted that "all press is good press," a principle that may have guided his Twitter campaign in the presidential election of 2016 (qtd. in Kruse, 2016): the mainstream media dutifully reposted Trump's tweets, often framing them as examples of outrageous, unpresidential behavior, but in so doing helping the candidate dominate the news cycle. As one *Politico* analyst noted, "flagrant provocations and the attendant bad publicity genuinely don't matter, so long as they serve the goal of owning the spotlight" (Kruse, 2016).

Part I

Building a Rhetorical/Ethical Network Theory

2 Reconnecting Rhetoric and Ethics

When the popular media talk about the ethics of social media as pertains to business, they often collapse ethics within the categories of legal or criminal lapses, as major violations of law, policy, or regulation: for example, security lapses or "breach of confidentiality, conflicts of interest, [and] misuse of company resources" (Lunday, 2010). In other words, ethics refers to major and usually clear-cut violations. The term ethics is not typically used to refer to everyday interactions or behaviors.

We see ethics as everyday because we see ethics as fundamental to all human interaction. Ethics pertains to character and credibility and to issues of trust, responsibility, honesty, and integrity—what in rhetoric is called *ethos*, the character of the speaker or writer. In taking this perspective on rhetoric and ethics, we are calling upon a rhetoric tradition that views the two arts—rhetoric and ethics—not as separate arts belonging to separate disciplines, but rather as an inextricably intertwined set of concerns fundamental to all communication interaction (Johnstone, 1980; Porter, 1998; McKee & Porter, 2009).

The crux of our position can be summed up in Quintilian's 1st-century definition of rhetoric as "A good man [or, we would add, person, organization, or machine] speaking well" (*Institutio*, 12.1.1). In that definition, we find Quintilian's insistence that in order to achieve effective rhetoric, the rhetor must, first, be a virtuous person (*vir bonus*) or else they will not have the rhetorical credibility (ethos) to compel an audience. This same principle applies to the collective, to the corporation, and to the machines we program to speak/write for us: To be effective, a corporation, organization, or AI machine must also "speak well."

As we discuss in this chapter, business professionals, corporate leadership, and the very company itself are impacted—long-term and short, directly and indirectly—by whether they "speak well" in the Quintilian sense of considering one's ethical obligations to a greater community. The questions Why are you communicating, for what purpose, and for whose good? carry considerations of ethics. Within this view, rhetoric and ethics are necessarily interrelated, overlapping arts. The one can't work without the other. We think that this has always been true historically about rhetoric and ethics, but in the social age, it becomes especially obvious if there is a credibility gap between what you say and what you do.

Our historical review and analysis in this chapter reconnects rhetoric and ethics and also recovers a number of key terms from the Western rhetorical tradition—particularly, ethos and *kairos*—that are important for developing an integrated rhetorical/ethical network approach to professional communication.

Rhetoric and Ethics in the Classical Western Tradition

What is the relationship between rhetoric, as the art of communication, and ethics, as the art of determining the right, the true, and the good? This is a question that Plato raised in 4th-century BCE Athens (particularly in his dialogues *Gorgias* and *Phaedrus*), that the Roman rhetorician Quintilian addressed in his 1st-century CE opus *Institutio Oratoria*, and that the New Rhetoricians revisited in the 1950s and 1960s (particularly Kenneth Burke and Richard Weaver).

The classical Western tradition of rhetoric and philosophy—the ongoing battle, really, between rhetoric and philosophy—invested thousands of years to dividing ethics and rhetoric into distinct arts—to such an extent that our fundamental framework for thinking about the two things is badly bifurcated. Thus, we feel it is necessary to spend some time in this chapter showing, first, how the two arts became separated historically and, second, how and why they should be reconnected—that is, in showing how ethics always involves communication, and how communication is always invested with an ethical component. To make this reconnection we do not need to go outside the rhetorical tradition. Rather, we are calling upon an aspect of the rhetorical tradition that has often been neglected and subordinated—the tradition of sophistic and civic rhetoric, which offers us a more complex, integrated view of rhetoric and ethics useful for the digital age.

When communication theory addresses ethics it often does so by assuming that the ethical inquiry and decision-making are prior to and separate from communication. Ethics refers to behavior, actions, events, and the process of determining what is the right or just thing to do in a particular circumstance. Communication refers to a second stage: how you explain, defend, or present your ethical behavior. Figure 2.1 represents this relationship.

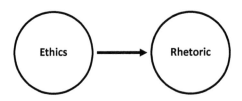

Figure 2.1 Traditional view of the relationship between ethics and rhetoric

We can see this view of ethics and rhetoric in the theory of Richard Weaver, whose 1953 work *The Ethics of Rhetoric* established this framework as authoritative. Weaver, one of the New Rhetoricians of the 1950s and 1960s, became known as the key spokesperson for the ethics of rhetoric—and yet his view positions rhetoric as secondary and subordinate to ethics.

In Weaver's framework, ethics (ideas about moral truth) come first, and then rhetoric's job is to represent those ideas in a clear and compelling manner. Rhetoric is certainly not unimportant in Weaver's model, but it serves a secondary and subordinate role, as the conveyor of moral truths established through other means (e.g., dialectic, revelation, scriptural exegesis, philosophical inquiry, scientific method). Ethics consists of universal, eternal truths that are not contingent upon culture or context. Ethics, in Weaver's view, and as Richard Johannesen (1978) explained, are "not to be altered by fads or the consensus of the moment" (p. 128) and the "ethicality of language is to be measured against a truth standard rooted in ideals, eternal values, essences, archetypes, and first principles" (p. 136). Rhetoric in this frame is purely instrumental rather than epistemic; it presents truth but does not contribute to the formation of knowledge or truth.

In this sense, Weaver's view of rhetoric is Platonic and separatist: seeing rhetoric as important and necessary for persuading the mob, but as secondary to dialectic, an inquiry method that is outside and prior to rhetoric, the method by which truly wise men (philosophers) come to understand the true, the just, the good, and then try to sell it, via rhetoric, to the ignorant mob or audience. In taking this stance, Weaver is calling upon a well-established rhetorical traditional—the Platonic tradition that sees rhetoric as secondary to philosophy, ethics, and dialectic inquiry.

But there is another, less well-established rhetoric tradition, one that we might call Isocratean or Quintilian, which offers us a different frame. As noted, the crux of our position can be summed up in Quintilian's definition of rhetoric as "the art of speaking well" (*Institutio*, 2.13.38) or "a good man speaking well" (*Institutio*, 12.1.1), *vir bonus dicendi peritus*. That definition insists that the rhetor must, first, be a virtuous person—*vir bonus*—or else they will not have the rhetorical credibility (ethos) to compel an audience (see Duffy, 2017). This different configuration is represented in Figure 2.2, which represents that though rhetoric and ethics are not the same—they do have distinct concerns—they are also strongly interrelated, and one is not prior to the other.

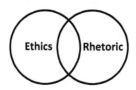

Figure 2.2 Sophistic view of rhetoric and ethics as intertwined arts

On a practical level, what does this diagram *mean*? Let's start by noting that "speaking well" carries a double meaning. First, it means speaking/writing effectively in the stylistic and aesthetic senses, as well as in the delivery sense: The rhetor crafts her language carefully, fluently, and concisely, choosing the appropriate words to convey the message and to instruct and compel the audience, and with a flair and nuance that also makes the message aesthetically pleasing, or as Cicero would say "delightful." The message is delivered at the right time and place, in a manner suitable to the message, the audience, and the setting. If it is a public speech, the rhetor speaks loud enough to be heard, but not too loud as to be shouting; she attends to questions of pace, rhythm, cadence, and emphasis in her speaking style; she uses visual supplements and/or gestures to complement and reinforce what she is saying. Everybody in professional communication understands that rhetoric has always been very much concerned with this manner of "speaking well." Rhetoric as delivery, style, voice, appearance, packaging.

The problem is that, historically, many have viewed rhetoric as concerned *only* with this—that is, as only the art of packaging, only concerned with style, arrangement, and delivery, "speaking well" only in the stylistic, aesthetic, and presentational senses. Hence the derogatory and popular notion of rhetoric as being "mere rhetoric": hollow and false, manipulative and misleading, lacking substance or truth. In other words, rhetoric as the opposite of ethics.

But "speaking well" has a second important meaning, a meaning that has not always been viewed as the purview of rhetoric but that is very much part of the classical rhetorical tradition, considered by Quintilian at some length (e.g., *Institutio*, 11.1.8–10) and by Cicero as well, in his 1st-century BCE *De Oratore*. The good speaker speaks with knowledge and expertise, and that expertise is very much guided by his/her public position and by her duties and obligation to the *polis*. The rhetor is speaking in favor of *the good*, of some good for the audience; the aim of the rhetorical act is, ultimately, the good of the audience, the good of state, or the good of the *polis*, some mutual good that is at the core of the speech. The "participation in civic life" is key to Quintilian's ideal for the orator (Walzer, 2003, p. 26; see also Walzer, 2006). The motivating force behind symbolic action is, or should be, a good, and so when rhetoric takes up the question of purpose—Why am I speaking or writing, or posting this YouTube video, or launching this marketing campaign?—it is interlaced with considerations of ethics.

We see this integrated view of the relationship between rhetoric and ethics emerge in some of the earliest works of sophistic rhetoric in 4th century BCE Athens.

According to Isocrates, the purpose of rhetoric is "the good of the state" and "the needs of the commonwealth" (*Panathenaicus*, 12). Isocrates' rhetoric emphasizes the importance of the character of the speaker as well as the good of the *polis*: "Mark you, the man who wishes to persuade people will not be negligent as to the matter of character; no, on the contrary, he will apply himself above all to establish a most honorable name among his fellow-citizens" (*Antidosis* 278). Isocrates has much to offer the modern communicator, a fact Charles Marsh (2013) recognized when he applied Isocrates' rhetoric framework in his book *Classical Rhetoric and Modern Public Relations: An Isocratean Model*.

In the Isocratean model, as opposed to the Platonic/Aristotelian model, rhetoric and ethics are very closely intertwined. Isocrates' focus is very much on the character of the rhetor, on building and maintaining productive relations (the phatic purpose), and on promoting justice. The ultimate goal of the rhetorical enterprise is social harmony, concord (*homonoia*), or what Aristotle in his 4th-century BCE teachings might call "the good of the state": "Isocrates linked rhetoric to the articulation of wise governance and civic conscience" (Poulakos, 2004, p. 75; see also de Romilly, 1958; Benoit, 1991). Put bluntly, your purpose as a rhetor—or as a public relations executive—is not only to persuade the audience to your message or to sell your product. Your purpose is to make society better, for everybody.

Socrates takes up this question in Plato's dialogue *Gorgias*, insisting that rhetoric must be about more than merely "flattery" or "base mob oratory" (as so he argues with Callicles). Socrates asks the very excellent question: Do orators speak "with a view to what is best, with the single aim of making the citizens as good as possible?"—or, like poets, do they sacrifice the common weal "to their own personal interest, behaving to those assemblies as to children, trying merely to gratify them?" (Plato, *Gorgias* 502e). That is *the* key question about rhetoric's relationship with ethics: Is rhetoric the false art of treating an audience like children in order to sway them, appealing to the base emotions of the mob, engaging in false flattery to secure a persuasive aim? In *Gorgias*, Plato leaves the question hanging—much to rhetoric's historical disadvantage—but Quintilian answers the question in *Institutio Oratoria*: No, these are the characteristics of a bad rhetoric, and do not represent how the art itself should be defined.

Vir bonus was central to Cicero's ethics of rhetoric, as well as Quintilian's. Cicero did not use the term ethos, but he did argue the importance of *dignitas*, "an idealistic quality associated with virtuous conduct and pristine values ... [and] entailing duty toward justice and loyalty to the State," and of *auctoritas*, or "the forceful weight of an individual's personality ... a type of long-range *ethos* ... a sustained reputation for public distinction and service" (Enos & McClaran, 1978, p. 102). In all of these frameworks—Isocrates', Cicero's, Quintilian's—there is a very tight relationship between the speech, the character of the speaker, and the intended outcome of the speech. Rhetoric is not just about the text and presentation of the speech.

As Richard Enos and Jeanne McClaran (1978) pointed out, the *vir bonus* ideal could easily degrade, slipping from its emphasis on genuine character and integrity to the appearance of such. However, the ideal for the orator was not only to seem to be a good person, but to actually be one: It is in that linkage between appearance and being, between *seem* and *be*, that credibility lies. As Quintilian puts it, "Eloquence requires the speaker to be a man of good character and of pleasing manners. The virtues which he ought to praise, if possible, in his client, he should possess or be thought to possess himself" (*Institutio*, 6.2.18). The key qualities of the effective rhetorician are wisdom (*phronesis* or *prudentia*), honesty, and integrity, both an understanding of "the good" and a primary intention to have the good of the *polis* as the aim of discourse. Thus, for Quintilian, the effective rhetor has a practical understanding of both politics and ethics.

Now it is certainly true that rhetoric can be used for deception, that rhetoric can mislead audiences, and that rhetoric can be used "to generate arguments on behalf of falsehood as well as truth" (Walzer, 2003, p. 32). Certainly, just as there can be bad doctors who do harmful things to patients, or scientists who do bad science, or poets who make bad poetry, there can be bad uses of rhetoric and bad rhetoricians. But, Quintilian wisely insists, just as we do not define the field of medicine by what bad doctors do, nor the field of poetry by bad poets, neither should we define the field of rhetoric by its false uses.

This framework we are recovering and espousing is not without controversy, nor without its detractors throughout the history of rhetoric. In fact, seeing rhetoric and ethics as interrelated and overlapping is traditionally *not* how the two arts have been configured, as our discussion of Richard Weaver's theory shows. Our purpose here is not to track the entire history of this split, but we will mention two notable and influential statements.

One place where this division is most strongly articulated and promoted is in Peter Ramus' influential treatise *Arguments in Rhetoric Against Quintilian* (1549/1986). Ramus was incensed about what he viewed as Quintilian's confusion between ethics and rhetoric (and also between logic and rhetoric). The art of thinking, he argued, should not be confused with the art of speaking or presenting; Quintilian, in Ramus' perspective, was muddled. "We should distinguish the art of rhetoric from the other arts, and make it a single one of the liberal arts, not a confused mixture of all arts [...] rhetoric is not an art which explains all the virtual qualities of character. Moral philosophers speculate appropriately and judiciously on the numerous problems involving the moral virtues [...] Quintilian's definition of the orator is as a result defective."

The sources of this division between rhetoric and ethics lie not with Ramus, but with earlier discussions about the proper scope of rhetoric, beginning probably with Plato's *Gorgias*. We can also see this split articulated in Augustine's *De Doctrina Christiana*, an influential 4th-century CE treatise distinguishing between *ars inuendi* and *ars proferendi*: the art of invention (Augustine was talking about scriptural interpretation) and the art of presentation. In Augustine's framework, the prelate must first interpret scripture and determine what is the lesson to be learned and the proper behavior to follow—that is the art of invention, which Augustine treats in Books I–III of *De Doctrina*. Then the prelate determines how best to preach the gospel to sinners and to the congregation—that is the art of rhetoric, which is an art of presentation and style, packaging the scriptural truth for presentation to different audiences (a discussion that Augustine published later, as Book IV of *De Doctrina*). Here we see the strict division represented in Figure 2.1: ethics (or knowledge or scriptural exegesis) comes first, rhetoric comes second.

Thus, the process of determining what is right, true, and just (ethics) is disconnected from preaching it or presenting it (rhetoric). Truth/ knowledge is discovered through some method prior to rhetoric— whether that method is scriptural exegesis, philosophical dialectic, scientific observation, data aggregation and analysis, or logic. You bring rhetoric to the scene later, as the instrumental means for presenting truth/ knowledge. There is the split between truth and presentation, between content and packaging.

For Augustine, Ramus, Weaver—and for many others adherents of this tradition—rhetoric is an art concerned *only* with style, arrangement, and delivery, "speaking well" only in the stylistic, aesthetic, and presentational senses. Ramus' insistence on that division between rhetoric and ethics of course became instantiated in the early configuration of the two disciplines and ultimately in the departmental structure of the modern university: Ethics is the job of the Philosophy Department, while the Department of English or the Department of Writing and Rhetoric attends to matters of aesthetics and style, or "writing" in the limited sense. We live with this distinction in the very structural framework of the modern Western university.

Cicero blamed Socrates/Plato for this division, presciently addressing Peter Ramus's and Richard Weaver's arguments:

> Socrates [Plato] separated the science of wise thinking from that of elegant speaking, though in reality they are closely linked together. [...] This is the source from which has sprung the undoubtedly absurd and unprofitable and reprehensible severance between the tongue and the brain, leading to our having one set of professors to teach us to think and another to teach us to speak.
>
> (*De Oratore*, 3.16.60–61)

We agree with Cicero. Dividing rhetoric and ethics is, in Cicero's words, an "absurd and unprofitable and reprehensible severance," one that needs to be challenged if we are going to have a useful, productive art of professional communication that combines elegant speaking (or writing) with moral thinking. Given the complexities of communication in a digital age, we need an integrated art of rhetoric and ethics more than ever.

Ethos

Central to an integrated view of rhetoric and ethics is the rhetorical appeal of ethos. Ethos—one of the three persuasive appeals discussed by Aristotle in *On Rhetoric*, along with logos (the appeal to reason) and pathos (the appeal to emotions)—was the appeal related to the credibility of the speaker: that is, to "the speaker's securing the trust and respect of an audience by representing him- or herself in the speech as knowledgeable, intelligent, competent, and concerned for the welfare of the audience" (Cherry, 1988, p. 256).

Ethos has long enjoyed a strong emphasis in professional communication theory and practice—though sometimes the ethical appeal has been disconnected from the qualities that, according to Aristotle, comprise the appeal. Aristotle identifies three particular qualities that comprise an effective ethos: "For the orator to produce conviction three qualities are necessary: good sense [*phronesis*, or practical wisdom], virtue [*arête*], goodwill [*eunoia*]" (*Rhetoric*, 2.1.5). For communicators to be effective, they must be viewed as credible, honest, just, wise, virtuous, and concerned with the goodwill of the audience. Ethos is one key rhetorical principle, though not the only one, where the concerns of rhetoric and ethics very much overlap and merge.

The focus on ethos carried into Roman rhetoric. Securing of good will (*conciliare*) is fundamental to Cicero's conception of ethos and of rhetoric overall (Enos, 2008, p. 127). The speaker or writer will not succeed in persuading the audience unless he (in Roman rhetoric it was "he") can demonstrate and embody excellent character, meaning primarily "an individual who was willing to act on ethical principles for the sake of justice" (Enos, 2008, p. 131).

The orator who hoped to persuade the audience should exhibit the quality of *eunoia* toward the audience, particularly at the beginning or end of a speech. What became known as the *captatio benevolentiae* ("capturing goodwill") was enshrined in Cicero's rhetoric as an important technique for building social and political alliances. *Benevolentia* included qualities and practices such as being polite, exhibiting a friendly disposition, being magnanimous, showing respect, and complimenting one's audience or interlocutor. And the place in a speech where this would be most effective was the *exordium*, the introduction, where, according to Cicero, the audience was to be made "attentive, docile, and well disposed" (*De Inventione*, 1.15; Donnelly, 1912). The *captatio* was secured through an appropriately respectful salutation and in the opening sentence of the speech or letter, where the rhetor expressed goodwill toward the addressee.

Cicero's *captatio benevolentiae* became a standard rhetorical technique in the medieval *ars dictaminis*, the art of letter writing (Murphy, 1974; Hildebrandt, 1988; Perelman, 1991). The Benedictine monk Alberic of Monte Cassino wrote about the importance of this rhetorical strategy in the late 11th century (Murphy, 1974, pp. 203–204). Many years later, this technique emerged in business communication in the form of the "positive buffer," the technique recommended for the genre of the "bad news message" as a way to buffer or mitigate unwanted news or information.

The technique works this way: Begin your letter (or email, video, or blog post) with what Cicero or Alberic would call a *captatio benevolentiae*, or expression of good will toward your audience. If you are giving someone bad news—alas, you did not get the job you applied for, we are denying your loan application—begin with a positive or encouraging expression, then tell them the bad news, then end with another positive buffer of some kind. Even very brief messages can follow this approach (see Table 2.1).

There are good ways and bad ways to do *captatio benevolentiae*. Some treatments can make the *captatio* overly mechanical or prescriptive (Murphy, 1974), in which case the *captatio* degrades from a general technique of persuasive ethos (a *techne*) into a prescriptive formula. That

Table 2.1 Structure of the classic bad news letter (applied to job rejection)

Section of Letter	Letter Content	Ethical Purpose (eunoia)
Positive buffer (+)	"Unfortunately at this time we have only one opening"	To show concern for audience, you wish the outcome had been different
Bad news (−)	"We are not able to offer you a position at this time"	To tell the reader the truth, even if the news is unwanted
Positive buffer (+)	"But we hope that you will consider applying again in the future"	To be encouraging about future possibilities, to maintain positive relations going forward
	"We thank you for your interest in our company and for taking the time to apply"	

is, instead of being treated as a quality of the speaker/writer and as a general principle to be artfully imitated (but not copied), the *captatio* became installed as a canned piece of discourse.

According to Murphy (1974), Hugh of Bologna's medieval treatise on letter writing is an example of the degraded kind of *techne*, an example of the art shifting away from classical *inventio* toward a kind of prescriptive *dispositio*, not merely providing "illustrative examples" but instead offering "phrases even paragraphs [...] to be used verbatim. [...] These are not suggestions for rhetorical invention, but are instead models for copying" (pp. 217–218). Murphy goes on to describe this as a shift from *inventio* to *reproductio*, from inventive art to copying—or at least from art to formulaic strategy. Rhetoric is supposed to be an art (*techne*), but, as demonstrated in this instance, can sometimes devolve into mechanical, formulaic strategy (*tribe*). This issue of *techne* (an art that is sensitive to context and audience) versus *tribe* (mechanical formula or rote copying) will come up again in our discussion in Chapter 7 of whether AI bots can do our communicating for us.

At this point we can see the ethical problem that has always plagued rhetoric, one that Plato noticed and abhorred: If *eunoia* is viewed as required pieces of text without (necessarily) an embodied connection to the rhetor, then we have an appearance versus reality gap, a credibility gap between the ethos of the text and the actual embodied ethos of the rhetor. The problem with Aristotle's rhetorical system, according to many scholars, is that it does not adequately address this problem: It "invites pretense and dissembling. [Aristotle's] emphasis on feigned *ethos* raises serious moral questions about his notion of ethical appeal" (Yoos, 1979; p. 42; Johnson, 1984). If the speaker is using *benevolentia* as only a rhetorical technique for persuasion, isn't that insincere? Isn't that false flattery? Isn't that manipulating the audience? The answer to that is, Yes, yes, and yes—*if* the speaker is using such strategies *merely* as a rhetorical technique to achieve his or her ends.

But the ethical problem of the ethical appeal—is it "feigned" or is it sincere?—melts away to some extent if we come back to our point that rhetoric is not an isolated or autonomous art but has an intimate relationship with the arts of ethics (and politics, too). The concept of ethos in Aristotle's *Rhetoric* is closely aligned with character and virtue as discussed in his *Nicomachean Ethics*, as both Christopher Johnstone (1980) and Porter (1998) have pointed out. Aristotle's treatment of persuasion in *Rhetoric* viewed *by itself* does suggest "a view of rhetoric that permits manipulation of the emotions in affecting judgment. This interpretation, however, fails to view the *Rhetoric* in the context of its companion work, the *Nicomachean Ethics*" (Johnstone, 1980, p. 9). When properly considered, "Aristotle's theory of rhetoric is grounded in and guided by the ethical principles developed in his moral theory" (Johnstone, 1980, p. 11). Here again, as in Quintilian's *Institutio Oratoria*, we see the importance of a linkage between rhetoric and ethics.

In short, Aristotle's *Rhetoric* needs to be read as linked with his key treatise on ethics, *Nicomachean Ethics*—and also, we would add, with his treatise *Politics*. The point of overlap between rhetoric and ethics has to do with the purpose of communication: Ultimately, why are we doing it? The ultimate aim of the speaker/writer must be the good of the *polis*, or what we might rephrase as the good of the audience (Porter, 1998, p. 37). In other words, goodwill cannot merely be a piece of canned text you drop mechanically into the *exordium*. It is, or should be, a quality rhetors possess, embody, and exhibit to others through the totality of their rhetorical actions.

It is important to note that in Book 2 of Aristotle's *Rhetoric*, ethos is not represented as just one thing. Rather Aristotle emphasizes three key qualities of ethos: *phronesis* (wisdom or practical judgment), *arete* (virtue, character), and *eunoia* (goodwill toward audience). Now it seems to us that many businesses try to achieve their ethos entirely on *eunoia* rather than also thinking about and practicing *arete*. In other words, the key here is that the goodwill you express must also be backed up by virtuous action and behavior. It's not enough simply to say you care about the community while you're dumping toxic chemicals in your neighbor's back yard. What you say and what you do—the totality of your symbolic actions—need to be consistent.

When Roger Goodell, President of the NFL, said that the NFL would crack down hard on players who committed acts of domestic violence—and then suspended Baltimore Ravens running back Ray Rice for only two games for knocking out his fiancé—there was a very clear disconnect between corporate words and corporate action. This is an example of what we mean by an inconsistency between *eunoia* and *arete*. This was rightly labeled hypocrisy, and, amid many other effects (such as signaling to domestic violence victims that crimes against them aren't that serious), it has the effect of harming one's ethos—in this case, Roger Goodell's individual ethos as well as the NFL's corporate image. Corporate ethics has to be more than "window dressing," as *Forbes* columnist Dina Medland (2015) puts it: "If you educate your employees in the best standards of behavior without a visible follow through in better business practices, all you teach them is to have absolutely no respect for your business." What you teach is that ethics is good PR, but that bottom-line financial outcomes matter more.

In short, within Isocrates' or Quintilian's conceptions, the rhetor is not supposed to fake being a virtuous speaker, the rhetor is supposed to be one—though classical rhetoricians like Cicero and Quintilian had to admit that rhetors could be insincere. (Of course.) But that was not how the art was defined or how it was supposed to work. Virtue must be integral to the art of rhetoric—a point that Quintilian emphasizes in Books 2.20, 12.1, and 12.2 of *Institutio Oratoria*.

Business research affirms the importance of corporate ethos overall: "Distrust has quantifiable impact on business performance [...] 63% of people who lack trust in an organization will refuse to buy products and services from it, 37% have shared negative comments online, and 18% have sold shares in a company they didn't trust" (Etlinger, 2015b, p. 9). Perhaps even more so in the social media age, consumers are especially quick to react negatively if they feel a company is acting hypocritically—as happened, for example, in 2012 to McDonald's when it launched the hashtag #McDStories (see Thomases, 2012; Lyon & Montgomery, 2013).

Certainly, a rhetorical strategy can always degrade into a thoughtless formula rather than a sincere expression—but the point of using a rhetorical strategy like *eunoia* or *benevolentia* is twofold: (1) To build concern for audience into your own thinking and feeling. Even if it is a formula, by repeating the formula you embrace and absorb the ethos it represents. You *become* that which you practice, imitate, repeat. (2) To show that you care enough about the audience to use the technique. Maybe you are "only" being polite, but the point is precisely that—you are taking the trouble to be polite, you are genuinely interested in maintaining good relations—and that is really the point being communicated.

The other way to look at ethos and *eunoia* is to see the ethical appeal as ethically and pedagogically formative: In the process of learning, practicing, and using the technique, the rhetor *becomes* the person who has goodwill toward audience. That is, repeatedly practicing goodwill until it achieves the status of *habitus* has the effect of instilling in the rhetor the quality of goodwill. Ethos is created in individual, discrete rhetorical events—but over time these discrete events have a collective force, creating a long-term ethos: "These proofs carry over into a rhetor's reputation and can be brought to subsequent rhetorical acts" (Enos, 2008). They constitute a "developing ethos," or what we might think of as an ongoing reputation or, in business, a corporate brand or image.

Would we say that someone who is polite to strangers is insincere? Yes, if we happen to know that the person is usually rude and just happens to be faking it to secure some benefit. But no, not if we know from experience that the person is always that way, if the person is being polite because they have learned to be polite, because they have learned that is what you are supposed to do, and because they have embraced that as their fundamental ethos in interacting with strangers. In such a case we would say, rather, that politeness is who the person *is*: she or he is *a polite person*, it is embodied in their character. That is, the virtue lies in the person or in the corporate brand; it is not merely a technique they are using in their discourse to manipulate an audience and secure an advantage.[1]

Two other aspects of ethos are important for our analysis in later chapters: ethos as collective, and ethos as complex and variable. First the collective: Ethos can refer to corporate image or identity as well as to individual identity. Every company has an ethos: that is, an image or identity that it projects to the public and becomes the face of the company. When an employee's actions hurt the company image, or when the company engages in behaviors that violate the social trust or that come across as hypocritical, that ethos is harmed—and the company must take steps to repair both their ethos and their relationship with the public.

Ethos also refers to identity or role as established through communication interactions, and this identity or role can change over time and in different rhetorical circumstances: In short, ethos is complex and variable. The ethos you have in one situation, for one kind of audience might be different than the one you have for another situation and audience. Your ethos as a private citizen, as a friend or family member, might be very different from your ethos as an employee of a company. Who you are as a private citizen is different from who you are as a spokesperson for your company, and yet the difference between these roles can become blurred, even indistinguishable, especially with social media usage, as we discuss in Chapter 5.

Changes in identity are also connected with uses of mobile technology. Because the cell phone is typically carried by the user and is, in a sense, attached to the user, almost becoming an embodied part of the user, its use and function can shift with the user's shifting identity. Or, conversely, the cell phone can prompt the user to shift identities. In Huatong Sun's (2009) study of mobile technology users, she described her close observation of one user ("Emma") during one four-hour period: "Emma was observed busily shifting her identities between a lover, a student, a niece, a common friend, and a close friend using a range of technologies. [...] Technologies make the emergence and co-presence of these identities in one locale possible, [...] her cell phone becomes a hub for her important relationships as well as a site for her various identities" (Sun, 2009, p. 257).

Kairos

Kairos, or timing, is another important concept from classical sophistic rhetoric that we want to recover for application to professional communication in the digital age—especially in regards to its connections with ethics. *Kairos* was not a principle emphasized in the Platonic philosophical tradition, which tended to focus on universals and timeless truths. But it was a key principle for the Sophists, and is certainly a principle relevant and important to understanding the ethics of digital rhetoric.

In rhetoric, *kairos* is typically defined as "the right time" but a better definition might be "opportune moment" (Poulakos, 1983; Kinneavy, 1986):

that is, the best time to speak or to write, or the opportune time to persuade an audience, or knowing what to say and how to say given the rhetorical situation (Kinneavy, 1986). *Kairos* in the rhetorical sense certainly includes considerations of chronological time—how quickly a company, for example, responds to a customer query. But *kairos* also includes the more contextual moment of speaking as well.

Kairos needs to be understood as *a form of knowledge* essential to rhetoric. Thomas Rickert (2013) described *kairos* as "a matter of making appropriate or fitting use of the opportunities that arise, whether they stem from the temporality of the situation or the governing proprieties of the culture in which the situation emerges" (p. 80). But as John Smith (2002) pointed out, there is an important difference between *chronos* (chronological time) and *kairos*: *kairos* refers to "a qualitative character of time" (p. 47) that pertains more to knowledge about cultural and historical moments that are imbued with audience attitudes, feelings, and emotions and that are very often tied to places and locations and to cultural memories, stories, and events.

For example: If a standup comedian in Cleveland refers to "burning river," that is an allusion with deep historical meaning for Clevelanders over age 50, a reference to the 1969 Cuyahoga River fire. The reference would likely draw a laugh in Cleveland, at least with older audiences, but likely be meaningless in another city.

On the other hand, if that comedian in Cleveland uses the phrase "toy gun" in a joke, that is decidedly not funny and will likely result in boos, or worse, because, whether or not the comedian knows it, in Cleveland that phrase is going to be viewed as a tasteless reference to the police shooting of 12-year-old Tamir Rice, a boy who in 2014 was shot in a Cleveland park playing with a toy gun. That event, a deeply painful and emotional one for Clevelanders, is not to be joked about—and even if the comedian's reference is unintentional, it is a serious misstep, a failure of kairotic knowledge. Knowing the audience's mood, attitude, state of mind, as well as knowing what the audience knows and doesn't know, and what its collective values are, is critical to effective communications.

What we see on social media, again and again, are missteps in the form of companies failing to acknowledge *kairos* as an important form of communication knowledge related to *ethos* and *eunoia* as well as to timing, appropriateness, audience, location, and culture. Ford's use of new vehicle images in its Boston Marathon tweet discussed in Chapter 1 constitutes a failure of *kairos* (in the sense of cultural moment) and a failure to understand community values.

The speed at which events and reactions to events happen online means that cultural attitudes, values, and emotions can shift, move, and morph rapidly. The crowd can assemble quickly (or disperse), become emotionally charged, shift allegiances, change attitudes, become hostile or friendly, an ally or enemy, all in the course of a few hours. What is deemed appropriate or harmless at one moment can become offensive, racist, or unjust in the next. The pre-programmed option of many social media management platforms—that allow for the composition of posts days and weeks before release on set dates (what some in the field call, disparagingly, the "set it and forget it" option)—can lead to problems because a post that seems appropriate one day may not be appropriate upon release. For example, the Twitter account of the *American Rifleman*, the magazine of the National Rifle Association (NRA), released a tweet on its account @NRA_Rifleman "Good morning, shooters. Happy Friday! Weekend plans?" on the morning after the movie theater shooting in Aurora, Colorado, in 2012 that killed 12 people and injured 70 others. Not surprisingly, this tweet was not well received.

Companies who maintain a strong social media presence have come to recognize the importance of virtual vigilance and attentiveness to these moments, and quick response to and intervention in crisis situations (e.g., negative messages going viral, trending). Given the centrality of *kairos* for effective and ethical communications (it is a key part of the network we describe in Chapter 4) and given the attentiveness to changing rhetorical situations *kairos* calls for, we wonder if artificial intelligent agents, AI chat bots and the like, can ever achieve the needed level of kairotic knowledge and audience awareness to communicate effectively. That is the challenge for AI's algorithmic programming, as we discuss in Chapter 7.

Kairos is an elusive concept because it seems to be one that is both unteachable and beyond the scope of rational analysis or prediction: How do you teach "good timing" or understanding when is the right time, moment, and place? We suggest, though, that the concept is amenable to analysis, and that it is essential to effective writing and communication on the internet. It requires attention to and deep attunement to audience, to community, to cultural Zeitgeist, and to the changing spirit, values, images, and attitudes of a particular time and place.

Kairos emphasizes the importance of time as a factor of rhetorical interaction. Interaction is fluid, it operates in a flow.[2] And, importantly for our purposes, *kairos* needs to be understood as a *form of knowledge* shaping how one views, understands, and experiences events—and as a *form of ethical knowledge*, insofar as *kairos* also involves cultural attitudes and values. Sensitivity to *kairos* is key to a rhetorical understanding of communicative events, especially ethically problematic social media events, and is a vital component of our rhetorical frame for understanding professional communication in the digital age.

Treatment of Ethics in Business Communication

What emerges then from our recovery of this sophistic, or Isocratean, or Quintilian view of rhetoric, for contemporary professional communication, is clear: You establish your credibility and reputation over time and through consistency of your public *ethos* or *auctoritas*. Your speech, your writing, your professional profiles, your posts, your YouTube videos, your tweets, your social media policies, your stated intentions, all your corporate communications must be consistent with your actions. And you must have the good of the audience, of the public, the state, the collective as your ultimate purpose.

We don't see very much business communication research addressing this important question about ethical motivation—*why* are you communicating?—that we see as fundamental to rhetoric and to communication. Ethics is just not discussed very much, at least not in business communication research.

Why not? Well, the terms ethics and rhetoric aren't hip. And they also have a long and troubled history, as we have seen—messy, complicated, maybe even embarrassing for purposes of business consulting. (Would you rather hire a business consultant who identifies her expertise as *rhetoric*, or an expert in *organizational communication research*?) This type of research is tapping into a different methodological and disciplinary paradigm, from communication theory, particularly organizational communication. And also—here we are hypothesizing—this disciplinary approach associates such terms with the outdated and now irrelevant humanities curriculum of Cicero and Quintilian. These articles are based on a social science approach toward communication, one that rejects a humanities approach, which rhetoric historically has been.

Business communication theorist Cynthia King (2010) recognized this problem, acknowledging that "those of us [in business communication] who study rhetoric are familiar with the fight to explain its rich theoretical traditions" (69). Like King, we would argue that these concepts still have continuing relevance and traction, and not simply as important terms but as interrelated concepts—as a coherent system for thinking about communication that is important to preserve. What is particularly important is maintaining the connection between rhetoric and ethics.

It is important to analyze and understand what motivates an act of business communication in the first place? *Why*, for example, are you writing that e-mail or leaving that voice mail or engaging the public on your Twitter site? Your motivation (purpose) vis-à-vis your audience's motivation is critical to understanding the discursive context and how you should approach it as a writer or speaker. What do you hope to achieve? What value lies in it for your audience? These are fundamental rhetoric questions that are also fundamental ethics questions: What is the "good" that a communication action aims for? Is that a "good" for the audience as well? What lies at the heart of any communication is a purpose connected with an ethical determination.

Don't get us wrong. We acknowledge that business is very definitely concerned about ethics. *The Journal of Business Ethics*, for instance, which publishes approximately 20 issues per year, thoroughly treats issues of business ethics. Ethics is not unhip for business, it is a very real and pressing concern. Ethics is certainly an important concern, but, our point is, it has been disconnected from business *communication*. The dominant frame in place is what we represent in Figure 2.1. Ethics is viewed as being about *behavior* rather than about *communication*. Business ethics takes up the question of what is the right ethical *action* or *behavior* to take, while business communication takes up the question of what is effective or ineffective *communication*. In short, the view of communication predominant in the field is instrumental (and Augustinian and Ramistic and Weaverean) and bifurcated: It sees rhetoric as the *saying*, not the *doing*; it sees ethics as about determining the right course of action while rhetoric is concerned with presenting it, arguing for it, and selling it. We need to change that framework.

Conclusion

Our goal in this chapter has been to put rhetoric and ethics back together: Thus, our book's subtitle: "a rhetorical and ethical approach." We have also wanted to rescue two key principles—*ethos, kairos*—that are critical to this merged approach. (These concepts and this overall rhetorical/ethical framework will be key to our discussions of professional communication cases and practices in later chapters.) In order to advance this approach, though, we needed to argue with the dominant Western rhetorical tradition, to change the dominant narrative, and to recover a lost, neglected view of the relationship between rhetoric and ethics, a view that we term sophistic and civic.

Our approach sees rhetoric as thoroughly enmeshed with ethics. We are not saying that ethics is a subfield of rhetoric (or, conversely, that rhetoric is a subfield of ethics), or that the one art precedes the other chronologically (i.e., you determine "the good" first, and then you persuade others to it). No, we are not seeing this from the standpoint of an Aristotelian tree diagram, nor from the standpoint of a chronological process (ethics first, rhetoric second). Rather, we are saying something more nuanced (Ramus would call it "a confused mixture"), something closer to how Quintilian configures the relationship, what we represent in Figure 2.2: Rhetoric and ethics are necessarily interrelated, overlapping arts; one can't work without the other, and they work conjointly. "Speaking well" includes one's ethical obligations as a citizen, to the community, to the good of the *polis*. If you're going to do rhetoric you necessarily have to put purpose and goals vis-à-vis audience on the table—and that brings you, inevitably, to ethics.

Notes

1 In addressing the problem of insincere rhetoric, Yumeng Liu (2004) emphasized the importance in Chinese historical rhetoric of the integration of one's
character and one's words—that is, consistency between the rhetor's pro-
jected ethos and the actual quality of the rhetor's character.
2 According to Plato, it was the 5–6th-century BCE Greek philosopher
Heraclitus of Ephesus who said, "You could not step twice into the same
river" (Plato, *Cratylus* 402a)—meaning that the world is in a constant state
of flux, and that certainly applies to social media interaction.

3 Ethics, Culture, and Phatic Communication

If we reconfigure professional communication as necessarily including issues of ethics and ethos, trust and credibility, goodwill for audience, and concern for the public good, then we have to reconfigure our rhetorical framework for talking about professional communication. What is the *purpose* of professional communication? For example, in business is it merely to *persuade* others—clients, business partners, potential consumers, the public—to purchase products and services? Quintilian was alert to the problem of defining rhetoric only as persuasion: Rhetoric must have an aim above and beyond mere persuasion because persuasion begs a question: Persuasion toward what end, and for whose good? A moral rhetoric, a true art, must have some "good," benefit, or value as its aim—and not just the self-serving good for the rhetor.

Traditionally, business and professional communication research and pedagogy has emphasized two main purposes for communication: the informative purpose or the persuasive purpose (or some combination of both). The foundations for this can be seen in the rhetorical frame of the Shannon-Weaver model (Shannon, 1948; Weaver & Shannon, 1963), which views communication primarily as the one-way transmission of information, encapsulated in a message, from the knowledgeable transmitter (encoder) to the uninformed receiver (decoder or audience)—or as the one-way effort at persuasion (see Figure 3.1).

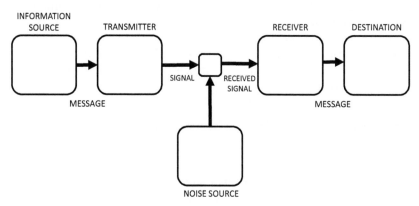

Figure 3.1 The Shannon-Weaver linear model of communication

This model has been often and soundly critiqued for many things, including for being simplistically one way, for failing to acknowledge and respect the contributions of the audience to knowledge construction, for underestimating the role of rhetorical context, and for being dismissive if not potentially manipulative of the audience. However, as George Lakoff and Mark Johnson (1980) pointed out, this one-way pipeline model is deeply embedded into everyday metaphors and ways of talking about communication and so has incredible power and influence over how we think. The one-way transmission model is, despite the many critiques, very much embedded into professional communication practice, as shown, for example, by traditional market research analysis where you analyze the audience only in order to better persuade it.

But there is another purpose to consider as well, one more in alignment with a sophistic theory of rhetoric and ethics—the phatic purpose. *Phatic* (from the Greek word *phanai*, to speak) refers to the rhetorical function of creating effective two-way communication channels to establish and maintain productive relationships, which are especially important in the age of digital rhetoric, social media, and global intercultural exchange (Miller, 2008; Bilandzic et al., 2009; Wang, Tucker, & Rihll, 2011).

What is the phatic function? Phatic refers to the purpose of building communication channels, keeping them open, and establishing ongoing and fruitful relationships (Porter, 2017). A phatic model posits a different end goal for discursive action—goodwill, trust, cooperation, partnership, harmony—and assumes a different kind of relationship, a dialogic and mutually beneficial relationship, between the company and its clients and customers. The core of the phatic function is the formation of an ethical relationship between rhetor and audience, and that relationship is very much based on ethos, the persuasive appeal having to do with the character and credibility of the rhetor.

In this chapter, we first define what is meant by *phatic communication* and the *phatic purpose* and consider its role in maintaining and building ethical relationships, a key purpose for professional communication. In developing this discussion, we consider questions of intercultural communication, which are particularly important given the global networks of communication enabled more easily and more ubiquitously by digital communications. Finally, we discuss several digital professional communication genres and venues for which the phatic function serves an especially vital role.

Historical Sources of Phatic Theory in Linguistics and Rhetoric

The concept of phatic communication was first articulated by the cultural anthropologist Bronislaw Malinowski (1923), who saw the phatic function as a feature of primitive languages in the respect that the peoples he studied used language, as he put it, as a mode of action as opposed to using language "to convey meaning" (p. 315). Malinowski saw "phatic communion" as a feature of primitive discourse, serving the end of "mere need of companionship."

> We use language exactly as savages do and our talk becomes the "phatic communion," which serves to establish personal bonds of union between people brought together by the mere need of companionship and does not serve any purpose of communicating ideas.
> (Malinowski, 1923, p. 316)

Malinowski sets the tone and framework for future discussions that view communication primarily in terms of a transmission or pipeline metaphor: The primary purpose of language is to convey meaning (information). And within that framework, phatic communication is non-relevant noise that potentially disturbs the clear transmission of information. Malinowski is clearly working in the racist, colonialist frame of his era, one dismissive of ancient, non-European people ("savages") and their communicative ethics ("the mere need for companionship"). He did not recognize, for example, how the African people of Kemet in ancient Egypt pursued a Maatian ethic that shaped their entire society, including communications, and how the values of community shape the discursive approaches to cultures throughout Africa today (Lehman, 2001; Karenga, 2004). Historical and contemporary cultures around the globe have values that have been and are shaped by the phatic function.

But in the Western tradition that has shaped so much of Euro-American professional communication practices, subsequent discussions of the phatic function in cultural anthropology and sociolinguistics[1] largely follow Malinowski's lead: The phatic function must be acknowledged, but is not all that important. At best, the phatic function is a secondary, supportive function of language, but it is not a primary purpose. But if an informative or persuasive communication is a means to some end, then what is the end exactly? Here is where discourse theory meets ethics: To ask the question, Why are we communicating? is to posit some end or outcome outside and beyond the communication itself.[2] It is that purpose outside discourse that Malinowski's linguistic framework neglects.

Not all linguistic treatments of the phatic function adhere to Malinowski's framework. John Laver (1975), for instance, demonstrated much greater respect for the phatic, developing a broader rhetorical view of it. In fact, Laver directly critiqued Malinowski's notion of phatic as "mere exchange of words" and saw a much larger and more important role for the phatic, particularly in professional communication. In this respect, Laver moved toward a more rhetorical sense of the phatic function, noting that the phatic function plays a key role in face-to-face organizational communication (especially in the opening and closing phases of interaction) and that bodily movement (gestures, facial expressions, head movements, physical distance from interlocutor, stance and posture, eye contact, etc.) plays an important role in establishing relations.

In face-to-face communication, there is an important embodied component of phatic communion, which the Roman rhetoricians Cicero and Quintilian would have treated under the canon of delivery (their notion of rhetoric was tied to the orator's public delivery of a speech to a large audience). Laver also noted that the phatic function serves an important heuristic or exploratory function, in the sense that interlocutors can use preliminary phatic communication to gauge the state of mind of the audience or interlocutor, the degree of friendliness and acceptance (or of resistance and hostility).

Feedback received in the preliminary phase can certainly influence what the speaker says next (and how they say it). Laver highlighted the importance of statements in which the speaker reminds the audience that they are together "bound in a web of social solidarity [...] by ties of common acquaintance" (p. 231). In other words, such speech is characterized by references to common acquaintances and social/group ties, which are important to establishing trust and social bonds within communication situations. Laver's understanding of the phatic function develops a social theory of the function useful for social media interaction, as we will discuss later in this chapter.

An ethical theory of rhetoric insists that creating harmony and positive relations, "establishing bonds of union," is precisely the point of communication—the end goal of it—rather than primarily the conveyance of information. Yes, conveying information is important, but we do that precisely for the ultimate goal of making things work better, creating felicitous relationships, and establishing a more perfect union. Companionship, harmony, friendship: These are not "mere" things. They are, in a sense, the whole point.

Where we see the phatic function in Western rhetoric is in a concept we discussed in Chapter 2: the classical Greek concept of *eunoia* or goodwill (*benevolentia* in Latin).[3] As Jacqueline de Romilly (1958) pointed out in her discussion of Isocrates' rhetoric, "*eunoia* is presented as an honorable aim in itself" (p. 96). And it exists in a very close relationship with *homonoia*, or concord, which is a kind of "mutual good will" (p. 98). That is to say, from a political standpoint, Isocratean rhetoric viewed concord or peace between neighboring city states, such as Athens and Sparta, as of critical importance. *Eunoia* is the basis for concord, and it is the responsibility of leaders to make sure that concord is established and maintained. The alternative—war—is a horror to no one's advantage ultimately.

A caution is in order: The rhetorical and ethical fallacy here would be to see the phatic function as simply an obligatory piece of language that the speaker or writer plugs into a discourse in order to achieve their persuasive or informative goal. Rather, in an Isocratean model, like that developed by Charles Marsh (2013), the phatic function needs to be viewed in a broader, more ethical sense as, first, the formation and maintenance of a positive relationship with those the rhetor interacts with, and, second, as fundamental to the rhetor's rhetorical identity (*ethos*), as their overall behavior and embodied practice as a rhetor.

This fallacy of seeing the phatic function as merely a piece of language conspires with the one-way instrumental/conduit view of communication that sees rhetoric as a toolbox of mostly stylistic techniques that writers/speakers use in their communications. And if rhetoric is no more than a toolbox of strategies, formulaic bits of texts dropped in for persuasive advantage, well, that is how we arrived at the popular definition of rhetoric as deception, manipulation, insincerity, dissembling, or lying.

But take the social turn and flip that around: What if the rhetor doesn't make rhetoric so much as *rhetoric makes the rhetor*—in the sense that the rhetor's ethos comes into being through discourse, through the discourse/s they are born into, through the discourse/s that interpellate them, through their symbolic interactions with others, through the rhetoric they practice. If the rhetor practices *eunoia* until it *becomes* them, then it is not simply a tool in their rhetorical toolbox. Rather, the quality is embodied; the rhetor *becomes* the good person who has goodwill toward audience. And that is what Quintilian means when he says rhetoric is the good person speaking well. Or what we mean by the professional communicator or corporation speaking well.

Cultural Variations for the Phatic Function: From Culture to Intercultural and Transcultural

The virtues of courtesy, politeness, friendliness, and the importance of building and maintaining goodwill in one's relations with others are universally valued, it is safe to say, though they may or may not take form as linguistic or rhetorical concepts per se. However, it is important to note that the particular standards, practices, and expectations for the phatic function—that is, the particulars for *how* the rhetor should develop and exhibit goodwill and build relations—can vary across cultures and contexts.

Meeting a stranger for the first time is an especially important and sensitive time for establishing good relations But what is considered "polite" in one culture might be considered "overly direct" or "overly polite," depending on cultural attitudes. In her study of business people in Romania and Europe generally, Irina Budrina (2012) found that Romanians and Europeans deemed the following introduction as "appropriately polite":

Hello, sir. My name is Adrian Popescu. I am very honored to meet you. Would it be possible for me to introduce myself to you?

However, U.S. business people reacted negatively to this same introduction, thinking it "overly polite" and not adequately direct (Budrina, 2012). This finding connects with other research indicating that European business people, particularly Eastern Europeans, prefer a higher degree of formality for initial contacts than would be considered normal or customary in US business contexts.

Politeness is a one quality fundamental to the phatic function. All cultures value "politeness," but the qualities for politeness and the customs associated with it can vary. Even within a broader culture, such as a national culture, there may be significant cultural differences among subgroups: differences related to, among many other factors, generation, gender, race and ethnicity, sexual orientation, economic status, and political orientation. Age and status differences are also key variables in determining what is appropriately polite.

Because customs and standards for politeness vary from culture to culture, enactments and embodiments of the phatic function vary as well. For example, according to Lin Tao (2012), the Chinese concept of *limao* includes politeness but also "respectfulness, modesty, attitudinal warmth, and refinement" (p. 188; see also Mao, 1994). Deference is also important as a way to "maintain harmony, eliminate conflict, and promote cooperation between people" (p. 191). Being modest, as opposed to boldly confident, is important. Being consistently polite is how one builds rhetorical credibility, i.e., "earns a good reputation" (Tao, 2012, p. 191).

Limao is related to the Japanese concept of *teinei*, but there are important differences across the two cultures, according to Tao (2012). In Tao's comparative study of 300 Japanese and Chinese students ages 17–28, she noted a keen sensitivity toward and awareness of false politeness: That is, the speaker who is pretending to be polite but is actually not polite. But she also noted some key differences between the Japanese and Chinese participants. The Japanese students placed a higher value on the quality and beauty of the language used and on the speaker's using the appropriate linguistic form for showing respect for the audience (particularly the audience's social standing) and occasion. In both groups, the women placed a higher value on politeness than did the men.

In another example, also drawn from Asian rhetorics and business practices, small talk is considered "essential for Chinese business people in creating a business atmosphere and establishing or enhancing business relationships" (Yang 2012, pp. 101–102). First, it is considered important to engage in small talk before one focuses on the business topic of a meeting or negotiation. In fact, according to McKay (2012) "unlike in the West, the creation of personal friendship is a prerequisite of doing business" in China. But how one engages in small talk and builds the relationship is also of utmost importance. Yang (2012) noted that if you are talking with a "business stranger," it is important to engage in work-related small talk (but not personal small talk) throughout the conversation. Personal small talk between strangers does not respect the personal distance and established relationship between speakers. That is, it would be overly intimate before one has established a long-term intimate relationship—and that could be perceived as inappropriate and impolite. It requires time to build the appropriate level of trust. Conversely, with someone who has become an established business partner it is appropriate, even necessary to engage in personal small talk at the opening stages of a conversation, though not in the negotiating stage. Thus, a U.S. business person who starts a conversation on an intimate, personable footing—a common strategy in conversations between U.S. Americans—may be perceived as breaking social rules and being impolite.

In face-to-face discourse, gestures, facial expressions, body language are all important components for building communication relationships—what in classical Roman rhetoric would be handled in the canon of delivery. For instance, in Japanese culture, *aizuchi* is certainly a phatic principle, referring to discourse and bodily behaviors (e.g., nodding, grunting, eye contact) that one uses in a conversation to signal the listener's presence, interest, and engagement with the speaker: "*Aizuchi* has a social function: to keep connectedness with others. The stage of connectedness is always characterized by a very high degree of alertness [and] confirmation of presence" (Radovanovic & Ragnedda, 2012, pp. 11–12). *Aizuchi* is an important component of Japanese interaction. Without it, an interlocutor will assume that that the listener is disengaged or uninterested in the conversation. We see an analogous form of this gesture on Facebook, where participants are expected to signal their presence by "liking" a friend's post.

In some cultures, silence is valued as a phatic strategy. For instance, in his comparative analysis of Arabic and English approaches to phatic discourse, Jamal al-Qinai (2011) pointed out that silence can be viewed as a phatic sign of respect in some cultures, but a sign of rudeness or disengagement in others. In Confucian Chinese rhetoric, according to Arabella Lyon's (2004) discussion of *The Analects*, stylistic glibness is something to be distrusted, and nonsense chatter—small talk?—is especially to be distrusted. Silence then is seen as "a positive tool for building relationships" (Lyon, 2004, p. 137) and as signaling that the listener wishes to place emphasis on actions rather than words and avoid using meaningless language as tool for manipulation.

In Confucian rhetoric, glib and aggressive styles of conversation or "sharp tongues" are to be avoided because what is valued is humility, a facet of *ren*, or true virtue: "the truly virtuous person [is] cautious and simple with words" (Xu, 2004, p. 123). Thus, a style of chatty, garrulous friendly discourse perhaps viewed as effective relationship building in one culture (e.g., a U.S. business culture) may be seen as nonsensical, disrespectful idiocy in another.

On a deeper level, we can see that the basis for Confucian rhetoric is the fundamental relationship between self and other, which should be governed by *shu*, "often translated as 'reciprocity' or as 'putting one-self in the other's place" (Mao, 2006, p. 102; see also Mao, 1994). In other words, the foundation and starting point for communication is a fundamental awareness and respect for the other. The quality of the interpersonal relationship matters here, but viewed in its social, political, and cultural context and, importantly, as integrally part of the tradition to which one belongs. *Shu*, then, serves as both a philosophical and rhetorical principle (thereby avoiding the fight between philosophy and rhetoric, and the tension between *seem* and *be*). *Shu* is a basis for both communication and for human relationships—after all, isn't that mainly how human relationships happen, through communication?—and a fundamental phatic principle for rhetoric. *Shu* is not something the rhetor "uses" in a discourse; it refers to the respectful and concerned nature of the rhetor's being-in-relationship-with others.

Rhetoric has always been attentive to issues of audience—"consider your audience" being one of the most important and consistent principles across rhetoric history and theory (Porter, 1992). And cultural difference is certainly a key feature of audience. Put simply, intercultural communication scholars such as those cited in this chapter emphasize as a basic principle that "cultural differences influence communication, behavior, and values" and must be accounted for—and these differences certainly "affect the way people communicate within social networking sites" (Sawyer & Chen, 2012, p. 152). Certainly, rhetoric must address the question of cultural difference.

And yet we have to be careful about how we approach the question. We have to be wary of defining culture narrowly in terms of national identity, of "placing too high a value on locating definitive culture" (Hunsinger, 2006, p. 31). As intercultural communication scholars point out, it is simplistic, even dangerous to define culture only by geographic regions or national boundary lines or to assume that all civilians of a given nationality share the same generic cultural habits, traits, values—e.g., "assuming all Brazilian citizens are alike" (Burnett, 2005).

Edward Hall's (1976) and Geert Hofstede's (2001) significant research on dimensions of culture was important for noting that there are cultural differences that must be accounted for in business communication—and for providing business communication and intercultural communication scholars with handy heuristics for describing such differences. But their categories were sometimes used simplistically, in essentialist ways, "flattening culture to reduced dimensions" (Hunsinger, 2006, p. 33), or what we could call simply cultural stereotyping: For example, it might be generally true to say the US is an individualist, low-context culture, while China is a collectivist, high-context culture, but be wary of how the generality operates in particular circumstances, because the generalization does not provide sufficient regard for cultural variation and hybridity, for cross-cultural interaction, for the movement of people across and between cultures, or for individual variations (see Triandis, 2004).

We can see the negative impact of flattening culture in Jakob Lauring's (2011) study of the impact of cultural stereotyping on team communications. His research site was a Saudi subsidiary of a Danish corporation in which there was frequent interaction between Danish managers and the subsidiary employees, who were of 14 different nationalities (but mostly from Saudi Arabia, India, Egypt, and the Philippines). One particularly important finding from Lauring's study is that the communication interactions did not merely reflect but actually constructed (in a mostly negative way), the cultures and identities for participants and for organizational culture. When participants relied on broad nationalistic generalizations about cultural identity ("Chinese culture," "German culture," "US culture") that led to stereotyping and grouping that ultimately resulted in dysfunctional cross-cultural exchange and impeded working relationships. What he observed was that the employees' use of culturally fixed categories led to team dysfunction—a cautionary point that confirms the importance of not essentializing or stereotyping cultural identity. Lauring called for "informal interaction practices" (p. 250) that aim at building trust. And he emphasized the importance of the "micro dynamics of human interaction" (p. 236), or the informal exchanges that build relationships in the first place. Such "micro-level strategic actions" (p. 235), or phatic interactions, have a significant effect on the quality and effectiveness of intercultural exchange.

Within national boundaries, there can be a diversity of cultures, or a hybridity of cultures. And across national boundaries, as people of various cultural backgrounds interact, they adapt to the new communities that they are forming, particularly on social media—and those new communities can develop their own values, conventions, and rhetorical principles. So we need a flexible view of culture, or as Hunsinger (2006) puts it, we need to focus less on *culture* (as a fixed, stable entity) and more on the *intercultural*, the various ways that cultural habits, practices, and values come into play—and sometimes lead to conflict or confusion in communication (p. 42).

Our framework for thinking about cross-cultural professional communication needs to shift from the Hofstedean approach that tends to represent *culture as fixed identity* of a person or group to a more flexible notion of *intercultural dynamic—how cultural differences interact in various communication contexts.* We need to look at rhetorical performance within communication events, or what Hunsinger called "cultural identity during discursive exchange" (p. 37).

Huatong Sun's important research (2006, 2012) on localization and cultural usability addressed this important distinction, cautioning us against making overly facile generalizations about culture based on broad national identities "while ignoring other subcultural factors […] including the messiness and complexity of local contexts […] and the actual practice of social activities" (Sun, 2006, p. 460). Sun pointed out, importantly, that technologies themselves are actants within communication contexts, influencing users and shaping how communication happens. In other words, *culture* in the broad sense, while important, is only one component of the *intercultural*. Sun's definition of culture includes a variety of factors influencing communication interaction, including: "broad sociocultural factors from national/ethnic culture (e.g., power distance, collectivism vs. individualism) and from subgroup culture (e.g., age group, gender, and organizational affiliation), individual factors (e.g., personal background, values, and interests), ways of life, daily activities, and interpretations of these" (p. 460). Notice that Sun's notion of culture includes gender and generation ("age group") as cultural components as well.

Sun's notion of culture is a more nuanced, rhetorically situated notion of culture that helps us avoid some of the dangerously broad generalizations that have been characteristic of intercultural communication theory based on Hofstede's and Hall's approaches. This is especially important with digitally networked, global communications where users cross many boundaries, including those of geography, culture, and language. Social networks themselves influence how intercultural communication happens: in the exchange between people of varying cultures, a new "third place" can emerge: a forum with its own hybrid cultural features and dimensions (Pfister & Soliz, 2011). The network is not simply a neutral technology for the passage of ideas. The network itself is an actant that changes the nature of interaction (as we discuss in more detail in Chapter 4).

A number of researchers in intercultural communication examining this hypothesis have noted that new media and social-mediated network interaction often, though not always, leads to more rapid cultural adaptation, for all participants in the interaction. Increasingly, these interactions take place on mobile devices, which make the interactions more frequent and more fully integrated into the lives of the users (Chen, 2012; Lebedko, 2014). These new networked media are influencing the process of globalization and, in doing so, are accelerating intercultural adaptation and cultural homogeneity.

But, running counter to the homogenizing impact of digital media are two factors. First, online networks enable those relocated from home communities to stay in touch more easily and more frequently. For example, Chen (2012) noted that international students studying abroad used online networks not only to assist their intercultural adaptation but also "to keep connected with those people they know in their home country in order to gain a sense of comfort in the new environment" (Chen, 2012, p. 6; see also Croucher, 2011). So there's the potential to keep more closely connected to one's home community and culture. But digital technologies and the online communities that form are also leading to the creation of new hybrid digital cultures and digital networks that operate according to different kinds of values and different notions of communication (Movius, 2010; Pfister & Soliz, 2011). This process is happening faster for younger adults in the millennial generation of 18–30.

Intercultural communication theory and research is rejecting the notion of culture as only or mainly the monolithic, fixed quality of a certain person or group—and is looking instead at cross-cultural interaction that addresses the local and contextual factors that shape communication. *Localization* is the key word here. The focus is not so much on identity apart from and prior to communication, but more so on identity-as-performed within communication networks and as influenced and shaped by other participants and by the design and affordances of the technology platform itself.

What does this mean, then, for the phatic purpose and professional communication in the digital age? Reciprocity and relationship building are key. As Ann Hill Duin and Joseph Moses (2015) articulate, the intercultural communication process—using the network theory of connectivism (Siemens, 2005)—is necessary to engage in a "reciprocal" process of "exchanging points of view." That is, the network must be created through exchange—exchange and interaction that is open to and accepting of differences, for the goal of establishing productive relationships.

Individuals understand meaning through increased recognition of intercultural patterns and by adapting and responding to the perspectives of others. Meaning-making is a reflective activity, but it is also a creative and reciprocal activity involving exchanging points-of-view (Duin & Moses, 2015, p. 41).

Localization from a business communication standpoint means strategically choosing which communities to participate in (or to form) and communicating "locally" within particular contexts of use. With online communication, platform selection is part of this. Facebook might be a popular social media option in the United States, but in many parts of the world other social media platforms have significantly more volume: e.g., Tencent QQ in China (where Facebook is banned), Cyworld in South Korea, Vkontakte in Russia, and Mixi in Japan. But simply picking the right social media platform (and, of course, language) in which to communicate online is not enough. Localization refers to cultural adaptation on a much deeper and broader rhetorical level, which means tailoring content and message to local social customs, habits, values, knowledge, and events (Solis, 2012), as we will show in the case of Taco Bell's social media usage presented in Chapter 6.

Phatic Communication and Digital Communications: Some Examples

In the cultural realm of digital social media, the phatic purpose of "staying in touch" is a worthy communication aim in its own right—and perhaps a baseline aim necessary for all other types of digitally-mediated social media interactions. The popularity of cell phone-based texting is one indicator of this value: How much texting has an informative or persuasive aim primarily versus how much of it serves the primary purpose of "staying in touch"? The latter is often the case. Facebook, Twitter, Instagram, and YouTube are social media sites whose popularity signals the inherent value of connectivity with others. Facebook in particular is testimony to the importance many people place on building and maintaining their social networks. The acts of friending, poking, liking, etc., are standard phatic techniques to maintain contact and to show "connected presence" (Miller, 2008, p. 394).

Danica Radovanovic and Massimo Ragnedda (2012) see the Facebook "poke" as the purest form of phatic confirmation of presence, signaling simply that "I am here." A "like" button serves a phatic function as well, but also signals confirmation or agreement. The motivation in such spaces is "less having something in particular to say (i.e., communicating some kind of information), as [...] the obligation or encouragement to say 'something' to maintain connections or audience, to let one's network know that one is still 'there'" (Miller, 2008, p. 393). While such phatic communications may be "content-less," they are by no means "meaning-less." They are important to maintaining what Vincent Miller (2008) called "mediated phatic sociability"; they are important to focusing on "the process of communication"; and they "potentially carry a lot more weight to them than the content itself suggests" (pp. 394–395). Sharing profiles, personal stories, anecdotes, thoughts, and pictures is a way to gain trust within the community.

Businesses have come to recognize the value of being on social media as way to interact with consumers and build brand and customer allegiance, as we describe in more detail in Chapter 6. The move by organizations to "go social" is not, of course, merely phatic; relationships matter, but so do sales (or, for non-profits, so do donations). So when Shell Oil hosts dialogue forums (see shelldialogues.com/forums), they are not seeking simply to connect with the public but they also, of course, want to present and argue for their own energy policies, build their company ethos, and, ultimately, drive sales (and guide government policy). But even with this profit-driven motive, the company is also engaging in a phatic function in an interactive social space that invites response and participation from the public. Such sites can certainly generate useful marketing information for companies by providing immediate public feedback for new products, campaigns, or initiatives, but that is not their only purpose.

The professional communicator working in this kind of social media environment functions more as a designer of interactive online spaces, as a public interlocutor, as an online community leader, and as participant in public discussion. The professional communicator working in these social spaces must learn how to design what Wang et al. (2011) refer to as a "phatic technology." A phatic technology is one that "serves to establish, develop, and maintain human relationships [...] to create a social context with the effect that its users form a social community based on a collection of interactional goals" (p. 44). They see the internet itself overall as a tool having a "strong phatic nature," primarily because of its "minimized time span between producers and users" (p. 49). What this means for professional communication is that instead of focusing on *creating information for users* the emphasis shifts more toward *creating communities of users*, communities that can share information and collaborate and crowdsource to solve problems. Further, communications that perhaps traditionally have been seen as insignificant "idle chatter" perhaps are "crucial to the strength of the ongoing social bond" (Gibbs, Vetere, Bunyan, & Howard, 2005).

For such spaces to work effectively, they have to be designed to function less like informative documents and more like communities, or even cultures, and they must be designed and adapted to specific cultures. Miller (2008) saw phatic discourse as even more than a function of language; he sees it as taking on the features of a culture:

> In phatic media culture, content is not king, but "keeping in touch" is. More important than anything said, it is the *connection* to the other that becomes significant, and the *exchange* of words becomes superfluous. Thus the text message, the short call, the brief email, the short blog update or comment, becomes part of *a mediated phatic sociability necessary to maintain a connected presence in an ever-expanding social network*.
>
> (Miller, 2008, p. 395, emphasis added)

Building relationships and "mediated phatic sociability" are essential for professional communicators working at the individual and the organizational level. To illustrate this point, we want to provide a few brief examples, considering email, virtual teamwork, and user help forums.

The business genre where people frequently violate principles of effective phatic communication is email. People are so flooded with email at work that they tend to rush, and when they rush they make mistakes. They forget to say "please" and "thank you." They write snarky emails. They send angry, ranting emails. They reply to the entire group when they thought they were writing to an individual. These are relatively minor, fixable mistakes but they matter as "micro-level social interactions" (Lauring, 2011) that significantly impact workplace relationships and communications (Mackiewicz, 2006; Rogerson-Revell, 2008; Zhu & White, 2009; Pullin, 2010; al-Qinai, 2011; Hudak & Maynard, 2011; McNely, 2011; Allen, Lehmann-Willenbrock, & Landowski, 2014; Kulkarni, 2014). What research shows generally is that such small exchanges, even when "content-less" (Miller, 2008), serve a vital role in the building of relationships, and are particularly important for establishing trust and social bonds for intercultural exchanges.

Building trust is a key component of the phatic function—and building trust is often cited as a key factor in intercultural communication and particularly for intercultural virtual teamwork (Rush Hovde, 2014). For a team to perform effectively and do its work as a team, it is vital to have social cohesion. For teams working in situations with weak structure (such as online teams), "trust is likely to have the greatest effect" on team performance (Jarvenpaa, Shaw, & Staples, 2004, p. 262). Some studies recommend face-to-face team meetings, if possible, "especially early in the process" (Rush Hovde, 2014, p. 245; Longo, 2014).

Of particular importance for virtual teamwork, but especially for intercultural virtual teamwork is "initial trust," building and establishing trust among team members at the beginning of a project—a point that recalls Cicero's advice about the importance of *captatio benevolentia* in the *exordium*. In their research, Jarvanpaa, Shaw, and Staples (2004) do not explicitly reference phatic communication, but that is what they are talking about when they emphasize the importance, first, of team members maintaining contact with others on the team: The first component of trust is simply signaling attentive presence to co-workers. Depending on the networks, this "presence" may be physical, textual, or virtual.

Trust is especially important in contexts operating with what Jarvanpaa et al. (2004) called "weak structure," teams that have very little shared social history, are not tied to a common physical location, or that are ad hoc and temporary. That description of weak structure resembles the teamwork context for many online professional communication courses. For example, Pavel Zemliansky's (2012) study of intercultural virtual teamwork (based on a classroom study involving students from the U.S. and Ukraine) found that "Teams which managed to establish more systematic and regular patterns of collaboration and information exchange produced better documents. [...] levels of frustration in those teams were lower because their members had developed multiple and redundant communication channels (email, Facebook, class wiki, and so on), which gave them the ability to restart communications quickly" (p. 282). The participants in the study reported "unanimously that social interactions and 'small talk' were extremely important" to their teamwork. Another key factor Zemliansky identified was selection of communication technology: Which technology would be most readily accessible to team members and be most helpful in building team identity and cohesion? In Zemliansky's study, different teams chose different technologies, selecting the ones that "gave them a more 'immediate' degree of contact and interaction" (p. 284) and allowed them to build "interpersonal relationships and trust" (p. 385).

Rather than serve as information providers (or merely as information providers), professional communicators need to create contact and interaction opportunities that enable people to build trust with each other as a community and with the individual or organization leading the conversations.

We can see this change in innumerable professional communication contexts, including in a long-time genre of professional communication, online user help documentation. In the old print realm, or even in the Web 1.0 realm, the model was more one-way information delivery: The technical writer would produce a piece of written documentation to assist users in installing, learning, and using a particular piece of technology or software, and that would be posted on a static web site. In more recent years, this online written document might be replaced (or supplemented) by a YouTube video providing a dynamic multimediated tutorial to help the user.

In the Web 2.0-based model, and on into the Web 3.0 and beyond, the technical writer—and she is not likely to be called that anymore, but is more likely to be called an "information developer" or "social media designer"—might produce the video but would also likely create and monitor a user help forum, based on a crowdsourcing model that enables users to help each other. Think, for example, of Adobe Customer Care on Twitter or Techsmith Community Support for Camtasia (which includes user blogs and Twitter and Facebook sites). Usually (not always) this multi-faceted crowdsourced approach provides more rapid and context-specific problem solving (Swarts, 2015).

The professional communicator in this realm is not so much creating help *documents* as designing and monitoring help *spaces*, networks, forums, and feeds—what John Law (2000) called "the construction of spatiality." The professional communicator functions more as an interactive space designer, as a remixer and redistributor, and as a curator of content, rather than a creator, of information resources. The job of content curation is a task traditionally associated with library science: maintaining, organizing, tagging, and editing content created by others. But helping users might also necessitate designing social games that enable users to interact socially in an engaging, compelling environment in order to learn a task or procedure (DeWinter & Moeller, 2014). The skill set needed for professional communicators may have more to do with writing compelling narratives and creating an engaging User Experience (UX) than with writing procedures or instructions (Redish & Barnum, 2011).

In many ways, the professional communicator designing help forums today is not a writer or even, perhaps, a designer, but more like a party-planner who has sent out invitations (come here if you have questions) and then, either through the original layout of the space and/or through circulating around with brief interactions here and there, helps facilitate the conversations that party attendees have among themselves.

People coming to a help forum certainly hope to receive information that solves their problem. Their primary purpose is not phatic social interaction; the social interaction is the means, not the end. As Jason Swarts (2015) noted, "Ultimately, visitors to the forums still expect their problems to get solved" (p. 185). But in interactive help forums, the forum functions as what Swarts (2015) called a "public sphere of performative help [...] a theater of proof, a sphere in which solutions are negotiated and resources are moved back and forth until the right balance is found, in the right moment that a solution works" (p. 176). This kind of online social interaction is the way that users seek help now, replacing the old document model of user help, though as Swarts pointed out, it "still follows the same underlying logic" (p. 176).

However, the role of the technical communicator in this rhetorical setting is not to create the definitive *help document* so much as it is to create the *help forum* that will promote the emergence of a solution in an "actor network." The kind of documentation that emerges from these forums is socially negotiated and constituted, less prescriptive and linear, and more open ended, more like "guidelines as opposed to instructions" (p. 183). In part, the skill required here involves deploying the wisdom of the crowd—designing a forum to maximize crowdsourcing, in other words. The communication model at work here is not a linear, expert-to-novice, Shannon-Weaver type of model for help; it is a network model in which the phatic function plays a significant role in maintaining the sociability of the network.

Notice, too, some other important features of this changed role: The professional communicator is often an engaged member of these communities, interacting with users, clients, the public, often in real time; is part of a team that works collectively within these communities; is interacting with participants from across the globe (requiring intercultural knowledge and intelligence); and, yes, still does provide direct instructional help and still does respond to users by posting help documents within the forums. So the old role of the technical documentation writer hasn't disappeared entirely, but is rather enfolded into a much broader responsibility. The phatic function is key in this context, as the means by which effective user help forums are built and nurtured.

Alex Hillman (2014) advised companies to stop hiring social media *managers* and instead hire social media *tummlers*. *Tummler* is a Yiddish word that refers to a performer or entertainer, particularly a comedian, whose function is to stimulate audience participation. In this context, the social media tummler is the community builder who encourages participation and audience interaction, serving not as the knowledge expert providing answers for the uninformed audience but as the catalyst for crowdsourced value.

Conclusion

From ancient communities to emerging ones today, from the home and public square to email and social media, and in rhetorics around the globe (e.g., Greco-Roman, Confucian, Maatian), we can see the phatic function as a major purpose of communication, including professional communication. Increasingly, professional communicators (as individuals and as organizations) need to write, interact, and design for phatic exchange in intersecting on-ground and online networks.

However, rather than seeing a particular communication as either phatic or not phatic, we would suggest this approach: While some communications may be purely phatic, almost all communications require some kind of phatic component to be effective. Even though the for-profit imperative has risen in many social media sites, the expectations and need for phatic engagement are still key. The phatic function should be regarded, then, as an important and necessary feature of all communications—even ones we may be inclined to view as purely informational (like user documentation)—and so should not be neglected in professional communication.

Further and importantly, the phatic is not merely something that we "add" to a communication—pleasantries and politenesses we merely drop in—but rather is a fundamental component of both the identity and character of the rhetor and of the communication context itself. For individuals and organizations, *eunoia*—the quality of having goodwill toward one's audiences—needs to be a fundamental and consistent set of behaviors that one practices and embraces as part of one's whole ethos-in-the-deep-sense rather than merely as a stylistic strategy that one selectively drops into a discourse to make the audience "attentive, docile, and well disposed" (Cicero, *De Inventione*, 1.15.20). Building relationships takes time and commitment, and it begins with and in every communicative action.

Notes

1 The notion of phatic function was further developed by the sociolinguist Roman Jakobson, who, in an influential 1960 paper, identified phatic as one of the six primary functions of discourse (Jakobson, 1960; Hébert, 2011; Wang et al., 2011). In his grammatical system (Systemic Functional Linguistics), M.A.K. Halliday used the term "interactional" instead of phatic, but, following in Malinowski's footsteps, he saw it as a function characteristic of a lower level of linguistic development. In Halliday's case, the phatic is characteristic of children's grammar, and the child's need to identify and reinforce relationships ("me and my mummy") (Halliday, 1976). In his influential treatise on purpose and aims for discourse, *A Theory of Discourse* (1971), James Kinneavy treated the phatic function as a kind of subfunction intended "merely to keep the channel open, as in introductions or some

seemingly trivial conversational crutches" (p. 59). In short, from this theoretical standpoint, phatic or interactional discourse is primitive, child-like, and trivial: "merely" keeping the channel open.

2 What is that goal? Aristotle provides one answer to this question in his ethical treatise *Nicomachean Ethics*, where he links the art of rhetoric to the social good: "Every art [e.g., rhetoric] and every inquiry, and similarly every action and pursuit, is thought to aim at some good" (*Nicomachean Ethics* 1.1). For Aristotle the greatest good for rhetoric and politics to aim for was "the good of the *polis*" (*Nicomachean Ethics* 1.2) and happiness for all. This is, for Aristotle, the final end, or ultimate cause, of rhetorical action (and for other arts as well, such as politics, music, sculpture). Peace, harmony, well-being, stability, happiness.

3 The phatic function has always been important in rhetoric, though the term *phatic* is rarely used in rhetoric. For example, Richard Lanham does not include the word *phatic* in his extensive *Handlist of Rhetorical Terms* (1991). Nor is there an entry for or mention of *phatic* in *The Encyclopedia of Rhetoric and Composition* (Enos, 1996).

4 Rhetorical Interaction and Networks

We begin not with the digital, nor with the contemporary, but rather with an historical example that illustrates the role of networks in rhetorical interactions.

In 1517, to protest the abuses of the Roman Catholic Vatican hierarchy, the German monk Martin Luther posted his *95 Theses* on the church door of All Saint's Church in Wittenberg, Germany. He also wrote a letter to his bishop informing him of his criticisms. The result of this dramatic act of rebellion was that ... well, nothing much happened. A few regional bishops were upset, and the Church hierarchy heard about Luther's protest and was upset. But Luther's message did not have dramatic reach or impact beyond the Church hierarchy.

From a communication standpoint, we might say that Luther chose the wrong medium to deliver his message: Posting his theses on the church door was performatively dramatic (it was a type of protest commonly done in those days), and writing a letter to his bishop was pragmatically circumspect and respectful, but as a strategic form of rhetorical delivery, his action was pretty feeble. From a business communication standpoint, you might say that Luther sent a letter instead of using social media.

But eventually, Luther did use social media, the social medium of his time—the printing press. When copies of Luther's message were printed and distributed, that is when things started to percolate. Between 1517 and 1520, Luther's thirty or so publications were reproduced in 300,000 copies, robust distribution for that time period (Eisenstein, 2005, p. 164). And when Luther's message was heard and discussed, distributed and redistributed, it had impact—a dramatic impact in Western Europe, promoting a religious upheaval that upset the existing power of the Church and spurred the Protestant Reformation.[1] It was also important, from the standpoint of access, that Luther's *95 Theses* were translated from their original language (Church Latin, which limited its audience to the clerical and intellectual class) to the vernacular languages of Europe, which made his ideas more widely accessible. The printing press, coupled with translation, enabled Luther to find a broad public audience for his message.

Notice that we have been referring to the *printing press* as the technology that enabled Luther to distribute his message—and in historical discussions, that is often what is referenced as a key agent enabling his critique. (For instance, Elizabeth Eisenstein's original treatise, upon which her 2005 book is based, is titled *The Printing Press as an Agent of Change*.) But that articulation misidentifies the revolution: Did the *printing press*, the machine, really upset the religious and political stability of Western Europe? Well, only in a manner of speaking. In this context, *printing press* is a type of trope: a synecdoche substituting a part for the whole.

So what is the whole? The whole is the *network*: that is, the printing press as it operated within an entire economic, political, infrastructural, and social assemblage that enabled, first, many copies to be made rapidly, then those copies to be distributed, and moved through the transportation system of Northern and Western Europe, based on various macro-economies of exchange between various municipalities and kingdoms, and on various micro-economies of exchange between booksellers, clerics, universities, students, and as impeded or assisted along the way by various laws and prohibitions.

The printing press was a vital technology for making copies more efficiently, but the printing press didn't do it alone; by itself, the printing press with its letter blocks and ink is not a *medium for distribution*. But the printing press network is. This printing press network included other support technologies and infrastructures such as horses, wagons, and boats; cities, towns, roads, rivers, canals; technologies for making ink and paper (and for making the printing press itself); book and pamphlet vendors; and money. In other words, there was an entire distribution network in place—a network of material things but also a network of laws, policies, codes (written and unwritten), pacts, treaties, monetary exchange systems, and agreements holding those material objects in a certain relationship—of which the printing press was an important piece, but only one piece—that enabled the distribution of Luther's critique.

And let's not forget people, whose movements and activities, beliefs and desires, hopes and fears, habits and personal fortunes (can they afford to buy books?), their level of education (can they read books?), not to mention their religions and beliefs (were they already predisposed to be critical of the Catholic hierarchy?), are also part of this network. And, finally, let's not forget Luther: His anger about the hypocrisy and abuse of indulgences was his motivation for writing and posting the 95 *Theses*.

So when people speak of how "the printing press" effected such widespread change, the printing press is a synecdoche of part for whole. We use the same kind of synecdoche today when we use the term *computer* or *digital* to mean not only that tablet that sits on our laps or the phone in our hands, but the entire social, political, and economic network, including the technological infrastructure, which enables us to use our computers to distribute messages to the world. *Computer* is often a synecdoche for *Internet*, or for the World Wide Web, or for social media or perhaps even for the whole nebulous thing, what we might simply call *the network.* The computer is a powerful technology to be sure—like a printing press with global broadcast functionality—but it is only one node in a vast network of multiple intersecting networks assisting human communication and interaction.

To be an effective communicator in this assemblage of networks means not only crafting a well-written (or spoken or multimodal) message, which our computer, as a communication production tool (and agent), helps us do. Just as importantly, we need to know how to *deliver* via the internet, which our computer, as a delivery tool (and agent), also helps us do. And it is not that we craft the message first and then decide how to deliver it. Rather, what we do is craft the message in a way that is appropriate for the delivery mechanism we know we are using and, beyond that, for the digital environment we are actually living in. The network makes us think about how our message will travel, where it will go (often without our intention), and that, in turn, influences our construction and design of the message.

To deliver our messages effectively in the digital age, we need to understand how the network works, how it has changed communication practices in dramatic and fundamental ways, how in fact it has changed us. Like Luther, we have to update our thinking about rhetoric and delivery to account for the social medium of our time. We have to stop nailing our papers on the church door and start thinking about how messages ought to be delivered to contemporary audiences using contemporary technologies—and thus, in turn, how our messages ought to be constructed and designed for digital delivery. We need a *network rhetoric theory*, a theory of communication specifically designed for human interaction via digital network and on social media. The purpose of this chapter is to develop such a rhetoric, building and expanding upon previous work on the rhetoric of networks.

Specifically, what we do in this chapter is:

- briefly consider the historical treatment of the rhetorical canon of delivery, arguing that we need an expanded theory of rhetorical delivery;
- explain why we think actor-network theory provides a useful basis for the construction of a network rhetoric theory; and
- build and present our own model for network rhetoric theory, which both arose from and shaped the cases we present in Chapters 5–7.

Recovering the Classical Canon of Delivery

As an art, rhetoric is concerned both with *making* an object (a communication message such as a report, a YouTube video, a business presentation, a tweet) and with *doing* something that has effect (e.g., creating value for some audience, building a relationship with someone, lodging a protest with Church authorities). In short, rhetoric is both a *saying* and a *doing*; it is both expression and action.

We know, this seems like a fairly innocuous, unsurprising, even obvious thing to say. But for much of the history of rhetoric, rhetoric theory and pedagogy have focused more on the making than the doing, more on the crafting of the message (*techne*) and not enough, we feel, on the action part (*praxis*). Aristotle's *Rhetoric*, historically one of the most influential rhetoric texts, treats rhetoric as a productive art: in his time and place, the art of making a speech. If you want to find Aristotle's theory of action, or *praxis*, you have to look in other works, like *Nicomachean Ethics* and *Politics*.

What does rhetoric *do* exactly? What work does it do in the world? What value does it create—and for whom? These are action/effect/doing kinds of questions, and we think the art of rhetoric does include these sorts of *praxis* concerns (see Zhao, 1991). Luther's impact was not just *writing* the message, it was also *posting* the message—and, even more importantly, posting it in a certain way, through the medium of the printing press and its distribution network. For that reason, the classical canon of delivery—*actio* in Roman rhetoric—is incredibly important, because delivery pertains to the interaction connection points linking any message with its action, effect, and interaction with audiences. We see understanding of network as a key concern of the rhetorical canon of delivery.

Delivery has always been part of rhetoric—it was one of the five classical canons of rhetoric, along with invention, arrangement, style, and memory—but it has always been an underappreciated and at times even despised and denigrated canon (Welch, 1999; Trimbur, 2000; Porter, 2009). In classical rhetoric and through most of the history of Western rhetoric, delivery referred to the oral/aural and bodily aspects of an oral speech or performance—i.e., to the speaker's voice (intonation, volume, rhythm) and to bodily movements and gestures. And that made sense in 4th-century BCE Athens, Greece, because in that time and place rhetoric was primarily the art of public speaking. Because delivery came to be associated almost exclusively with speech situations and with functions of the speaker's body (voice, gestures), it seemed less relevant later in the history of rhetoric, if not irrelevant, to writing and the world of print culture.

Aristotle was one of delivery's early and most influential denigrators. He saw delivery functioning "in the same way as acting [...] a matter of natural talent and largely not reducible to artistic rule" (*Rhetoric* 3.1.7). Aristotle's dismissal of delivery provided the dominant cue for Western thought in regard to the canon: that is, delivery is a matter of "natural talent" and is "unworthy" of serious intellectual treatment, even though, ironically, "we cannot do without it."

> Besides, delivery is—very properly—not regarded as an elevated subject of inquiry. Still, the whole business of rhetoric being concerned

with appearances, we must pay attention to the subject of delivery, unworthy though it is, because we cannot do without it.

(Aristotle, Rhetoric, 3.1.7)

The Greek orator Demosthenes offers us a very different view of delivery. According to Quintilian, when Demosthenes was asked to name the three most important components of rhetoric, he responded, "Delivery, delivery, delivery" (*Institutio*, 11.3.6). In counterresponse to Aristotle, Quintilian not only saw delivery as important, but as integrally related to speaker credibility and persuasive force. In *Institutio Oratoria* (95 CE), Quintilian provided a detailed and embodied view of delivery (11.3), focusing mainly on voice and bodily movement of the speaker: the quality of voice and the position and carriage of the body (including discussion of hands, neck, eyes, head, and, interestingly, dress), as both relate to the emotional force of the oration. Quintilian noted the important connection between delivery and the character of the speaker (*ethos*) and the emotional depth and appeal of the presentation (*pathos*).

In other words, delivery has a lot to do with persuasion. For example, Quintilian told us, a demeanor exuding modesty can be persuasive with judges in a legal matter, just as much as "a toga sitting well upon the shoulder" (*Institutio*, 11.3.161), but the demeanor only achieves the desired effect if the emotion is sincere, the facts are compelling, and the argument sound: "All emotional appeals will inevitably fall flat, unless they are given the fire that voice, look, and the whole carriage of the body can give them" (*Institutio*, 11.3.2). Quintilian's point here is that the body is an integral part of rhetorical action. The sincerity of one's commitment and the appropriate coordination of one's thoughts, feelings, and bodily expressions are important to rhetorical effect. Embodiment is part of character, and character, ethos, is fundamental to rhetoric (as we discussed in Chapter 2).

While Quintilian's approach to delivery is more expansive and respectful than Aristotle's, it is still very minor compared to his treatment of the other canons. Perhaps because delivery came to be associated exclusively with the art of public speaking, delivery was easy to ignore in the age of print and writing. With some notable exceptions (e.g., Welch, 1999; Trimbur, 2000; Buchanan, 2005; Eisenstein, 2005; Brooke, 2009; Porter, 2009; Morey, 2016), there is not very much discussion about rhetorical delivery for writing or print, and much less for digital writing.

But things have changed. To understand how communication works in the digital age, we have to evolve beyond both oral and print models. As Porter (2009) put it, we need "an expanded and retheorized notion of delivery designed for the distinctive rhetorical dynamics of Internet-based communication. We need a robust theory of digital delivery to help us navigate [...] rhetorical complexities in the digital age" (pp. 207–208). An "expanded and retheorized notion of delivery" means knowing how audiences are likely to access, engage, and interact on networks, which pertains in critical ways to the rhetorical decisions writers make about informational content, design, style, etc. The kind of knowledge we are talking about requires deep understanding of the rhetoric of networks.

Understanding Networks

As John Jones (2015) noted, and as our Martin Luther example shows, "Networks are not new to human experience. As long as people have existed together in society, networks of relations have existed." Jones provided an example of a map showing the railroad network in Massachusetts in 1879, a network that connected towns and cities across the state, at that time a new technology network serving as a key means for human travel and communication (and, of course, for the delivery of U.S. mail). In the 19th century, the development and expansion of railway technology dramatically increased the speed of human travel as well as the speed of communication transmission.

However, as Jones also noted, digital networking is something qualitatively different: "Digital networking technologies allow for a dramatic increase in the level of complexity that networks can support, represented by either the number of nodes in the network or the density of their interactions" (Jones, 2015). And, in addition to complexity and density, we would add two characteristics to Jones' list, speed/synchronicity and mobility/pervasiveness: Digital technology dramatically increases the speed of communication across networks, making communicative interactions synchronous (more or less), and wireless digital technology coupled with smartphone technology increases the mobility and pervasiveness of communication: The network enables communication to be delivered instantaneously (more or less), without wires, right to the device in our hand, where we can see and read the message immediately in real time (more or less). This set of changes is more than simply an upgrade on the old network systems of roads, rail lines, and even phone lines. This combination of changes—complexity, density, volume, synchronicity/immediacy, mobility, multimodality—results in a substantive deep change in the nature of interaction, and that is having dramatic effects on cognition, culture, politics—everything.

Contemporary rhetoric and communication scholars—such as Jones, and others whom we will discuss momentarily, particularly those in the fields of computers and composition and technical communication—have recognized the significance of these changes and for more than 30 years have built a body of theory and research showing how technology changes communication practices and, more specifically, how digitally-mediated network interaction changes writing practices. We gratefully acknowledge and build from this important work, particularly theory and research that has used actor-network theory.[2]

Our overall approach to network is based mainly on actor-network theory (ANT) as developed and described by Bruno Latour, most explicitly in his book *Reassembling the Social* (2005).[3] Applying actor-network theory requires us to shift the traditional focuses of rhetoric. If we apply an ANT perspective, we do not study writers, texts, or genres as isolated objects. Rather, we are interested in the larger rhetorical social scene: in the collections and interactions of various communicators and texts who come together (perhaps only briefly) in a common social media space, for a common purpose, defined by a common marker (e.g., the hashtag, the keyword), topic, or event (e.g., an offensive tweet). From an ANT perspective, we focus on the flow, distribution, and circulation of texts, not just the texts as isolated rhetorical objects.

The other key feature of actor-network theory is its focus on the participatory role of technology: how technology itself exercises a substantive influence on human affairs, often independent from, and even at odds with, human designs, goals, and intentions. In *Aramis, or the Love of Technology* (1996a), a fictional narrative building off the Frankenstein motif (and its precursor, the Greek mythic legend of Prometheus), Latour explores and demonstrates how a new technology—Aramis, a new French railway system—takes on a spirit and identity of its own and becomes an actant, an interactor in the developing political conversation about its design, development, and funding (see also Latour, 1996b).

Latourian actor-network theory acknowledges the role of technology as an actant, and that is the key reason we use it as our framework and methodology for developing a network rhetoric. However, our approach is also thoroughly informed by, and borrows from, other kinds of models that acknowledge network connectivity, particularly the metaphors of ecology and activity system as developed within the field of rhetoric/composition.

Alternate Models of Network: From Context to Ecology, System, Network

The shift toward a network model of communication aligns with historical developments in rhetoric theory since the New Rhetoric movement of the 1950s and 1960s. Scholars of the mid-20th-century New Rhetoric (such as Kenneth Burke, Richard Weaver, Chaim Perelman and Lucie Olbrechts-Tyteca, Lloyd Bitzer, and others) began by critiquing the narrow formalist focus on the textual elements of communication—that is, the obsessive New Critical focus on linguistic features of *the text*. As they pointed out, the text by itself does not carry all the meaning necessary for communication interaction. New Rhetoricians rediscovered and recovered the classical emphasis on *context*: the importance of occasion, audience, venue, and genre (see, for example, Bitzer, 1968). The New Rhetoricians did not abandon the focus on the made text, but they insisted on focusing on the text-in-context: that is, the text as arising from a certain motive or exigency, as having a certain intention or purpose, and as being directed toward some audience.

In the 1980s and 1990s, there was a further shift in rhetoric theory: Rhetoric took what was later called "the social turn," a poststructural shift toward emphasizing the broader social scenes for rhetorical inter-action, including, in the 1980s, constructs such as *discipline, community* (or *discourse community*), and *culture*, and then, in the 1990s, *hyper-text, rhizome, system* (or *activity system*), and *ecology*.[4] Such concepts, as deployed in rhetoric theory, recognize that rhetoric must account for more than merely (a) the individual writer/communicator producing the isolated written text or speech, or even (b) the immediate rhetorical oc-casion or context. Rhetoric must also account for the larger social scene and cultural forces that significantly shape rhetorical activity, and that communication interaction both constructs and operates within. Rheto-ric in the 1980s and 1990s was already moving toward network theory.

In digital rhetoric, there are various kinds of systemic and circula-tory metaphors in play describing this larger social scene, including *sys-tem* (Ehninger, 1968; Jung, 2014); *activity system* (activity theorists in general, including Engeström, 1996; Russell, 1997; Engeström, 2001); *ecology* (Cooper, 1986; Nardi & O'Day, 1999; Edbauer, 2005; Brooke, 2009; Chaput, 2010); *hypertext* (Bolter, 1991; Johnson-Eilola, 1997); *rhizome* (Deleuze & Guattari, 1987; Johnson-Eilola & Kimme Hea, 2003; McCoy & Rowan, 2011; Gartler, 2017); *datacloud* (Johnson-Eilola, 2005); *assemblage* (Bennett, 2010); and *network* (Latour, 2005; Spinuzzi, 2008; Castells, 2010; Jones, 2015; Read & Swarts, 2015). Are these constructs all versions of the same essential thing, or are there distinct differences that are important to acknowledge? What are the affordances (and impedances) of one model/metaphor versus another?

In common parlance, the term *network* implies circuits and wires, non-living, non-breathing material objects that are more or less stati-cally constructed as a medium or container for communication—and that is the chief danger of using network as the operative metaphor. Many rhetoric theorists prefer the term *ecology* because it puts some life into the scene, emphasizing the network as an embodied lifeworld of moving, breathing actants (e.g., Cooper, 1986; Rice, 2005; Brooke, 2009). It also forefronts the importance of change, circulation, and in-teraction, how messages move and intersect vibrantly to change eco-logies. Ecology acknowledges the importance of non-human actants, most especially the natural world in which we live. The natural world is not a fixed given either; it, too, changes based on interactions and inter-ruptions that change the nature of the ecology.

In *Information Ecologies* (1999), Bonnie Nardi and Vicki O'Day argued for the value of the ecology metaphor in regards to informa-tion and computing systems, because it emphasizes the organic and evolutionary qualities of how systems operate. They worried about the technocentric nature of the system metaphor, which can "leave us with a sense of the inexorability of technological change [and] does not address with enough force the possibility of local and particular change" (p. 43). The ecological perspective, a more biological and environmental metaphor, views the actants in their environment as providing a shaping force on the system. The other problem they saw with the system metaphor is that it tends to "wash out the distinctions among different local settings" (p. 47). With the ecology metaphor, Nardi and O'Day argued, "the spotlight is not on technology, but on human activities that are served by technology" (p. 49). In addition, ecology "suggests diversity ... [and] implies continual evolution" (p. 56).

In *Lingua Fracta* (2009), Collin Brooke provided a useful summary and synthesis of the ecology model as used in writing studies, beginning with Marilyn Cooper's influential 1986 article on "The Ecology of Writing." Brooke sees the ecology metaphor as particularly well suited to understanding and producing new media discourse. Both Brooke and Cooper see the key affordance of the ecology model as moving beyond "the individual writer and her immediate context" (Cooper, 1986, p. 368), as acknowledging "the constant motion of an ecological system" (p. 38), and of calling attention to how the system itself ("other writers and writings in the systems," p. 368) shapes production within the system. Our notion of network carries with it all these qualities of the ecology metaphor, which we also see as affordances of a Latourian network metaphor.

Activity theory, particularly as articulated by Yrjö Engeström, is also relevant to this discussion. According to Engeström (1996; 2001; see also Russell, 1997), activity theory posits that the individual operates within a "collective activity system," which is how we think of networks. The activity system in this construction is not simply the physical network of wires, poles, and electrical impulses moving across and between nodes (servers, computers), but is also the social network, that is, the people who participate in the network, and also, and most importantly, the practices, actions, and *activities* that they produce within the system. Systems include both nodes (points of origination) and links (points of connection). The network includes actors and interactions. And networks are by no means isolated, autonomous units (at least as articulated by third-generation activity theorists such as Engeström): Systems overlap and intersect, merge, split, and collapse. They can represent tightly bounded communities of practice with well-established patterns, even rules for interaction. Or they can be very loose groups of people who come and go, joining, participating, leaving, coming back at regular intervals, inventing conventions as they go and changing them rapidly.

In *Network* (2008), Clay Spinuzzi provided a comprehensive, reflective discussion of the differences and common ground between activity-systems theory and actor-network theory. Like Spinuzzi, we are aware of the complications and potential traps of using network as a guiding concept. He argued for the affordances of the term *network*, as long as network is not misunderstood as synonymous with technical infrastructure. Spinuzzi made the important point that some network configurations can, over time, appear to become fixed and stable: "The longer these networks are, the more entities that are enrolled in them, the stronger and more durable they become" (p. 39)—and that feature is what leads, no doubt, to the notion that networks are fixed and stable. Spinuzzi noted one key affordance of the activity systems approach to networks: that it "demands the foregrounding of human beings and their labor and requires ways to account for change-in-stability" (pp. 7–8), what Spinuzzi referred to as an "arborescent, evolutionary explanation" that, to us, strongly resembles the ecology and rhizome metaphors as discussed by others in the field.

We find much of value in both the constructs of ecology and activity system. But ultimately, we feel that the term *network* has singular affordances that make it a preferable metaphor—and a preferable methodology—for understanding professional communication in the digital age. We do realize though that if we use network we had better be wary of how we use the term—and of how others might understand it. We mean network in an ecological sense as a living, breathing, moving changing ecology. We need to make sure "to add the dimension of movement back into our discussions of rhetoric" (Edbauer, 2005, p. 20). And we also take from activity systems theory the importance of the focus on activities, actions, interactions as they unfold within systems.

Why do we prefer the actor-network version of the network metaphor? For several reasons: because

- ANT treats technology as a participant actant, as having its own agency apart from human desires, goals, and intentions. This is an affordance we discuss in more detail below—and it is a particularly important affordance in anticipation of the development of AI communication bots (as we discuss in Chapter 7).
- ANT does not assume that the network is a stable reality—a wooden stage onto which the players enter, state their lines, and exit. Rather, it sees the network as itself socially—or, we would say, rhetorically—constituted. The network is not a stable a priori ground; it is itself in a state of flux. As Law (2004), put it, the "major ontological categories (for instance 'technology' and 'society,' 'human' and 'non-human') are treated as effects or outcomes, rather than as explanatory resources" (p. 157). This is a key distinction between actor-network theory and other theories that tend to treat the network and/or the social group as a methodologically stable ground (e.g., Castells, 2010).

- Methodologically, ANT is "better equipped to deal with mess, confusion and relative disorder" (Law, 2004, p. 2), and, we would add, to deal with the flux and instability of systems. ANT understands probabilistic knowledge. It eschews master narratives (or what Law, 2004, called "the single smooth narrative," p. 74). And it is also highly suspicious of prediction. ANT understands that reality flows and changes, and that efforts to fix actors or actions, or networks or social groups, as stable entities is methodologically flawed.
- ANT is a postmodern theory (versus a modernist theory) that better understands how language works to mediate and construct our world—and in that respect, it aligns better with a postmodern social view of rhetoric, and with a rhetorical perspective overall. ANT is aware of *time* as a factor of rhetorical analysis, a point we discuss below.
- More pragmatically, *network* is a recognized and commonly used metaphor for digitally-mediated communication in the popular media and in the world of business and professional communication.

An ANT Approach to Network

What are the characteristics of an actor-network approach? In this next section, we lay out in more detail the features of an ANT approach, also acknowledging some of the issues and problems inherent in this approach.

Of course, ANT focuses first and foremost on networks. But any network is itself comprised of and intersects with multiple other networks operating at multiple levels of granularity, as John Law (2000) explained in his discussion of an important 15th-century Portuguese technology, the carrack or sailing vessel:

> What is the ANT analysis of this technology [the carrack]? [...] Unsurprisingly, it pictures it as a network. [...] For instance, a vessel can be imagined as a network: a network of hull, spars, sails, ropes, guns, food stores, sleeping quarters—not to mention its human crew. On the other hand, if one turns up the magnification, then the *navigational system*—its Ephemerides, its astrolabe or quadrant, its slate for calculations, its charts, its trained navigator, not to mention its stars, recruited to the system and playing their role—can also be treated as a network. Then again, one can turn down the magnification and think about (say) the Portuguese *imperial system as a whole*, with its ports and entrepots, its vessels, its military dispositions, its markets, its merchants and its principles as a network in which things more or less stayed in place.
>
> (Law, 2000)

Law's example of the carrack, which recalls our discussion of Luther's network at the beginning of the chapter, notes that any technology is itself comprised of multiple technologies operating in multiple networks. The point is that any technology operates within "an array of relations" (Law, 2000)—and for an advanced technology system, such as 16th-century Portuguese shipping—the technology is not simply the machine, the sailing vessel. Rather, the operation of the machine depends on an entire system of support ("the imperial system as a whole"), that includes infrastructural elements such as vessels, ports, and marketplaces as well as regulatory mechanisms such as treaties, laws, and monetary exchanges systems. The system holds in place and works

> So long as the relations between it and its neighbouring entities hold steady. The navigators, the Arab competitors, the winds and the currents, the crew, the stores to feed the crew, the guns: if this network holds steady then so does the vessel. It doesn't founder, turning into matchwood on some tropical reef. It doesn't get seized by pirates and taken to the Arabian Sea. It doesn't sail on, lost, until the crew are broken down by disease and hunger. The vessel is an effect of its relations with other entities.
>
> (Law, 2000)

The reduction of the network to a single technology, the carrack or sailing vessel, is like the synecdoche of the printing press: For simplicity's sake, we use the lone technical object to stand for the whole—but in so doing, the danger is that we lose sight of the whole, "the array of relations" that is the network. We begin to believe, wrongly, that the printing press—or Facebook—is the agent of change.

Similarly, it is a fallacy to isolate the human agent from the scene: Human agency of various kinds operates at various levels to hold the operation of the technology in place: Somebody is charged with purchasing and collecting "the stores to feed the crew," without which the vessel can't do its job. As critical theorists would point out, it is human manual labor that often goes unrecognized, the people who do the hard work that makes network linkages work: e.g., the driver of the carriage who delivers the *95 Theses* from one town to the next, the construction worker who builds the cell towers for internet and cell phone transition, the IT person who maintains security checks on a campus wireless network.

From a practical standpoint, it is methodologically difficult to look at all these various moving pieces at the same time—and that is why, no doubt, we use synecdoche to help control the narrative and make analysis and discussion feel more manageable. But we can't let the synecdoche lead us to forget the operation of the network and the complexity of its moving parts. Actor-network theory helps us keep that balance in place: If you are looking at the larger system ("the internet"), don't forget the smaller pieces, multiple subsystems, and human microactions that hold that system in place. If you are looking at the smaller pieces (somebody's tweet), don't forget the larger system, which shaped the production of that tweet, even if that larger system is not the focus of your full analysis.

As a rhetorical methodology, actor-network theory is useful for studying digital communication practices within social groups—and, importantly, for studying how communication practices enact change (or not). ANT takes a broad social perspective on human action and interaction—while at the same time remaining vigilant, even suspicious, of sociological methods that tend to isolate and freeze "the group" as an object for study. As Latour (2005) cautioned, "there is no group, only group formation" (p. 27), meaning that groups are neither isolated nor static; they are constantly in a state of flux: "there is no relevant group that can be said to make up social aggregates, no established component that can be used as an incontrovertible starting point" (p. 29).

ANT notices that there is an innate problem in studying groups, a kind of Heisenberg Uncertainty Principle as applied to sociological analysis. The Heisenberg Uncertainty Principle in science says that you can't simultaneously measure an object's position and velocity: As soon as you collect data about it, the "it" has moved onto something else, it has changed. It is an object in motion, so you can't really capture the object's position and speed, at least not precisely. Same thing applies to studying social groups. As soon as you write a marketing report about millennials' political views, the millennials have aged and changed. Your study, which was based on only partial data anyway, represents a view from yesterday, not today. It's the problem of studying the moving target.

In *Reassembling the Social* (2005), Latour argued that the social unit is created by discursive interaction; social units do not pre-exist the discourse that brings them into being and that sustains them (and that changes them). He concluded that this discovery renders the social group unhelpful, or at least suspect, as a grounding for scientific inquiry. This may be a distressing claim to a sociologist or anthropologist, but not particularly so for a rhetorician. The term *public* (or the term *society* or any comparable social concept for that matter) is a social construct—and *the public* as an entity is constantly morphing and changing. The term is fluid, it moves and shifts, and it participates in relations of power; any effort to stabilize the meaning of the term precisely is doomed to fail. But that does not have to be regarded as a problem: It is a feature of complex human systems built upon communication interaction. (Welcome to rhetoric.) To say that a term has fluctuating, unstable meanings is not to say that a term is meaningless (an equation that too many radical skeptics make). Far from it. From a rhetorical standpoint, a term can certainly be traced and its many uses (plural) classified and understood. The anxiety of uncertainty, instability, and flux is a stress only for those methods whose idol is precise meaning or certain prediction.

Actor-network theory views the social system or network as the key focus for investigation. At the same time, it stresses that the social system is not an *a priori* object or pre-existing communication interaction; rather, the social system comes into being through communication, and develops/changes as interaction happens. In this sense, then, Facebook and Twitter are not networks; rather, they are platforms, that is, digital places or *venues* that enable the formation of networks. Each platform sits in the same place in the sense that its address (URL) is fixed, but in all the important rhetorical respects the platforms are in motion.

Why is this distinction between *platform/venue* and *network* important? Because it helps us understand why linear transmission models of persuasion or information, still framing how many professionals approach communication, are limited. It helps explain the emergence of unplanned events, unexpected results, surprising moments. As Engeström (1996) put it, sometimes "the puppet surprises the puppeteer" (p. 261). As Lucy Suchman (1987) put it, sometimes there is a gap between the plans and intentions of the designer and the actions of the user. As we would put it, communication is not simply transmitting information (or intention) from Point A to Point B. Communication involves an interaction and negotiation among participants. And while this interaction may be somewhat predictable, and while we sometimes achieve our intended communication objectives, we don't always, and that is because circumstances and networks are in a state of constant change, and people are diverse. Our communication efforts are always running a bit behind: We are always, in our heads, addressing yesterday's audience on yesterday's network. As Latour (1996b) explained, "there is a yawning gulf separating the agent from structure, the individual from society" (p. 232). We think this was and is true in the world of print, too, but the gulf is even more obvious and evident in the world of the digital network, because cultural change happens so much more rapidly.

In focusing on network, we are not abandoning the focus on discrete rhetorical actors and actions—not at all—but we are saying that in order to understand the quality and effectiveness of such events, we need to look at those events as appearing and operating within an array of relations—whether we call it *system*, *ecology*, or *network*. We have to move well beyond linguistic or discourse analysis, and even beyond contextual rhetorical analysis, to look at networks. ANT proceeds inductively and ethnographically, tracking connections and interactions between participants to uncover significant assemblages that come together to form networks (Jung, 2014).

The network is not a pre-existing place or thing, it is not a container through which communications flow: that is the pipeline metaphor, the transmission model of communication (represented in Figure 3.1), a model that has always maintained considerable power over people's thinking about how communication works. ANT flips that model around to say: Networks are spaces created through people's interactions (Law, 2002). To be sure, there are stable material objects and places—e.g., my laptop computer, my social media account on Twitter, the Facebook URL—but that is not the same as the social network. The problem is confusing the objects and spaces as the network, instead of as merely interactant components within the network.

But even the technology is not perfectly stable. When it enters into a new array of relations the technology itself can change in unexpected ways. Think of the lead water pipes in Flint, Michigan: Are those lead pipes a static technology? Well, yes and no. They are still composed of lead and they still carry water (potable or not is a different matter) to the people of Flint. They are, in one sense, the same pipes now as when they were installed. But with the change of source of the water running through them (the State of Michigan changed the water source from Lake Huron to the far more polluted Flint River) and the discontinued use of a pipe protecting chemical, the pipes changed dramatically: from a relatively safe delivery technology supporting human life into a poisonous threat. MySpace changed dramatically, too: In 2005, it was the most used social media network, but a combination of factors changed that, including the widely publicized news in 2009 of MySpace closing the accounts of 90,000 registered sex offenders who many feared (fairly or not) were using the space for potentially predatory purposes. By 2015, with the combination of bad publicity and the rise of Facebook, MySpace had become one of the least used social media sites. Same pipes perhaps, but a very different network.

We could say that "nearly everything is a network" (Jones, 2015)—or, at least, that everything is connected within a network, or rather multiple networks. A network simply refers to the connectedness—communication or interaction connectedness—of people and objects. Networks are constantly changing, new ones emerge, old ones disappear, participants come and go. The problem with any static, print diagrammatic representation of networks is that it will fail to represent motion, movement, and change over time. What is really needed to represent the network (which a print book can't provide) is a dynamic video.

Also important to actor-network theory—and this is a point emphasized by Jane Bennett in *Vibrant Matter* (2010)—the network or assemblage itself exerts its own influence, it comes to have a life and intention of its own that may not be in concert with the goals and intentions of the human participants (either as individuals or in the collective). "Objects too have agency," argued Latour (2005, p. 63). In Latour's *Aramis*, the machine—the design for a new commuter railway system that is partly built but then abandoned—comes to life: It becomes a character in the novel, with its own desires, hopes, intentions, and even its own voice, reflecting on its own existence and interacting with the human participants (who mostly do not recognize that the machine is a living thing). In Latour's *Aramis*, we of course see a re-telling of Mary Shelley's *Frankenstein*, the story of the scientist Viktor Frankenstein, who creates a monster that he first loves, but then eventually rejects and abandons. Actor-network theory takes an expensive view of actants, including objects (like texts and images) and technologies and even historical traces as actants "capable of influencing how information is processed by the network" (Jones, 2015).

We invoke actor network theory because its frame of thinking exposes something important methodologically about our thinking about online communications: Maybe analyses of social media have been looking at the wrong things in the wrong way. Maybe we have been looking at the objects in the network rather than at the network itself. Maybe we have been looking at objects as isolated events instead of at the interactions between and among objects in a discursive flow. Maybe we have been looking at interactions locally and currently instead of globally, historically, and diachronically. (We include ourselves in this "we." At times, and in previous publications, and perhaps even in this book, we have certainly performed rhetorical analysis of isolated events and texts, perhaps neglecting to see the event or text from a network perspective.) That is why we—collectively as scholars, as professionals, as communicators, as professional communicators—need a different methodological frame or lens to redirect our attention to what is really happening. That is what our network model, Figure 4.4, attempts to capture.

We respect Latour's warning about the perils of studying interaction: "any given interaction seems to overflow with elements which are already in the situation coming from some other time, some other place, and generated by some other agency" (Latour, 2005, p. 166), which is why it is important when studying interaction to bring a deep consciousness of the larger contexts, histories, and forces that are always at play in any interaction.

We need to be wary of a trap within Latour's own articulation of actor-network theory: his tendency toward a kind of radical agnosticism. Aren't all perspectives biased? Can we ever really know anything? Certainly, all perspectives are biased, but bias does not preclude knowledge-making. Using a methodological frame or perspective means that you bring a bias to the study, a bias that inevitably privileges some data over other data. The solution here is to be aware of and transparent about the bias of the methodology, and to be critical and humble about the results it produces, acknowledging the gaps and, what Latour called, the "uncertainties" (p. 170). In our own case analyses in Chapters 5–7, we aim to do that, to acknowledge what we are and are not looking at in depth in the networks we study and thus what knowledge we can and cannot make from the analyses.

What Latour articulated in *Reassembling the Social* is a kind of postmodern methodology that is more attentive to change, to fluidity, to diversity, and to power relations, that is more humble about its results, that is more suspicious about the groundings for its approach, and that eschews positivistic certainty in favor of rhetorical probability, than the older, modernist methodologies that tended to rely on fixities like the author, the text, the audience, the group, or the activity system. (In our view, activity theory tends toward a naivete about power, about certainty, and about predictability.) As his book title suggests, Latour is not trying to destroy or dismiss the social; he is trying to *reassemble* it along different lines.

Here is where it helps to bring rhetoric to the postmodern social science methodology Latour offers us. Rhetoric has always dealt with the problem of context: The art is based on the rhetor understanding her context, and yet context changes, shifts, morphs, constantly. And so the effective rhetor needs to be in close touch with changing historical circumstances, changing audience attitudes and emotions, changing cultural memes and moments—and even more than that, the challenge of addressing the diverse audience: People are different. The rhetorical strategy that works for Person A is a colossal failure for Person B. Past experience provides some help and guidance, but with every new communication, the rhetor enters/creates a new contextual moment. That is the rhetorical nature of communication: It is slippery. This uncertainty is a problem only if your standard for knowledge is a scientific standard of predictive, epistemic knowledge—but that is not the kind of knowledge that rhetoric is. Like other social arts (politics, law, ethics), rhetoric operates in the realm of probability, probable knowledge, productive knowledge (*techne*), practical wisdom (*phronesis*), and practical knowledge (*praxis*) (a realm, by the way, that artificial intelligent agents struggle in, as we discuss in Chapter 7).

The fallacy we see repeated over and over—the fallacy that ANT addresses—is the modernist assumption that the network pre-exists as a stable, monolithic entity that participants then join (or leave). That is the fallacy of viewing Twitter or Facebook or Instagram as the network; seeing the business organization as the overseer of the corporate account on that network; and seeing customers as more or less passive members who join the stable network. This modernist, arhetorical view of networks is what feeds the myth of control: If networks are nice, neat, cool, fun (pick your adjective) locations—properties, as it were, that we own and control—then we can determine what happens there.

Partly, too, this is the persistence of the single authorship model of writing working in concert with a transmission model of communication—in this case, the single author being the corporation who creates discourse and the consumer who passively receives it. The linear sender-receiver model misses a crucial quality of how discourse operates: "sender-receiver models [...] tend to identify a kind of homeostatic relationship, which simultaneously abstracts the operation of social links and circulation" (Edbauer, 2005, p. 6).

This linear model stands in opposition to an ecological or network model that sees writing "as an activity through which a person [or corporation] is continually engaged with a variety of socially constituted systems" (Cooper, 1986, p. 367)—and these systems "are made and remade by writers in the act of writing" (Cooper, 1986, p. 368). In other words, these systems "change social reality" and do not merely reflect or represent it.

ANT provides us with a very different kind of rhetorical model, one that begins by acknowledging that networks are created and built through communication interactions, some of which are brief and momentary and others of which go viral—but what happens in these networks can quickly move outside the control of any given individual or company. Although companies have come to realize this—"How do we control what happens to our hashtag!"—at the same time, they still hope to control. They often continue to manage their social media marketing according to a stable systems model that doesn't sufficiently account for the rapid fluidity and spreadability of Web 2.0 communications, especially with mobile technologies.

In short, companies and business professionals need a different network model to work with—not a one-way broadcast model, but a post-human rhetorically-alert network model that accounts, first, for the speed and spread and two-way (multi-way, more accurately) nature of social media and, second, that accounts for the complex interactions of human and non-human actors in both online and on-ground interactions as these events spread virally and unfold rapidly over time.

A Rhetoric Network Model for Professional Communication

Let us turn now to how actor-network theory can be transformed into an operational model useful for understanding and analyzing networked professional communication.

Discussions of communication lapses in business, particularly in popular media, often focus on the communication *event or action*—that is, a problematic moment when somebody did something wrong, focusing mainly either on the wrongful discourse (e.g., Justine Sacco's racist tweet; Ford Motor Company's insensitive tweet) or focusing on the writer, the person or corporation who erred (Sacco, Ford): Was Sacco's tweet a joke or not? Was Ford's apology for its lapse adequate or not? In other words, the focus falls on the discursive event, on the offending text, or on the person or corporation who does something wrong. In other words, the frame for understanding these events is an individualist frame that focuses on actor-action (see Figure 4.1).

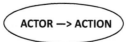

Figure 4.1 Actor-action as primary focus for rhetorical or ethical analysis

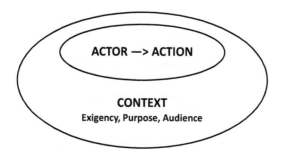

Figure 4.2 Actor-action in its immediate rhetorical context

This frame aligns with the traditional focus of post-Enlightenment, modernist rhetoric on the made object (the text) or on the agent producing it (the writer, the communicator). It, too, is an individualist focus. If we were to put this in theological terms, as Luther might do, the popular media focuses on the sin, on the sinner, or both—probably because that is the focus that garners the most attention.

For a network form of rhetorical analysis this focus on the actor/action remains important, but it is not enough by itself to explain the dynamics of the system. What is also needed is a broader perspective that includes *context*: that is, the cultural moment, audience, exigence, purpose, constraints, etc., for a particular discursive event (Bitzer, 1968). As we discussed earlier, one of the key contributions of the New Rhetoric was to reconstitute rhetoric as fundamentally a contextual art that has to account for how context—and most importantly, the factor of audience—affects communication interaction. Figure 4.2 adds context to our map—and key to context is *audience*. Every communication (or at least every effective one) needs to consider audience as a key factor, and that is certainly one of our key points about phatic communication: Interaction is primarily about building and maintaining relations with audiences within contexts.

But now we need to shift to the elements that a Latourian actor-network perspective emphasizes, starting with the technology/ies involved, what in information and communication theory is typically termed ICT (information communication technology)—the technical infrastructure part of network, the platform or venue for interaction. For our purposes, though, we refer to this infrastructure as CT, Communication

Technology, because the technologies are not merely or only transmitting information. Figure 4.3 adds this element.

In our explanation of the components of the network and in our representation in Figure 4.4, what is important to note is the multilayered nature of elements and the many simultaneous roles, the way, for example, that audience and CTs are actors too. In addition, we of course need to view discursive events as part of a larger network or system. There is not just the isolated event, the agent, and the immediate context, but, as shown in Figure 4.4, a much broader network involving context-in-a-broader-sense (historical and cultural background); near-time and far-time responses to the event; and multiple agents who contribute to the event, shaping past, present, and future understandings, interpretations, and actions.

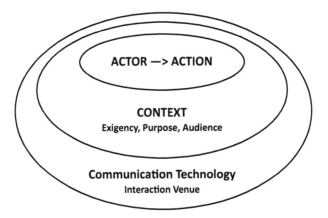

Figure 4.3 The influence of Communication Technology (CT)

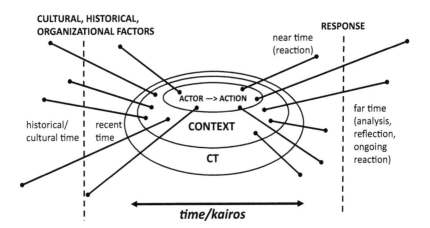

Figure 4.4 Rhetorical action/interaction from a network perspective, unfolding and changing over time

Figure 4.4 represents our network perspective on rhetorical activity, a perspective insisting that for us to understand a rhetorical or ethical event or moment, we must first start by not viewing it as isolated. That event exists in an immediate rhetorical context, but also within broader contexts—the history of the company as employee-owned, for example, the global crisis on AIDs, the new European laws on privacy—contexts like these all shape interactions, the actions and reactions in the network.

Responses are, of course, the immediate reaction to the event, what we call near time (e.g., the twitterstorm following an offensive tweet) and the longer-term analysis and ongoing reflection (e.g., retrospective media pieces, scholarly reports). A network perspective recognizes that a network is ever-shifting and changing, a system unfolding over, across and within time, where views of action and agent herself changes.

In taking this network perspective, we are not excusing the actions and responsibilities of individuals or of corporations within the network. What we are saying, though, is that the network does exert an influence on human (and machine) action—and that individual and corporate collective rhetorical/ethical actions need to be understood and evaluated within that network, that "array of relations," an array that involves both human and non-human agents.

There are three important characteristics of this view of network that are important to highlight:

- this model treats technology itself not as merely instrumental but as an active participant, or actant, in the network, one exercising ethical and rhetorical intention;
- this model represents the virality and spreadability of interaction; and
- this model emphasizes the importance of time—and time in its various manifestations (e.g., cultural time, immediate past time, immediate response time).

Below we discuss each of these features of the model in more detail.

Technology as Participant Actant Exercising Rhetorical and Ethical Intention

Notice that technology is a very prominent character in this diagram. Technology exerts its own power and influence, often apart from, or even contrary to, the wishes and intentions of the technology creators and designers, as Latour (1996a; 1996b) and Bennett (2010) have strongly argued.

This view of technology-as-actant stands in opposition to what Andrew Feenberg (1991) terms the *instrumental view of technology*, which presumes that technologies are neutral objects that serve human interests, mere tools that humans simply use and control. We see an example of an instrumental viewpoint expressed by Archer Taylor in reference to the printing press:

> The powers which shape men's lives may be expressed in books and type, but by and of itself printing [...] is only a tool, an instrument, and the multiplication of tools and instruments does not of itself affect intellectual and spiritual life.
>
> (Archer Taylor, 1941, qtd. in Eisenstein, 2005, p. 308)

According to Taylor, printing is "only a tool, an instrument" that "does not of itself affect intellectual and spiritual life." Now that may be true if we regard the printing press as a technology detached from its context and use—but if we look at the printing press as operating in an entire network, as we did with our Luther example, then we would arrive at a very different conclusion.

The instrumental view certainly does acknowledge that there can be problems with technology, but is optimistic about the human ability to solve those problems, in three respects:

- through testing and improvement of design, flaws can be fixed;
- even with flaws, the technology can perform far better than humans at the same task; and
- if the designers themselves are guided by the high moral principles, those principles will be installed in the design.

Connecting the instrumental view to question of rhetoric and communication, you can see that it fails to account fully for the complexity of communication: different audiences, different cultures, the multiplicity of meanings inherent (and unavoidable) in all language use. In regards to ethics, instrumentalism is naive about power and control: it assumes the designer (a) has full control/agency over machine, and (b) has good intentions and high ethical standards. From the standpoint of methodology, it relies too much on lab testing and does not sufficiently respect field testing, which would reveal problems with onground, in-situ use.

Feenberg contrasted the instrumental view with the *substantive view*, which argues that technologies substantially change human thought and behavior, so much so that the technology becomes, in a sense, the all-powerful force in human-technological interaction. You see this view in overly optimistic claims for what a technology will do (with computers all students will love learning!) and in overly pessimistic claims as well (computers are killing books!). Technologies certainly do exert powerful influences in the network. But they don't do it alone.

Given the limitations of an instrumental view or a substantive view, Feenberg adopted a third position, what he calls the *critical view*: technology is not simply a neutral tool or instrumental factor, nor is it an all-shaping substantive power. Rather, humans both shape and are shaped by the technologies they use.

History is, of course, replete with examples of the profound influence of technology on human society. For example, Jeffrey Pruchnic (2014) noted, the development of large mechanical clocks during the late medieval period was not a neutral technological development helping citizens keep track of time. Rather, clocks changed people's attitudes toward time: the introduction of mechanical public clocks provided a secular, shared sense of time that replaced two older systems of time keeping: (1) the seasonal or circadian time of planting and harvesting, and (2) the authority of Church time (division of day into prayer periods). In other words, mechanical clock technology was not simply a new way of keeping time; it did not simply make the status quo more timely. The public clocks introduced a new sense of time altogether, a new political authority for timekeeping. The clock—and, again, *the clock* is a synecdoche standing for a larger whole—introduced a system that upset the existing order and eventually replaced the established customs and authorities.

As the mechanical clock example shows, networks or assemblages are not simply human communities but also include objects working as actants—a point particularly important for understanding digital media ethics where often CT exerts an effect beyond what any individual human agent in the assemblage intends or anticipates. Twitterstorms occur not just because of the humans who tweet and retweet but also because of the connectivity across digital devices that has created the conditions for such a viral network to occur.

The instrumental view of technology, so pervasive in popular discussions of technology development, leads to the set of beliefs that says, in effect, technology serves human needs, it is controllable, and it is ethically neutral. Historians and philosophers of technology—like Bruno Latour, Jeffrey Pruchnic, Luciano Floridi, and others working in the field of Machine Ethics—by and large espouse a critical framework viewing technology not as neutral but as imbued with ethics: that is, when you program a machine, you are necessarily and inevitably building ethical choices within it. There is no such thing as a neutral algorithm.

Machine Ethics[5] is an emergent subarea of the philosophy of science and technology that focuses on questions related to the design of artificial intelligence machines, aka robots, that can replicate human actions, including communication actions (see, for example, Floridi & Sanders, 2004; Grodzinsky, Miller, & Wolf, 2008; Torrance, 2008; Adam, 2008; Wallach & Allen, 2009; Crnkovic & Çürüklü, 2012; Floridi, 2014; Alač, 2016; Etzioni & Etzioni, 2016). The key question Machine Ethics asks is: What are the moral and ethical implications of assigning robots to these formerly human functions? To the extent that Machine Ethics focuses on AI communication, it very much overlaps with our rhetorical-ethical theory and with our network frame.

Isaac Asmiov's 1942 short story "Runaround"—later collected in his 1950 book of short stories, *I, Robot*—is regarded as key literary source for Machine Ethics, as Asimov's work fictionally deals with the question of machine ethics. The robots in Asimov's collection of stories are programmed according to the "Three Laws of Robotics," an ethical system programmed into every robot. These three laws are an algorithm essentially functioning to determine robot action—to guarantee ethical behavior, as it were. (The First Principle is "A robot may not injure a human being or, through inaction, allow a human being to come to harm.") However, these ethical precepts quickly run into problems whenever robots engage real human situations. As Asimov shows, the laws often fail to address the complexity of the situation at hand, or they come into conflict with one another, and those fissures or gaps in the ethical code result in dilemmas, the problems that the stories address. To put this another way, when placed into contextual (rhetorical) situations, the algorithms that control robot behavior run into trouble, because the algorithms do not anticipate the diversity of human situations.

A key defining philosophical source for Machine Ethics is Martin Heidegger's 1954 essay "The Question Concerning Technology" (Heidegger, 1977). In that essay, Heidegger built the argument that technology should not be regarded as neutral. A technology, any technology, is designed and built by humans and is thereby invested with human values. Conversely, the instrumental view focuses on what the machine does, how it operates: the bottle opener, when deployed correctly, opens a bottle, and we are able to drink from the bottle—and that is assumed to be a useful, good thing. The instrumental view looks at the immediate end, what Aristotle calls the *causa efficiens*, the efficient or immediate outcome, or what we might think of as short-term results.

Instrumentalism looks at technology—or, really, any newly designed system (say, a disruptive innovation such as Uber or Airbnb)—from the framework of optimistic neutrality. It's new! It's different! If we use it properly, it can help us! Such a framework (*gestell*, in Heidegger's theory) certainly does admit that there can be unethical, malevolent uses, misuses of technology—but only if bad people misuse the good technology. In other words, the badness or goodness of any technology lies in its human use; the technology itself is neutral.

But what Heidegger, Feenberg, and others term the *critical framework* examines the technology in its context of use, looking at the why, the purpose: For what end does the technology exist? As Heidegger asked: What about the *causa finalis*, the ultimate end of the technology, the purpose it achieves within human society? What changes does the technology enact in us, as humans, and is that what we want? To focus on *causa finalis*, ultimate or long-term consequences, is to raise the question of ethics. *Cui bono?* What good and whose good was the technology designed/intended to promote? And, an important follow-up question, how is the technology actually being used, and what are the results of that use?

Uber, for example, may result in lower costs for people seeking a ride across town, but at what cost to systems designed to recognize and protect both workers and consumers? Ultimately, is society better off with thousands or even millions of people working as "independent contractors" in the so-called "share" economy who do not share any of the benefits of employment, at least as manifest in the United States (e.g., health benefits, workers compensation, retirement)? This critical view does not see technology as simply the machine abstracted from use, as simply the plastic, wires, tubes, resistors, circuits, metal (or the app to connect drivers and ride-seekers); it sees technology in its context of use, as participating in human-computer interaction and, in doing so, effecting fundamental changes in humans, in society, in culture, and in reality.

The Internet itself is a good example of how the original intentions of designers can be thwarted by users. As Manuel Castells (2010) pointed out, the first computer network, ARPANET, went on line on September 1, 1969. This network, which linked the US Department of Defense with four research universities (UCLA, Stanford, UC-Santa Barbara, and the University of Utah), represented a cooperative effort between university-based research and the U.S. Department of Defense. It was intended as a computing tool to support university scientists with federal Defense Department grants and to facilitate their communications with Defense Department personnel (Castells, 2010, pp. 45–46). But then something interesting happened: "scientists starting to use it for their own communication purposes, including a science fiction enthusiasts' messaging network," and then, soon thereafter, "personal chatting" (Castells, 2010, p. 46). Users discovered that this network was a great tool for sending messages to one another.

This difference between *causa efficiens* and *causa finalis* does appear in popular culture, particularly in the realm of science fiction. For example, in the 1993 film *Jurassic Park*, the chaos theory mathematician, Ian Malcolm, challenges John Hammond's rationale for creating dinosaurs in Jurassic Park: "Your scientists were so preoccupied with *whether or not they could* [make dinosaurs] that they *didn't* stop to think if they *should*." This distinction between *can* and *should*—a key question for the philosophy of science and technology development—translates neatly into Heigeggerian terms. Malcolm is saying, in effect, "you focused on *causa efficiens*, but you neglected *causa finalis*. And, as a result of your intellectual, methodological, and ethical failing, your dinosaurs will eat you."

Heidegger pointed out that the very term *technology* has its roots in the classical Greek concept of *techne*, or art: the art of making or producing something. In ancient Greek thought, rhetoric is a *techne*, or art of production: specifically, producing a speech that will have a persuasive effect on some audience in order to achieve some good for the *polis*. *Techne* is a form of knowledge—though not a scientific form (*episteme*). Rather, *techne* is a knowing-how kind of knowledge, and in the act of making something lies an important distinction between *causa efficiens* (how will my speech persuade this audience?) and *causa finalis* (what larger good will changing the audience achieve?).

To raise questions about *causa finalis* should not be viewed as technophobia or hostility to technology development. It is, rather, a view that is critical about, but not hostile to, technology development: It advises us to be circumspectly cautious about development, but especially suspicious about exaggerated claims regarding benefits. AI, whether in self-driving cars or social media chat bots, is not necessarily bad, but you can't approach it naively: You have to be aware of how context changes things. What is acceptable today could be taboo tomorrow. When designs go "out there" in the network, they inevitably change. To the degree that they are adaptive/responsive to their environments and to the immense variety of users, they can change in harmfully unintended ways. Users can change meaning, the context can change meaning, the technologies can change meaning, as evidenced in the case of Justine Sacco, discussed in Chapter 5, and the case of Microsoft's Tay, discussed in Chapter 7.

We find the critical theory of technology highly compatible with the networked theory of rhetorical communication. First, it acknowledges the complexity and nuance of communication. Communication is not just processing information or delivering data from point A to point B. You are creating value and creating relationships through interaction with human and non-human agents throughout the system. Second, and this is where actor-network theory comes in, the network itself is an actant, an active agent that exercises its own distinct power within a communication system like the internet. That network can change, modify, or undercut designer intentions.

Problems can arise, though, if our habits, dispositions, and cultural values have not quite caught up with the technologies we are using. New technologies can be disruptive, forcing us to change our attitudes—or not, if we choose to be resistant. Some people adapt quickly, coming to appreciate the affordances of the new technology, learning to deploy it to advantage—and learning to work with or around its impedances. Other people do not adapt so quickly: they retreat to the older familiar technologies, or they struggle to become proficient with the new.

Our attitudes and values, our expectations and assumptions about communication, might still be hanging back there in an earlier age: We live in the age of the mechanical clock, but maybe our daily lives are still organized according to seasonal and circadian rhythms. We live in the digital age, but maybe some of us are hanging back in the age of broadcast media; or, perhaps for others, in the age of the business telephone call and the face-to-face meeting. And we carry with us attitudes, values, and ethics from older, even ancient traditions, philosophical and religious traditions such as Enlightenment philosophy, Greek democracy, Christianity, Confucianism, 18th-century federalism, Jeffersonian democracy, communalism, socialism, Marxism, Buddhism; notions of justice, truth, privacy, good manners; social and tribal customs that go back millennia.

This out-of-synchness with technology is certainly *age related*, we would say: It is to be expected that older generations developed their communication proficiencies with older technologies, and so bring their prior experience with them to new communication venues. But we would not say it is *age determined*; that is, the ability to adapt and adjust is tied more to one's attitudes than to one's age, to a person's capacity to adapt to changing technology, even to welcome it.

But it's not just humans adapting to the technologies and technological networks we've created. It's also, as AI developers working on new deep learning projects explain, the technologies, the computer networks, that also need to and do adapt to the humans they interact with. As a network theory, ANT helps us avoid the fallacies of both instrumentalism and substantialism. ANT provides a critical view in the sense that it sees technology development as neither innately good nor innately bad, but as possibly either, or even both at the same time, depending on the circumstances of its development. Objects participate actively as actants in the social world, and exert an effect, but they do not determine the social world.

Third, and perhaps most importantly for our study, ANT views technologies as actants imbued with ethical and rhetorical intentions. Technologies do not simply perform the tasks imagined by their creators and designers, and they do not simply and unproblematically reflect the values and ethics of their well-intentioned creators and designers. When technologies go "out" in the world, into contexts of human use, they change. They perform in ways their designers did not imagine or intend: as did Tay, as did ARPANET, as did Frankenstein, as did the robots in Asimov's *I, Robot*. If designers only think about *causa efficiens*, but neglect *causa finalis*, then they are not thinking thoroughly or critically enough.

Virality, Spreadability. Multimodality

The internet is not just a pipeline, a neutral medium for delivering messages dutifully from companies to consumers. It is not simply another broadcast medium. And it does not simply, dutifully serve and reinforce existing rhetorical relationships, ethical systems, institutions, and power structures. Rather, the internet, or rather the assemblage of human interactions on the internet, is changing culture and "transforming existing social norms and institutions" (Nahon & Hemsley, 2013, p. 3).

It has created a "social infrastructure" that fundamentally changes the nature of rhetorical interactions and in so doing, over time, changes attitudes, rhetorical interactions, and ethical standards. As we discussed in Chapter 1, the qualities of *virality* and *spreadability*, when combined with the *multimodal functionality* of digital discourse, creates a distinctive kind of rhetorical interaction.

To illustrate this point, we refer back to our FedEx example of the video posted to YouTube "FedEx Guy Throwing My Computer Monitor," from Chapter 1. Before the internet, the web, social media platforms, and the ubiquity of smart phones (at least in the United States), the customer who watched his new computer monitor get pitched over the fence would have had little recourse but a letter of complaint. FedEx might have responded with a letter of apology, perhaps even offering to replace the monitor, but that would have been the end of it. But with digital networks audiences are larger and thus the potential for response is larger as well.

One key to the difference between the old print model and the new social media model is, as we have discussed, speed and reach. How broadly and quickly is the communication dispersed? Virality isn't new—information certainly spreads via print, as we saw with Luther, or broadcast media— but the speed and extent of the spread is what has changed dramatically. Another key to digital virality is multimodality: It is possible to spread images and video quickly, and thus postings have an immediate and profound visual impact that rises to the status of visual *evidence*, and is thus much more than a merely textual account.

Another key feature of spreadability is that information can flow from one medium to another: For instance, a tweet that goes viral in the afternoon can be picked up and reported that evening on nightly television news and then be printed and distributed in the newspaper for print or online distribution the following morning. An example would be the video postings of the 2011 student protest at the University of California-Davis and the subsequent pepper spraying of students, which was not reported by broadcast news until the event had already reached a saturation point on social networks, through postings and repostings of ad hoc videos created by student protesters. It was the social media postings that actually pushed the broadcast media, forcing them to cover a story that might have otherwise been ignored.

Perhaps more so than with pre-digital communication networks, the digitization of professional communication means that the connections throughout the network have the potential to extend and connect in more ways and to shape more widely more aspects of the network. One letter from an upset customer probably isn't going to change company practice, but 15 million views on YouTube and the accompanying news reports will. According to Nahon & Hemsley (2013), virality drives institutions and businesses "to be more accountable, transparent, and participatory; virality also pushes institutions to become more social [...] finding ways to engage with their citizens and consumers" (p. 122). Accountable, transparent, and participatory are also expectations or values: People expect businesses to be responsible, accountable, and trustworthy—to have integrity, in other words. And when there is a gap between the saying and the doing, between the expressed ethos and the behavior, then the public acts with outrage. The bigger the company, or the bigger the gap, the larger the extent of the outrage and protest.

One last important point: Our diagram in Figure 4.4 looks static because of the constraints of print publication. The elements look set on the page in such a way that elements on the left side—Historical, Cultural, Organizational contexts—look far removed from responses positioned on the right side. This leaves the impression that these elements only connect through mediated means—through, say, the original actor and action—but they also connect with each other. Organizations change, unfolding histories change, cultural moments arise from the interanimation of actors throughout the network. The spread and scope and speed of digital media impact that tremendously.

Time

As we discussed in Chapter 2, the ancient sophistic concept of *kairos* is critical to our theory reconnecting ethics to rhetoric—but it is also important to our conception of network. *Kairos* means the opportune moment for rhetorical interaction (Poulakos, 1983; Kinneavy, 1986). It includes the notion of chronological, linear time, but as John Smith (2002) pointed out, *kairos* means much more than that: It also refers to "a qualitative character of time" (p. 47) that pertains more to knowledge about cultural and historical moments that are imbued with audience attitudes, feelings, and emotions and that are very often tied to places and locations and to cultural memories, stories, and events.

In Figure 4.4, time—as pictured by the arrow at the bottom—refers overall to the flow of the network, and to its changing character. It moves. (If we could put video in the book, we would design our diagram as a dynamic video showing movement.) Time in the chronological sense has both backward and forward effects. Cultural and historical time in the sense of past events, experiences, attitudes, habits, and practices carries forward and continues to have force and exercise influence on our interactions. And as new interactions generate responses, those responses have short-term and long-term effects on the network, changing its conception and structure. As new actors engage, participate, leave, new actors come on board, there is a flow of discourse, and the elements of the network change. This dynamic flow is a critical aspect of Latourian analysis.

Sarah Read and Jason Swarts (2015) recognize the importance of *when* as part of a Latourian rhetorical analysis in their network analysis of the CIRCUIT studio (a digital media research lab supporting the design of hardware, software, and games at North Carolina State University). What Read and Swarts noticed in their research study was that "CIRCUIT transformed or multiplied into new objects" over three distinct periods during the time of their analysis. As a network and as a concept CIRCUIT developed a life and identity of its own apart from actions and intentions of individual contributors to it. As new human actors first engaged the system, then departed, to be replaced by new actors, all contributing to the emerging conception of CIRCUIT, "the actors facilitated a transformation that allowed the CIRCUIT concept to gradually materialize and have budgetary effects" (p. 34). But in a second stage of development, due to new actors engaging in interaction, CIRCUIT changed and developed both a new conception and a new network structure. And then it entered yet a third, new stage of network configuration.

In each stage, the very identity of CIRCUIT changed—and in each new phase, each new *when*, the configuration of the network also changed. Read and Swarts concluded their analysis by noting the affordances of an ANT approach to network analysis: "A Latourian analysis and a network analysis offer an outlook on networked phenomena as flows, or interactions, between actors that give rise to a networked object while being a thing in itself that affords the flow" (p. 38). The name of the thing might stay the same—CIRCUIT—but that does not mean the thing is a stable, fixed entity from a rhetorical standpoint: The meaning of the concept and the structure of the network change because of network interaction. As a methodology, ANT is designed to notice the complexity that time—understood in its broader, sophistic senses—introduces.

As we have said, *kairos* needs to be understood as a *form of rhetorical knowledge* shaping how one views, understands, and experiences events—and as a *form of ethical knowledge*, too, insofar as *kairos* also involves cultural attitudes and values. Sensitivity to *kairos* is key to a rhetorical understanding of communicative events as they unfold, move, and change, especially ethically problematic social media events, and is a vital component of our network model. It is this flow that makes network interaction so complicated—and interesting, we think—but it is also this flow and unpredictability that raises the most serious challenge for AI-based professional communication.

Conclusion

Our ANT-based network model is certainly a framework for rhetorical analysis—a type that examines how agents and objects coalesce and interact rhetorically in digitally mediated social spaces, aka, within networks. That is the rhetorical frame that we think has the greatest explanatory power and usefulness for describing how professionals communicate in the digital age.

The key, of course, is network—but network understood in a certain way. The network is not simply the technological infrastructure, a mass of wires, computers, towers, electrical impulses. It is not a pipeline. The Internet is not just a neutral medium for delivery of messages from Point A to Point B. Nor is the internet the only part of the network. The network as we are constructing it is a highly social, highly dialectic, dramatically instantaneous (and yet infused with an archival permanence) form of human interaction that creates a new kind of rhetorical dynamic leading to, as we discuss in upcoming chapters, new questions and new kinds of ethical responsibilities and obligations. The key contribution of this model is that it calls attention to the various factors that impact communication interaction—particularly historical and cultural factors, CT agency, and *kairos*.

To the extent that they focus only on isolated elements—e.g., the text, the writer/communicator, the technological medium—traditional models for understanding communication are not adequate for understanding the complex dynamic of social media communications. The model we offer in Figure 4.4, based on actor-network theory, acknowledges the networked nature of communications while at the same time (we hope) providing a framework that is manageable and usable as a methodological tool for rhetorical analysis. One of the criticisms of ANT is that while it might offer conceptual depth and complexity, it is hard to use; it is not something you can actually deploy as a method. Through our ANT-inspired network rhetoric approach to case analysis in the following chapters, we hope to show this is not the case. A network rhetoric theory has much to offer our understandings of and our practices of professional communication

While the actor-network model may be newish, the rhetorical canon for it is not: Knowledge of the network is critical to the rhetorical canon of delivery. And while traditionally the canon of delivery was not regarded as significant, not requiring any special talent, and certainly not a form of knowledge, like Luther we have to change our thinking about that. Network knowledge is fundamental to delivery and essential for rhetorically effective professional communication.

Notes

1 Historian Elizabeth Eisenstein (2005) stops just short of saying that the printing press caused the Protestant Reformation in Europe. But she does say that the printing press was hugely influential, and that the Reformation could not have happened the way it did without the printing press. It is not clear that Luther really wanted a public audience, at least not at first. According to Eisenstein (2005) Luther was reluctant to have his *95 Theses* widely distributed (p. 169). But "it was largely because traditional forms of theological disputation had been transformed by entirely new publicity techniques that the act of the German monk had such a far-reaching effect" (p. 171).

2 Two important works developing a network theory approach are Manuel Castells' *The Rise of the Network Society* (2nd ed., 2010) and Clay Spinuzzi's *Network: Theorizing Knowledge Work in Telecommunications* (2008). However, we are especially indebted to Sarah Read and Jason Swarts' 2015 article "Visualizing and Tracing: Research Methodologies for the Study of Networked, Sociotechnical Activity, Otherwise Known as Knowledge Work," in which Read and Swarts demonstrate how actor-network theory is a particularly appropriate methodology for studying network interaction in workplaces. As Read and Swarts point out, studying professional communication from the standpoint of network theory has been a "common frame" for understanding workplace communication (p. 15; see for example Nardi, Whittaker, & Schwarz, 2002; Johnson-Eilola, 2005; Spinuzzi, 2008).

3 Bruno Latour's ANT methodology is explicitly articulated in his book *Reassembling the Social* (2005), but this theory is implicitly developed in an earlier work: *Aramis, or the Love of Technology* (1996a). Our work also draws methodologically from John Law, particularly his article "Objects, Spaces, and Others" (2000) and his book *After Method* (2004).

4 Even earlier, in his 1968 article "On Systems of Rhetoric," Douglas Ehninger recognized the need for rhetoric to develop a systems perspective. He saw this perspective as chiefly a historical and cultural one. A rhetorical system refers to "the rhetoric embodied collectively in the treatises of a given place of period" (p. 131), as a general "social and intellectual mileu" (p. 132). In *The Archaeology of Knowledge* (1972), Michel Foucault argued for the importance of the discursive formation—a poststructural precursor to the actor-network model—as a key force of social power controlling the production of discourse within a given milieu.

5 Machine Ethics emerged as a formal field of inquiry in the early 2000s. In 2005, the AAAI (Association for the Advancement of Artificial Intelligence) sponsored a Symposium on Machine Ethics. And in 2009, Oxford University Press published an important work titled *Moral Machines: Teaching Robots Right from Wrong* (Wallach & Allen, 2009). The work of scholars in Machine Ethics can be found in journals such as *AI and Society* and *Ethics and Information Technology.*

Part II

Cases of Network Interaction

5 Employee Use of Social Media and Corporate Response

As Augie Ray (2012a), Director of Social Media at Prudential Financial, noted, "Social media will continue to challenge and change laws, regulations, business practices and the nature of the employee/employer relationship. Until the dust settles—and that will not be for many years—employers and employees alike are better off proceeding with caution. There are many landmines waiting for companies and workers in our new and evolving social era." There are indeed "many landmines waiting for companies and workers" on social media networks. The intense use of social media by companies and employees raises complex rhetorical and ethical issues that help shape and expose company culture and communication strategy, particularly when examining corporate response to employee use and misuse of social media.

Cases of employees getting themselves or their employers into legal, ethical, and reputational controversies because of social media missteps abound. Promotional photos used at the wrong time (Ford's Boston Marathon bombing tweet), cheery greetings tone-deaf to events of the day (the National Rifle Association's "Good morning, shooters" after the 2012 theater shootings), ill-conceived hashtags that are appropriated to unintended uses (#McDStories)—the examples go on and on.

Of course, long before the advent of social media, employees could intentionally or unintentionally harm company reputation and embarrass companies. But with social media the extent and velocity of embarrassment are significantly more dramatic: The twitterstorm happens immediately, offensive events go viral within hours (companies certainly don't want the embarrassing point to be "trending"), and aired dirty laundry stretches across the entire internet and globe. In addition, the public can more readily and instantly mock, remix, refute, and parody the corporate response—and that then becomes a new problem. The digital network changes the fundamental rhetorical nature of such events and, thus, requires a different kind of thinking in response.

Often, the immediate corporate response to an employee social media misstep (made as an individual or on behalf of the company) is to fire the employee(s) responsible. And maybe sometimes such an action is justified. But is it always? Should an employee be fired over one tweet even if that tweet is made on a personal account and not on company time? Do employees have the right to express their own opinions (and make their own mistakes) on social media without fear of retribution from employers? How should companies respond to employees who commit missteps on social media—whether they are missteps done directly on behalf of the company or done as a person who also happens to work at the company? When and where in the intersecting online and onground networks are people *employees*, and when are they *individuals* who have rights of privacy and expression beyond their work lives? When faced with employee use of social media, how much should a company try to make employees conform to expectations, and how much should a company aim instead to change itself and its own corporate culture?

In this chapter, using the rhetoric network theory articulated in previous chapters, we present and analyze three cases of employee use of social media and corporate responses: (1) the well-publicized case of Justine Sacco, her ill-conceived tweet, her firing for that tweet, and how the company interpreted her role as a communicator; (2) a case drawn from our interview with the President and CEO of a U.S. textile company, who found himself faced with an employee blogging derogatory statements about a named company executive in a public blog; and (3) a case drawn from our interview with an HR executive of a U.S. candy-making company that is making the transition into social media, including changing how it interacts with former employees. Our analysis includes insights shared with us by the Director of Ethics for a US subsidiary of a multinational manufacturing company.

These cases show different approaches to corporate response to employee (mis)use of social media and different strategies for handling relationships and building organizational ethos. How companies and company executives choose to respond, or not, to employee use of social media reveals important considerations for rhetoric and ethics in a circulatory, networked culture.

The Case of Justine Sacco & IAC

Justine Sacco was the senior director of corporate communications for IAC, a media and internet company that in 2013 managed more than 150 brands and corporations. On December 20, 2013, on an airline trip from London to South Africa to visit family, Sacco sent the following tweet from her personal Twitter account:

Going to Africa. Hope I don't get AIDS. Just kidding. I'm white!

Sacco, it seems, had little idea how offensive and insulting her tweet was, how clearly it showed her white, western-centric positioning, her racism, and her callousness toward a global health crisis that has devastated millions of individuals and their families, especially in Africa. In 2013 worldwide, there were 1.3 million deaths from AIDS, 35 million people living with HIV, and 2.1 million new HIV infections (Avert, 2016), and roughly two-thirds of all AIDS deaths and HIV infections were in Africa (WHO, 2016). In addition, because of the imbalance of wealth in the world, the percentage of people receiving antiretroviral treatment is higher in majority white populations in the United States and Europe. AIDS is no joke—and to imply that it is and that it is a disease that only affects black people is problematic at best.

But, immersed in her privileged positioning, Sacco seems to have been oblivious to how wrong-headed her tweet was on so many levels. Instead, she typed that exclamation point, posted her tweet, and then turned off her phone and was in the air for ten hours. Unbeknownst to her, but perhaps not surprising, while she was flying, her tweet garnered a lot of attention. In fact, without her knowing it, she became the focal point of a global twitterstorm.

Sam Biddle, an editor at the time for Gawker Media's *Valleywag*, was the first to retweet Sacco's tweet to his 15,000 followers and to post it on his blog. As he explained a year after the event, "As soon as I saw the tweet, I posted it. I barely needed to write anything to go with it: This woman's job was carefully managing the words of a large tech-media conglomerate, and she'd worded something terribly" (Biddle, 2014). Sacco's post was retweeted extensively, trended highest worldwide, and two new hashtags developed: #HasJustineLanded and the much more widely and still used #HasJustineLandedYet. Many people found themselves glued to Twitter waiting to find out what would happen to Sacco when she landed.

As with any twitterstorm—worldwide events of public criticism and/ or shaming (see Ronson, 2015a)—the tweets came fast and furious. Justine's unintended global audience responded loudly, pointing out the racism and biased privilege in Justine's tweet and sharing how upset her tweet made them feel. In addition to criticizing Sacco, many responded by mentioning her company IAC and its CEO Barry Diller as well:

> #IAC needs to fire this racist, stupid bitch!

> #TWIT insult a continent, racially profile them & mock AIDS? Thank You Barry Diller & IAC !NEXT!!

> Aside this ignoramous it speaks volumes of IAC who employed her Awareness raised about AIDS/HIV

Sacco's tweet and the underlying attitudes that its content reveals are problematic in so many ways, it would have been hard for any company to ignore. But perhaps because of its very mission—managing corporate brands—the trending tweets certainly got IAC's immediate attention.

Even *before* Sacco landed, IAC sent the following statement to Biddle and *Valleywag* about Sacco's tweet: "This is an outrageous, offensive comment that does not reflect the views and values of IAC. Unfortunately, the employee in question is unreachable on an international flight, but this is a very serious matter and we are taking appropriate action" (qtd. in Biddle, 2013). When Sacco landed, she learned she was in deep trouble at work, was the subject of CNN news stories (Stelter, 2013), and had her Twitter feed, which had only 174 followers, read through by thousands (many who pointed out other inappropriate tweets made months and years earlier). Not surprisingly, Sacco deleted her Twitter account soon after landing.

The next day, Sacco released a public apology in a South African newspaper, "Words cannot express how sorry I am, and how necessary it is for me to apologize to the people of South Africa, who I have offended due to a needless and careless tweet" (qtd. in Dimitrova, Rahmanzadeh, & Lipman, 2013). IAC also released a statement:

> The offensive comment does not reflect the views and values of IAC. We take this issue very seriously, and we have parted ways with the *employee* in question.
>
> There is no excuse for the hateful statements that have been made and we condemn them unequivocally. We hope, however, that time and action, and the forgiving human spirit, will not result in the wholesale condemnation of an *individual* who we have otherwise known to be a decent person at core.
>
> (qtd. in Biddle, 2013, emphasis added)

Tellingly, in this posting IAC moved from calling Sacco an *employee* (which she had been for two years) to an *individual*, a point we discuss in more detail below.

Sacco's tweet was certainly careless, insensitive, and offensive, demonstrating Sacco's privileged positioning and her (intentional or unintentional) racism. There's a lot that could be examined in this case in terms of network interactions. For example, after the event a great deal was written about the actor (Sacco's white and wealthy identity and positioning), about the action (whether Sacco's tweet was a joke, as she claimed, or not), and about the response (whether Sacco was—and continues to be—a victim of excessive and undeserved shaming) (e.g., Blanchfield, 2015; Ronson, 2015a,b). In our discussion here, we want to take a new tack and examine Sacco's case through the lens of employer and employee interactions in the network. When an employee makes a social media misstep, what factors should be considered when weighing possible responses? How does a company determine an ethical and appropriate response?

Examining the Actor and Audience Perception: Role Boundaries

A key factor to consider when examining the action of a social media misstep is to identify what role the person is in when communicating—a question that pertains centrally to our point, in Chapter 2, that ethos can vary from context to context. As the Director of Ethics for a multi-national corporation with 80,000 employees around the world and 12,000 in the United States explained to us in an interview[1]:

> Most of the ethical issues we [company management] face have to do with professional roles. How a person is functioning and how they are holding themselves out when they communicate is of great importance to us. So when we look at the policies we have, it's clear that they're trying to make a distinction between whether or not a person is authorized to communicate on behalf of the corporation or whether or not they are acting in their private capacity to communicate. [...] It's a question of role: In what role is the person operating in?
>
> And also what do people outside our company—what is a reasonable expectation for them to understand what role that person is speaking in? [...] It's hard to talk about professional ethics without defining what a role is and what a professional role is versus a private role is. Who are you acting on behalf of, and who do people perceive you as acting on behalf of? What is your role, what is your obligation in this particular capacity?
>
> (Interview, October 21, 2015)

Here is where the question of ethos comes into play. Was Justine Sacco an employee, or a private citizen, or some blend of both when she sent that tweet? Clearly her company considered her an employee and then, once fired, as an individual. But was she tweeting in her role as a public relations executive at the time of that tweet? What if she'd made that comment orally on the plane to a few people or via a telephone call and it never was recorded digitally and thus never available for ubiquitous copying and sharing? Does the very public nature of social media and its velocity (Ridolfo & DeVoss, 2009) and spreadability (Jenkins, Ford, & Green, 2013) change when and in what role a person communicates? With social media, can we ever not be employees? The blurring of role boundaries—when is a person an employee and when is she a private individual—has always occurred in business, but with digital media those boundaries are blurring even more.

As the Director of Ethics explained, if two employees get in a fight on a Saturday night at a bar "we'd say, not our problem. That is clearly on somebody else's turf; you were not operating in your capacity as an employee." But if those same employees take to fighting and attacking each other in social media, then that's different because then "it's being viewed by other employees in the workplace and that is a workplace threat. That is something that we have to take seriously" (Interview, October 21, 2015).

Although Justine Sacco was not fighting with anyone, the analogy applies. Because Sacco was a public relations executive charged with overseeing communications for IAC and their many clients, her digital communications, once retweeted beyond her immediate circle, were being viewed in a very public forum. IAC had to take her tweets and the public reaction to them seriously. If Sacco had been in some other role for IAC than communications—if she'd been, say, part of building maintenance or IT—would her tweet have garnered the firestorm it did, and would IAC have reacted as they did?

In addition to determining the public-private roles of individuals when communicating, the relationship of the individual to the company and how audiences will perceive that individual's communications matters. As the Director of Ethics explained using a non-digital example, if an executive of the company goes to a political rally wearing the company polo shirt with the name and logo prominently displayed, people may think that the political views expressed are the views of the company, too, given the executive's leadership position.

But if an hourly employee, one who is not publicly visible as a representative of the company, wears the same shirt to a political rally, that act of wearing, while still, perhaps, against company policy, is less of a problem since that hourly employee would be less likely to be seen as representing the company. Every individual, then, has private roles and employee roles (see Figure 5.1), but depending on the nature of the person's job, the degree of overlap could be significantly higher.

For Sacco, because of her job as a public relations executive, there was a great deal more overlap between her employee role and her private role (see Figure 5.2). Given her ethos, her identity, status, and position in the company, she had less latitude in exercising her rights as a private citizen.

In addition to all of the other ethical missteps Sacco made in the content and delivery of her tweet, she also failed to recognize how intertwined

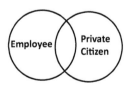

Figure 5.1 Employee and citizen roles mostly distinct

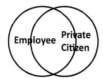

Figure 5.2 Employee and citizen roles extensively intertwined

her roles were. In a sense, because of the nature of her position, she could never *not* be seen as an employee in her publicly available communications. And the way the social network operates also creates a stronger connection between personal and employee roles. Sacco was not speaking to a small group of colleagues standing around the water cooler; she was not texting to a few friends; she was tweeting on a broadly public platform—and that changed the nature of the entire network.

The Role of the CT and Public Response

The nature of the communication technology (CT) also shapes the network. Sacco's tweet was publicly available for worldwide distribution. Biddle was the one to first repost her message, and there are certainly ethical considerations involved in his decision to retweet her post, an action he reflects on in a *Valleywag* piece one year after the event (Biddle, 2014). Legally, he could post her tweet because of Twitter's terms of service, which, at the time, allowed for copying and distributing of tweets (the terms have since changed), but was it an ethical course of action? In pondering the ethics of his decision, Biddle (2014) recognized that it was a "dicey" decision, one fraught with "swamps and thorns. Biddle concluded that he would do it again even though he "was surprised to see how quickly her life was upended" (qtd. in Ronson 2015b).

Sacco's life was upended in part because of the very nature of Twitter itself, how its global, public reach, and its communicative immediacy, enabled the mob to form, and, rereading the tweets, it was indeed a mob mentality out to ridicule and vilify Sacco (perhaps deservedly, as some commentators pointed out). The storm that ensued isn't just Sacco's or Biddle's responsibility—at least not primarily—because everyone who participated in the storm as poster and onlooker was an actor in the network. What had started as a single action—Sacco sending a single tweet—became a network of thousands of interrelated actions. Each person who participated in the twitterstorm was an actor but so too was (and is) the technological medium. As one user noted in a tweet in the midst of the storm, "I remember when you could be utterly stupid without the whole world finding out."

The other technological factor here involves preservation/copying of the event and its publication and distribution. In other words, what is different here is not just the role or location of the employee, but the capturability (copying and archiving) of the event via digital technology, the shareability (pasting) of it via social media, and the velocity and virality of its spread through social media (Ridolfo & DeVoss, 2009; Jenkins, Ford, & Green, 2013). Because of the incredible breadth and speed of distribution of networked CTs, Sacco's communication to 174 followers gets broadcast in just a few clicks worldwide. In that sort of massively public forum, the chances of someone being able to step away from an employee role and from employment ramifications for inappropriate communications are slim.

The Ethics of Corporate Response

Within professional communication, the organization is also always a key actor in the network. IAC's response was shaped by the public outcry but also played a role in the shaping of that discourse as well. IAC certainly responded swiftly—firing Sacco less than 24 hours after the tweet was sent. In relation to ethics and ethos, it is helpful to consider whether, in their handling of the Sacco case, IAC was a good company speaking well. Judging by the *chronos* of the event, it seems that could be a debatable point.

While Sacco was still in the air, IAC posted, as we quoted earlier, that her tweet was an "outrageous, offensive comment that does not reflect the views and values of IAC" and that "this is a very serious matter and we are taking appropriate action." They do not specify at what time this "action" happened, but early the next day, IAC announced that they had fired Sacco. Clearly, IAC was a company seeking to cut ties and establish distance as quickly as possible: Sacco's brand had gone bad and they didn't want that to tarnish their own or their clients' brands.

Given the swiftness of their action, it seems IAC made up its mind to fire Sacco even before she landed. They certainly did not give her much time to discuss and reflect with them her side of the story. We have not spoken with anyone at IAC, but we also wonder whether their own company culture and their own social media policy might have contributed to the problem? In pondering that question, we first must make clear that Sacco's biases arising from her white privilege and her economic privilege are, of course, the foundational causes of this whole case, but there are ways in which other factors contributed and ways in which too this case is instructive for considering employer and employee relations and questions of company culture.

In this case, what does IAC's move to fire quickly say about their own ethical culture at the time? Are their actions ones of a company that takes responsibility for its employees and the culture it itself has perhaps fostered, or is it a company seemingly willing to sacrifice responsibility and fairness (to the employee) in the interest of brand protection? The company's own ethos comes into question here, we feel. We do not necessarily disagree with IAC's decision in this case, given how egregious Sacco's tweet was, but we do raise questions about the company's decision-making process, the *how* of the decision within the network.

Given the type of company IAC is and Sacco's specific job at the company, it makes good business sense that they would want to cut ties as quickly as possible. Would you want to hire a company to manage your brand in a global marketplace if its own public relations executive communicates so ineffectively in digital media? But when thinking about the role of employees and employers and recognizing the widespread prevalence of social media missteps, was such an immediate firing the ethical thing to do?

The Director of Ethics, who has worked in ethics and industry for decades, reflected on a change he has noticed in perhaps too-swift corporate reactions to employee actions:

> I found that human resource departments are very quick to fire people in some part because of the fast-moving nature of the modern world. Communications go out quickly, people react quickly, reputations are made and lost quickly. And there's the sense that HR has to react quickly. I don't know if we have to. [...]I've really tried to highlight that the person who has made that mistake is tactically the one you want around because (1) they would probably be willing to talk about their story and be a good learning example, and (2) they're never going to make that mistake again.
>
> (Interview, October 21, 2015)

In the immediate response to an event, firing may seem the best way to go, but when time is factored in, it may not be the best course of action. In other words, companies need to be cautious about the rush to judgment. Figuring out where the line crossings are and what the consequences for those crossings will be is tricky for both companies and employees.

Another way to consider this issue, the Director of Ethics explained to us, is to look at what claims a company makes on an employee. Using the Navy as a comparison, the Director described how "The Navy makes claim to the whole person upfront. You do these kinds of stupid things in civilian clothes out in town [...] they're going to come after you. [...] Companies don't do that. They don't say that your moral character matters. They don't make a claim on the whole person." Companies are not the military and thus cannot ever have "full claim" on a person, but companies are increasingly showing concern about employee non-work behavior that could impact the company, as the Director of Ethics explained:

> What exactly is our [the company's] moral claim over a person who goes out, gets drunk, and runs their own car into a tree? I'm not sure we have one, but I definitely sense that at companies [the thinking is] your private behavior could reflect on us, and just the fact that it could gives us some authority to make employment decisions based on that outside behavior.
>
> I see in social media people are definitely starting to blur that line, and I don't think they're thinking through that properly. It feels like a wave—one of those things where overreach is becoming the norm in a lot of different areas of public and private life. It scares me a little.
>
> (Interview, October 21, 2015)

Employee surveillance (or workplace monitoring) is centuries old; however, with digital technologies, it is much easier to implement. From video and audio surveillance to monitoring of online activities and use of global positioning systems to track movement, employees worldwide are subject to intense scrutiny by employers. What employers are allowed to do and not do in tracking their employees at work and away from work varies a great deal by country and is shaped not just by regional and national laws and regulations but also by differing cultural perspectives on privacy (Kidwell & Sprague, 2009).[2]

Companies, like all organizations, also have unique cultures and how much a company chooses to consider employee's social media actions depends on the company culture. Understanding corporate policies and corporate culture is helpful for clarifying the often-blurry situations created by employee social media usage and corporate response. We would argue that an ethical responsibility of any company is to ensure that policies—legal, ethical, specific to company culture—are communicated clearly to employees. But it is important to recognize that the best policies in the world will never be able to address every situation that may arise. Policies around social media usage continually evolve with new situations and new technologies arising often faster than the policies can be revised. In these revisions, what sometimes can happen, as noted by the Director of Ethics, is an expansion of the overlap between what is company business and what is personal, private business. In other words, "overreach."

In the United States, some companies have developed overly broad social media policies that restrict employees from posting (on company or personal accounts) anything that might harm the company, the company's reputation, etc. Such overly broad policies, ones that say such things as employees may not post negative information about the company, have been struck down by the National Labor Relations Board (2015) in numerous cases. Employees have the right to discuss wages and work-ing conditions among fellow employees if the goal or *possible* goal is concerted action, but "an employee's comments on social media are gen-erally not protected if they are mere gripes not made in relation to group activity among employees" (NLRB, 2015). And if an employee posts really offensive and problematic comments, as Justine Sacco did, that is not protected under U.S. law, and companies may, legally, fire that employee.

Reflecting on the company role in the Sacco case, we don't know at the time of her tweet whether IAC had a social media policy for em-ployees and, if they did, what those were. But we can ask some critical questions: Had IAC communicated to employees their expectations for social media usage—and for different categories of employee? Had they made clear what they would view as company business, and what was personal, private business? Corporate policies shape network commu-nications, helping employees situate their practices so they align with company expectations and company culture.[3]

Regardless of what policies they may or may not have had at the time, IAC clearly was taking the approach that Sacco as an employee was a liability and they took immediate action to distance themselves from her.

The Case of the Blogger at Sunbury Textile Mills

IAC's response to Justine Sacco's tweet was to fire her, and that is often the response of companies. But one chief executive officer and president we interviewed chose a different approach, one based not just on the immediate context of the event but much more on the historical context and culture of his company.

Henry Truslow IV is CEO and President of Sunbury Textile Mills, which in some form has been running since its founding in 1890 in Sunbury, Pennsylvania (Sunbury, 2016).[4] Sunbury employs about 200 people at its mill in Sunbury and at its design and marketing center in New York City.

One day in 2014, Truslow received a call from one of his Senior Executives who asked Truslow to Google the executive's name, which Truslow did. One of the top links returned was an anonymous blog with many posts that were, in Truslow's words, "very derogatory and slan-derous" to the Senior Executive and "it was obvious the blog was written by somebody in the company, an employee." The Senior Executive told Truslow that something had to be done about this, and Truslow agreed, but he wasn't at first sure what to do.

When Truslow consulted with company lawyers, they told him there was nothing he could to the employee based on their reading of recent U.S. National Labor Relations Board (NLRB) rulings. But Truslow felt strongly that for the good of the company, "I can't do nothing" (Interview, October 15, 2015).

He also understood the difference between law and ethics: Perhaps, there was no legal course of action he could take, but there were many possible ethical actions that could be taken in response to the situation. As the leader of the company, responsible for both the individuals in his employment and the culture and brand of his company, he set out to restore company ethos and in doing so, although he would not recognize it in these terms, he set out to be Quintilian's good man speaking well for the greater community.

Truslow also recognized that even if legally he could punish the blogger, he did not want to. Prosecuting or firing someone for slander mattered less to him then (re)establishing clearly for all in the company the company ethos. Given the type of company he ran—one where the average employee had 20 years of experience and one that was set up as an Employee Stock Ownership Plan (ESOP)—he felt that prosecution and firing were not the ethical responses. All employees were owners of the company, and as co-owners, he felt it more important that all work together. What Truslow decided was needed instead was a communal response and a communal consideration of what the company stands for. Truslow's response, then, was shaped very much by the broader historical and cultural context in which his company operated.

"It Hurts Us Universally": Appealing to Communal Values

It is also important to point out what Truslow did *not* do: He did not respond via writing, by blogging, posting to social media, or sending an email; he did not issue an executive memo condemning the blog postings. Rather, he responded to the situation face-to-face, in person via a meeting with employees based on his understandings of company culture. Because of the nature of the posts, Truslow deduced that the employee was at management headquarters, so he traveled from his base at the mill to the management NYC offices. He explained his visit simply by saying that he wanted to talk with everyone at that office.

When employees came into the presentation room, Truslow had a projector, and he broadcast the blog post on a big screen:

> I said, "We're here to talk about something that I never imagined in my career that I'd be talking with you all about. But somebody in this room has taken it upon themselves to write slanderous and defaming comments in a blog." And the whole time I'm talking to them I'm going slowly through the thing, so they're reading it while they hear me speak.
>
> I said, 'Whoever has written this. I still can't believe this person is in this room. I'm not pointing fingers and I have no idea: I don't

want to know who did it. But what I want everybody to know is that whoever has written this—the obvious person it hurts is [the Senior Executive] because it's slanderous toward him. But beyond this it hurts every single person in this room. It hurts every single person in the factory. It hurts our customers, and it hurts our company. So it hurts us universally.

(Interview, October 15, 2015)

Truslow emphasized to employees that he did not want to engage in a "witch hunt" because that would be counterproductive and that he simply hoped that whoever wrote the blog post would consider taking it down. Truslow hoped his talk would have the desired effect: "I was hoping that night it would be taken down. Once everyone got home, whoever had written it would take it down. [But] I woke up the next morning and checked online and the damn thing was still up, so I was like, 'Oh, damn, it didn't work.'" (Interview, October 15, 2015). But then on the second day after the presentation the blog posts were taken down.

Truslow surmised this: "Everybody in the office, that's all they were talking about—so the next day we think that the person in the office didn't take it down because they wanted to gauge the reaction of all the other people" (Interview, October 15, 2015). What Truslow realized was that it wasn't his statement that swayed the anonymous blogger. Rather, it was the collective comments of the community:

[I did what I did] in an effort to right the ship and correct a wrong [...] We're 200 employees total—it's a very tight group, we have a good culture. I don't think it's much beyond that. [I said to them] this is just wrong and we've got to get it straightened up. I just laid it out for them and let them influence each other. And the proof was in the pudding—it took 48 hours instead of 24.

(Interview, October 15, 2015)

What did not work in this case was a top-down executive order. What did work was the appeal to collective values that resulted in collective action. Now, certainly Truslow did wield his power as CEO and President. He called all New York City employees to an unscheduled meeting—a significant act in itself—and he spoke passionately about what Sunbury Mills stands for, about what he felt was right and wrong in this situation, and about how, from his perspective, the whole community is hurt by the blog posting. By appealing to collective company values, Truslow set out not to fire the employee involved, as IAC did with Sacco, but rather to change employee behavior to align more with company culture. In a sense, he set out to raise the anonymous blogger's awareness of the company culture.

In this case, what we also see is the importance of making a strategic network shift. The blogging employee started his complaint in one network, an online social media network. But what the CEO did was shift the grounding of the network, moving to a more traditional onground network, the employees at the New York City office assembled as a group on a particular day. Now, those two different networks are certainly connected and overlapping. But what the CEO realized, innately, is that the best response to the problematic situation was to make the appeal in the second, more traditional network. We also see that his top-down appeal did not actually work in the way that he hoped. But it did work in an unexpected, indirect way: His appeal affected the network—and then the operation of the network, the values of the community, made the difference.

Sometimes such an approach is an appropriate response, and it works. Sometimes, however, what's needed is not employee change per se, but company cultural change.

The Case of World's Finest Chocolate and Adapting to Greater Transparency

World's Finest Chocolate is a family-owned chocolate company based in Chicago, Illinois. Founded as a cocoa distribution company in 1922 by brothers Edmond and Arnold Opler, in 1939 it began manufacturing chocolate products, and in 1949 it launched chocolate product fundraising. Today, the company CEO is Eddie Opler, the third generation to run the family business, and the company is often recognized for being one of the leaders in the chocolate and product fundraising fields. World's Finest Chocolate employs about 300 people, nearly all at its headquarters and production plant in Chicago. It has been recognized as one of the top 100 places to work by *The Chicago Tribune* (World's Finest Chocolate, 2016).

As part of our research to learn more about corporate response to employee use of social media, we interviewed Anthony Gargiulo Jr., Vice President of Human Resources at World's Finest Chocolate. Gargiulo described how at World's Finest Chocolate (WFC) they have not encountered any problematic usage of social media by current employees because employees mostly post about "a Christmas lunch or a summer picnic type of thing. So we look on those things as positive—they generate interest in the company and they generally give a good impression of the company. So we haven't had to address anything that's been problematic so far" (Interview, January 29, 2016).

The "so far" is key in Gargiulo's response, and perhaps arises from his role in HR and the responsibility he has for building and maintaining productive relations with not only current employees but also potential and former employees. Gargiulo recognized the impact social media and other digital technologies are having on employee-employer relations and that to stay responsive, companies need to continually assess their communication strategies and be willing and prepared to change company culture.

> What I would tell you is that World's Finest Chocolate has kind of been on a journey now as the third generation has taken over. We were a very paternalistic company in the past. My boss would agree with everything I'm saying here because we've talked about it a lot. In the past it was like, "We'll take care of you. Keep your head down and just do your job." To now we're at the point where we want—we make sure when we communicate with people we're doing it more on an interactive basis versus telling people things. What comes with that is a certain evolution in transparency. We're definitely on a path to being more transparent in how we communicate and share things.
>
> (Interview, January 29, 2016)

To provide an example of this changing culture of greater transparency, Gargiulo pointed to WFC's recent foray into the social media platform Glass Door. Founded in 2007, Glass Door is a site where job applicants, employees, and former employees can post anonymous reviews about a company's interview and hiring processes, working conditions, salaries, etc. When a company gets a certain number of reviews, they are able, if they wish, to post a company profile and set up interactive and public responding with the anonymous reviewers.

At the time of our interview, WFC had just started in Glass Door, but, as Gargiulo noted, "for our boss [CEO Eddie Opler] to agree to engage in Glass Door was a big thing" (Interview, January 29, 2016). In Glass Door, World's Finest Chocolate is recognized as an "Engaged Employer" because of their commitment to respond to and to consider anonymous reviews. Such engagement, particularly with former employees, is a key for changing company culture.

In his role at the company, Gargiulo advocated that the company embrace feedback and criticism so as to be open to change.

> I think too you have to be comfortable with the realization that no work place is perfect. I think Bill Gates used to say, "Your most unhappy customers are your greatest source of learning." You can use that feedback in these different mediums to improve things. We do the same thing internally. We have an exit interview process that we did not have before. We make sure that that feedback is shared with the manager and the manager's manager when somebody leaves. We look at that not to go after somebody or to take points away from a manager or to give negative feedback, but for what we can learn from it.
>
> (Interview, January 29, 2016)

With this cultural mindset, if someone says something negative about the company it's not necessarily the employee who needs to change, but rather the company. This is particularly important when applied to social media, as Gargiulo described:

> That's the other point here that I think we have to consider as we think about social media interaction. We're a company, and what we want to do is build trust with our employees. So everything we do, whether it's a program, an action, or a decision that we're making, we're asking ourselves, is it building trust? It might be a decision that's not a good decision for the employee [such as being fired] but we have to ask ourselves how you communicate with employees. [...]
> And just being respectful that employees have the right to talk about their working conditions. And you know what? If enough of them are talking negatively about it, then we need to look at what we're doing. We need to take their feedback and figure out what are we doing wrong? I try not to be defensive but just say if there is some criticism and pushback, let's engage and try to get to the bottom of whatever the problem might be.
>
> (Interview, January 29, 2016)

Gargiulo's and WFC's emphasis on trust highlights the role of phatic communications. All communications must build trust and must build relationships, even with employees as they are leaving (of their own volition or through termination). In an age of social media, building and maintaining good will and trust is especially crucial.

Rather than continue business as usual and not necessarily respond to employee comments, many companies are making the move to transparency that World's Finest Chocolate is doing. Changing company culture, making it more responsive to the changing dyadic dynamic of digital communications, changes interactions throughout the network, enabling companies to build and maintain relations with employees and enabling companies to adapt to new and emerging communication contexts.

Conclusion

All these cases highlight the interconnected interactions in the rhetorical network. As Justine Sacco found out so brutally, communicative actors never act in isolation; as Henry Truslow IV discovered, company values and expectations need to be clearly articulated so as to influence communications throughout the network; and World's Finest Chocolate recognized the need to transform company culture and communications so as to adapt to the new CTs shaping professional communication.

More generally, for professionals, these cases show the importance for both employees and employers to consider carefully the roles someone is in when communicating and how someone's message may circulate and be viewed by the public. Employees need to reflect on their position in the company and consider when and if they can ever really just be a private citizen when posting to public media. The higher up in the company the employee sits, the greater the likelihood that their writing/speech will be viewed as representing the company. But, as we have discussed, the *where* matters, too: On publicly available platforms, the networks of private citizen and employee are more likely to be interconnected and thus the role boundaries blurred.

Employers need to articulate as clearly as possible for themselves and their employees what some of the role boundaries might be, showcasing in social media policies or in employee handbooks when someone is an employee, when is someone a private citizen, and when such roles might blur. With more foresight from both employees and employers the chances of situations such as Justine Sacco's and IAC's will, most likely, be lessened.

Second, companies need to recognize that their ethos—both with employees and with the public—is shaped in part by how they choose to respond to employee use of social media. What constitutes appropriate communications and appropriate responses to employee social media usage depends on the culture of the company. What we see in these three cases are three possible approaches a company may take: (1) cut ties with the employee so that the now former employee is not company responsibility, (2) seek to change the employee so the employee aligns more with company culture, and (3) seek to change the company so the company's culture adapts to changing contexts and changing relationships needed with employees and with the public.

Companies sometimes approach social media crises as PR events to be managed, controlled, or stifled as quickly as possible—but that instinct may be misguided given the circulatory nature of digital communications and given the rhetorical demands of ethos. Rather than trying to silence the event—hard to do on social media, in any case—perhaps the smarter corporate response is to turn the event into an opportunity to build corporate ethos by demonstrating integrity, leadership, *phronesis, eunoia?*

Certainly, in some instances, firing an employee is not only a legal action but an ethical one as well, but we would argue that companies and their employees would be better served to never rush to judgment and rush to react. *Phronesis*, or practical wisdom, also applies here.

One of the key qualities of ethos in Aristotle's *Rhetoric, phronesis* refers to one's ability to deliberate wisely, given competing options, and to arrive at a careful, thoughtful, reflective judgment about what to do and how to do it. With the speed of digital communications comes an intense pressure to act and act quickly, but taking time to analyze a case, from many angles, within many contexts, and forward and backward in time, is essential. With such a careful and multifaceted network analysis, the chance for ethical decisions to be made will be greater, thus serving both employees and employers better and strengthening individual and corporate ethos.

Given the complexity and reach of social media, companies and employees will certainly face communication quandaries and potential internal and external communication crises. But by approaching the analysis of communicative events with a networked frame of analysis that takes in local and broader contexts and that looks both forward and backward in time and across intersecting networks, employees and companies will be better positioned to make decisions and to take actions that either align with a company culture they wish to maintain or that effect change so as to help companies and employees adapt to changing environments.

Notes

1 The Director of Ethics we interviewed spoke to us with permission of his company but as an individual and not in his official capacity as an employee of the large multinational corporation for which he works. His views represent his own perspective and opinions and not necessarily those of his company.

2 Governments also conduct surveillance and monitoring of digital communications, censoring platforms, filtering content, and prosecuting communications deemed illegal, as, for example, the global research by the OpenNet Initiative showed (OpenNet Initiative, 2016).

3 For a sample listing of non-profit, government, and corporate policies from the United States and other countries, see the Social Media Database provided by Social Media Governance (2016). As social media advisors have noted, organizational policies need to reflect organizational culture, and for global companies that may mean variations by region and by country so as to be sensitive to different cultural contexts (e.g., Hallett et al., 2013).

4 Henry Truslow IV is author Heidi McKee's cousin. We did not plan to interview family members for this project, but upon hearing about our research, Heidi's cousin said, "I have a story for you," and we listened.

6 Social Listening
An Ethical and Organizational Shift

Corporate communications in social media continue to evolve. As Roger Sametz (2010), President and CEO of Sametz Blackstone Associates, recognized, "The notion that you can manage your brand by simply crafting messages onto print and digital materials and then handing them down from headquarters is becoming more outdated every day. Today, monologues need to be replaced by dialogues; formal market research needs to be paired with attentive listening." When social media first emerged in the early 2000s, for-profit and non-profit organizations and their marketing divisions often approached these spaces with a one-way, broadcast communication mindset, a monologic mindset: Organization creates message, organization sends out message, consumers or members see message, consumers are persuaded to purchase products, or members are persuaded to donate. Communications on platforms like Facebook and then eventually Twitter and Instagram were viewed mainly from the perspective of the old broadcast media model—as akin to radio, television, magazine and newspaper ads, and billboards (Grunig 2009; Sametz, 2010). The benefits of social media were perceived mainly as reach (drive up those likes!), speed (the message could get out faster), and improved corporate research (social media provided data mining opportunities to track views, clicks, purchases, and link trails by target demographics). For for-profit organizations in particular, consumers on social media were viewed just as that—consumers, largely passive recipients of company messaging and company products.

But the paradigm for corporate (and non-profit) social media communications has shifted with some recognition, finally, that social media has its own distinct dynamic that is quite different from broadcast media. Most simply put, it is a two-way rather than one-way communication medium, it is interactive, and it is dialogic—or, at least, has dialogic potential (Childers, 1989). The full implications of that distinction for businesses have become much clearer. The consumer is now a prosumer or even a produser, according to Axel Bruns (2009), meaning instead of being a relatively silent and passive viewer, buyer, and user of advertised products; the consumer can now be (potentially) more fully an agent in the communicative network, someone who engages corporations in real-time and ongoing conversations and who at times even actually helps make things: In a very real sense, online participants can create or help create digital content. The innovative company that understands this new paradigm knows how to encourage customer engagement and participation (in its various forms) and knows how to leverage consumer *knowledge*, not simply for the purpose of marketing but to actually change organizational culture and structure in many areas, including public relations, customer service, marketing, product development, operations, and research.

Clearly, social media are changing the communication dynamic between corporations and their customers—at least for those companies that are truly and significantly trying to become (what is the current buzz phrase in business) "a social company." But what does this social engagement with customers look like, and, even more importantly, is it actually changing company-consumer interactions and rhetorical and ethical relationships, and even corporate behavior?

Becoming a social company requires much more than simply changing marketing strategies or hiring a new department of social media writers. This change requires deep retooling of corporate structure and operations, a fundamental shift in corporate culture that goes beyond simply a new approach to public relations. It's not just that the PR department needs to pursue customer relationship management, or CRM (Tarpening, 2015), but the whole company does. Companies who have successfully gone social have been able to change their fundamental culture and posture: putting *relationships*, not selling, at the fore and emphasizing *listening* rather than pitching. As a business tip column in Bloomberg put it: "If you've been pondering how best to use CRM in your business, you may want to begin with where it's headed (two-way communication) rather than where it has been (one-way messaging). Start by listening rather than talking and responding rather than pitching" (McKee, 2012). Social media listening, or simply *social listening*, has become key for corporate communications (Snyder, 2011; Jaume, 2013; Edwards, 2014).

Social listening involves listening across many channels, some more potentially problematic than others. One significant area is qualitative, direct engagement where an employee, as a representative of the company, communicates with members of the public, writes replies, and communicates directly. And then, the employee reflects on and shares those communications with others in the company so as to develop insights for company action. The other significant area, and the more potentially problematic one, is data analytics. Through their own in-house systems or by using services provided by third-party platforms, companies collect data of all sorts on consumers. They monitor social media communications through stream aggregation and content analysis using aggregation platforms such as Hootsuite, GNIP, and Netbase, to collect data and apply algorithms and analytics. Companies can, of course, track the conversations on their own managed sites, but they can also pull in mentions of their company name and products from other sites. This large online data aggregation—which is often coupled with data compiled from off-line interactions such as swipes of loyalty cards, locations of point-of-sale purchases, and even, now, biometric data from wearables—raises a number of ethical issues regarding privacy of data.

How a company collects data, informs customers of that data collection, provides users the opportunity to opt out, and protects and disseminates that data are important ethical considerations that are being examined by academic researchers, by legislative and legal bodies, and in industry and consulting organizations (e.g., Kerr, Steeves, & Lucock, 2009; Etlinger, 2015a; Etlinger, 2015b; Information Accountability Foundation, 2015; European Commission, 2016). In other venues, we too have researched the ethical implications of big data collection and privacy (McKee, 2011) and the importance of ethical interactions with research participants online (McKee & Porter, 2009).

Big data certainly influences and shapes consumer and corporate communications, and much could be written about the important role of and the often-troubling ethics of big data. But in our analysis in this chapter, we wish to focus on the phatic function and how companies organize themselves (or not) to listen to customers in a way that increases the potential for reciprocity in networked interactions. We examine communicative exchange to explore how corporate listening offers the potential for an ethic of reciprocity.

All organizational actions are, of course, shaped by organizational *ethos*. The ethical mindset a company brings to bear is key. Are customers merely data providers to be "mined," or are they real people with whom to interact? Is corporate listening just another term for nodding and taking, like a pickpocket who engages in conversation to steal one's wallet? Or is engagement with customers guided by a more rhetorical and reciprocal phatic ethic, with the aim to build and sustain relationships? And what does a company do with the information it gathers from its conversations with customers on social media? How a company understands and enacts corporate listening—what ethic it brings to the rhetorical act of listening—is the focus of this chapter.

In our discussion that follows, we focus primarily on the communications of one U.S.-based company (Taco Bell), but the implications of an ethic of social listening apply to non-profits and to companies in non-U.S. contexts. The cultures to which a company would be listening and adapting would be different than the 18–24-year-old U.S. audience we use as an example in this chapter, but the approaches for analyzing and adapting communications in the social network would apply.

We certainly acknowledge the profit-driven motive that necessarily underlies all corporate action. Even socially responsible companies that donate to charities and create foundations do so not only because they want to do good in the world, but also, of course, to showcase what a socially responsible company they are, building a corporate ethos, which may, in turn, build stronger relationships that may, eventually, lead to more sales. But even with the profit-driven motive, we advance the viewpoint that corporate communications—at least in the direct interaction of company to customer—can be ethical, and that commensurability with the social good (as defined by particular and specific cultural groups) is not only possible but essential. From our perspective, for-profit companies can be ethical and moral, even as they pursue profit. Key to ethics in a social media age is to engage in phatic communications via listening that transforms not just communication practices at the point of platform with users—the tweet, post, video—but that also transforms the company. What does a company *do* with what they have learned from listening to consumers? How do they change themselves—their organizational structure or culture?

We begin by briefly overviewing listening from a rhetorical perspective and its role in building the phatic function. We then present a case analysis of one company, Taco Bell, drawing from an interview with Rob Poetsch, the Director of Public Affairs and Engagement for Taco Bell, who describes the impact corporate listening has had not just on customer-corporate relations but also on the organizational structure and culture of whole company. We trace how Taco Bell listens to and interacts with customers so as to build phatic relationships that shape the entire communicative network and that may, in their responsiveness to customers, show an ethical reciprocity. We conclude by reflecting on the role of corporate ethos and corporate structure in rhetorical networks, examining the question: Can the social network have the effect of changing corporate ethos, corporate structure, and corporate sense of mission? Our answer: Possibly yes.

An Overview of Social Listening

When social listening for companies first emerged in the early 2000s, it was based on the older model of data mining designed for traditional web platforms. The goal for corporations was to gather as much data as possible from consumers so as to send them targeted advertising; building long-term relationships or using the data for improving company products and services was just not part of the equation for most companies. As Susan Etlinger, an Industry Analyst for the Altimeter Group, explained in an interview with us:

> The reason that a lot of this stuff started with advertising was because that was the business model that would be funded by start-ups in the 90s. A lot of the ways we first did business in social was simply due to what business models would be funded by venture capitalists and

private equity. If we can get more eyeballs, then we can make more money. But then smart people started figuring out we can use this [data] to find product defects and to find supply chain issues and we can use it to find competitive opportunities and customer service opportunities, so it has spread across organizations. Social, digital engagement has become more embedded throughout the business.

(Interview, April 29, 2016)

Admittedly, for many companies today the targeted-advertising model is still very much the norm. For these companies, *social listening* is just a nicer sounding phrase for what is really traditional marketing research and sales. But other companies, those that are often awarded for their social media strategies, recognize that social listening provides opportunities to improve and develop customer relationships, and they have moved away from one-way marketing and advertising toward a fuller, reciprocal engagement, using listening to benefit customers in meaningful ways and, as Etlinger described, embedding insights from listening throughout the organization.

But what exactly does it mean *to listen*? Listening is a fundamental literacy skill, on the same level with reading, writing, and speaking. And of course it is also a fundamental communication skill necessary for engaging and interacting with others on social media and throughout onground and online networks of communication.

In the Western classical rhetoric tradition, listening has been mostly neglected (until fairly recently[1]). The tradition mainly focused on speaking and writing, on oral and written literacy, with rhetoric defined as "discovering the available means of persuasion" (Aristotle) and as "the good man speaking well" (Quintilian). Numerous rhetoric scholars have noted that the classical tradition has not given sufficient attention to listening as a rhetorical skill (Ratcliffe, 1999; Glenn & Ratcliffe, 2011a; Glenn & Ratcliffe, 2011b; Lipari, 2012). In fact, the tradition has viewed silence as the characteristic of the passive audience-to-be-persuaded-or-informed: That is, it is the speaker who speaks and it is the audience that is silent and listening.[2]

As discussed in Chapter 2, business communication has traditionally emphasized two main purposes for communication: the informative purpose or the persuasive purpose (or some combination of both). And in this respect, business communication has often adopted the rhetorical frame of the Shannon-Weaver model (represented in Figure 3.1). But there is another purpose to consider as well, one that aligns with a customer relationship model—the phatic. *Phatic* (as we discussed in Chapter 3) refers to the rhetorical function of creating effective two-way communication channels to establish and maintain productive relationships.

If social media require us to rethink communication along phatic lines, tailored to the cultures and communities in which the communication occurs, this also presages a new role for listening in and by organizations.

Social listening does not serve merely as the instrument for an organization to simply transmit its message and assert its will; social listening must reconceive itself as phatic, as relationship building, A rhetorical/ethical approach to listening, one that takes account of the ethical obligations involved, views listening as necessarily part of a dialogic exchange—and the phrase *dialogic listening* captures the fundamental nature of that exchange (Johannesen, 1971; Cornwell & Orbe, 1999). In this model, listening means an active, engaged, and attentive effort to understand what others are saying, with an overall attitude of respect, and with an openness to change. We have to be listening for more than merely "self-interested intent" (Ratcliffe, 1999), that is, we can't be listening to or analyzing the audience *only* to figure out how better to persuade them to our position or product.

Authenticity is also a key quality of dialogic communication, meaning that the listener is genuinely engaged with the speaker, is present and attentive, is interested in what she/he is saying, is focused on the topic or issue at hand, and is committed to having a productive exchange. It means, conversely, that the listener is not "insincere, pretending interest in a speaker's ideas and feelings when not actually caring; feigning interest in a person's problems, activities, etc. while not actually interested or concerned ... [or] 'using' the other person for selfish and/or concealed reasons" (Floyd, 2010, p. 130).

Certainly, corporations are in business to sell their products and services, certainly, they are self-interested—as are we all—but, as many have learned with relationship marketing, interactive communication has to be more than simply that. The relationship cannot involve deception or pretense; there needs to be some kind of mutual value—reciprocity—in the interactive exchange between speakers and listeners. As Shara Clark, past president of the Cincinnati Chapter of the Public Relations Society of America and a social media consultant, explained to us in an interview,

> Social media is about this two-way conversation and being authentic and opening those barriers a little bit. [...] Just getting advertised to feels not relationship-driven. It doesn't have that same two-way authentic relationship feel. It has this, "I'm being advertised to" kind of feel.
>
> (Interview, September 9, 2015)

A good rhetoric always involves an economic exchange of value between speakers and audiences—and so the good of the customer, the good of the public must be a priority. Of course, the public customer knows that, ultimately, the corporation has a commercial agenda: selling a product or service. And so any attempt at interpersonal listening and communication runs the risk of *seeming* to be deceptive and manipulative: I am engaging you, pretending to be interested and engaged, purely for the purpose of selling you something.

When is engaged listening genuine and authentic and when is it not? At this point, we can see the ethical problem that has always plagued rhetoric: When is a speaker's or listener's rhetorical action sincere versus when is it feigned for the purpose of persuasion? One answer to that question lies in time: Richard Johannesen (1971) talked about the importance of time as a characteristic of dialogic communication (p. 381). It takes time to build the trust necessary for a truly dialogic interaction, and the time expended is also a mark of commitment: That is, the listener is not simply here for the moment, but is in it for the long haul. Has the speaker built up a history of credibility, trust, and sustained commitment over time? Has the corporation established a reputation for honesty and transparency in dealing with customers and the public, in admitting mistakes and problems, and in addressing issues quickly and effectively, with customers' best interests at heart? And, perhaps most importantly, has the corporation exhibited an openness to change: that is, a willingness to change its operations, to improve its products and services, and perhaps even to admit mistakes or even to say, no, this product that we sell is maybe not the best one for you? When a corporation exhibits that kind of rhetorical behavior over time, then it establishes an ethos as a responsive, caring company, not as one just out to make a profit.

Can you fake dialogic listening? Sure, faking is very easy to do in the short run or in a single email or tweet, or even in a single ad campaign. But achieving genuine credibility requires sustained commitment over time to an ethos of authenticity. As we discussed in Chapter 2, the rhetor's ethos comes into being through discourse, through their symbolic interactions with others, and through the rhetoric they practice and embody. And so for a corporation to achieve that level of authenticity requires a commitment to consistent behavior, at which point the corporation is not faking being an engaged, trustworthy entity, they have actually *become* one. Listening is not simply a tool in their rhetoric toolbox, pulled out at the point of messaging, but, rather, true listening—genuine engagement with and consideration for audience—is embedded throughout the organizational network.

The two-way symmetrical model helps explains how organizations need to change not only their public relations strategy, but also their foundational ethic in the age of social media. Going social requires that a business think about interaction—at all levels of the network—differently pursuing a model that emphasizes *two-way symmetrical interaction for a phatic purpose* and that is shaped by an ethic of dialogic listening and reciprocity.

The Case of Taco Bell: Social Listening in Action

One example of a company that has been highly successful at dialogic listening and reciprocal relationship engagement with customers is Taco Bell. Taco Bell (parent company Yum! Brands) is a restaurant chain headquartered in Irvine, California, with more than 6,000 restaurants worldwide (most in the U.S. and most run by independent franchisees) and with over 170,000 employees. Taco Bell is active on social media with widely followed accounts, including (as of January 2017) Twitter with 1.8 million followers, Facebook with10.4 million likes, and Instagram with 1 million followers.

Taco Bell is frequently cited as a model for how to enact effective corporate social media interaction. The company was awarded Advertising Age's 2013 Marketer of the Year award (Morrison, 2013). Social media experts, marketing communications analysts, and media reviewers consistently have high praise for Taco Bell. Comments such as the following are typical: "Taco Bell has built an incredibly strong social media presence—one of the best I've ever seen. Just take one look at their social media channels and you can see that they seem to be doing everything right" (Parent, 2013). And "whenever the next app or social media platform arises, we can count on Taco Bell to set the benchmark as to how to best utilize the platform" (lotus823, 2013, 2015). In short, Taco Bell is "killing it with social media" (Parent, 2013).

Here is a sample exchange between Taco Bell and one of its customers on Twitter (Stopera, 2012):

> @tacobell Hi, I FUCKING LOVE THE DORITOS TACO ITS SO FUCKING GOOD MYSELF
>
> @[customer twitter account] You're right, Tyler. #DoritosLocos-Tacos are f***ing good.

This Twitter interaction is not your typical corporate public communications—how often do you see large U.S. corporations writing f***ing to a customer?—but what this exchange shows is Taco Bell's approach to social media. Taco Bell's social media team offers personal and fairly immediate response to a customer, using the customer's own language, creating rapport, and embracing the customer's ethos, even if it is not the kind of officially sanctioned ethos that a corporation would typically embrace in a public forum. Taco Bell is responding to the customer as a friend or social peer might respond.

Ethic of Friendship

That ethic of friendship is key to Taco Bell's social media strategy. Rob Poetsch explained in an interview with us the philosophy behind their approach:

> We always want to be relevant with that 20-something. So whatever generation is in their 20's is where we aspire to be and that's where our customers aspire to be, it's a mindset demographic [...] We focus on communicating with our fans—our most passionate fans—as a

friend. Our social media team, instead of acting like a corporation, is very, very conscious of acting like a friend. And they do that in a way that is endemic to every platform that we're on.

(Interview, February 25, 2016)

Taco Bell's demographic—those in their 20s and teenagers who aspire to that mindset—seem to be responding positively to this approach. Taco Bell's various social media accounts are filled with millions of fans who interact regularly and who often write things like, "I LOVE YOU, TACO BELL!!!" and "Taco Bell at 10:21pm Fucking Awesome." Fans post photos of their wedding parties, senior high school prom pre-parties, and the like being held at Taco Bell. They feel connected to Taco Bell and want to share that connection with the company and with millions of other fans. As Poetsch described, "We are constantly amazed by the means to which people go to express their passion for the brand. We had a fan make a prom dress out of Taco Bell taco wrappers. It was amazing! We didn't ask her to do it. I think the beauty of it is—we embrace the people who love our brand. We don't really try to make them do things that they wouldn't do. We try to be authentic."

Like many corporations, Taco Bell did not begin its social media interactions with this approach. As Poetsch explained to us (Interview, February 25, 2016), when Taco Bell started on social media they were more interested in "protecting the brand." But then eventually they saw "opportunities to engage in a proactive grand engagement level." This move from brand protection to brand engagement changed what Taco Bell posted online: They moved from advertising to experience sharing.

When we first started, like many brands, we took content and we repurposed it. So we'd take, like, POP [point of purchase marketing] from a restaurant or a digital channel and crop it and put it in a Facebook post. And that was before we had this strategy of acting like a friend. You're not going to sell your friends a taco. But you're going to share with them experiences. So if you look at our channels—our Instagram channel, our Snapchat stories—they're much more about experiences than they are about marketing. We really don't try to sell people in those channels: We want to connect with them.

(Poetsch interview, February 25, 2016)

Taco Bell shifted to a more phatic purpose for social media, one that involved "connecting" with people and "understand[ing] what people are saying" in order to enact change in the company and the brand itself. They moved from broadcast and brand-centric marketing communications to more dialogic and whole-network engagements with their target age group.

As one millennial media analyst explained, "Taco Bell is clearly targeting those of us in the 18–34 age group, which is by far their strongest customer demographic. This allows the company to dig in and become part of the community, instead of trying to please everyone. The result is a voice that sounds more like one of your friends than it does a major American corporation" (Parent, 2013). Another explained, "Whichever public relations intern or team of meticulous, well-trained professionals is in charge of @TacoBell is doing a bang-up job with a clever combination of retweets, sassy comebacks, hashtags and whimsical life advice. We kind of, a little bit, maybe want Taco Bell to be our best friend" (Boboltz, 2014).

Listening to Learn and Take Action

To be that friend, Taco Bell does a lot of listening, but listening of a certain kind, an active listening. Further, they have taken the extra step of rebuilding their corporate organizational structure to make sure that what they hear gets distributed throughout the company so that customers' perspectives can influence all aspects of the company.

> We have a social listening platform that's designed by NetBase. We have a social listening room—we have a team of analysts that do that. But then the magic happens when you get the data and you get the context and you get the insights around it and then you're able to take action. We do that every day. We have what we call the daily stand-up. It's a 15-minute meeting open to everyone in the organization, including our agencies and our franchisees. We want this to be a download process—here's what's going on with our brand, our competitors, trends, things that are going on in the food industry. And we quickly go through those conversations in both social and earned media and produce a pretty simple report. And then from that meeting we make a determination if there's any action we need to take.
>
> (Interview, February 25, 2016)

Part of what helps Taco Bell succeed in social media communications is that the company has an integrated structure for listening (a social listening room) and an organized process for distributing listening results across the company (a daily 15-min stand-up) to make sure that the results of listening are heard immediately and shared widely across all areas of the company.

For many large companies, their organization structure is often distributed and siloed with only a few key connectors across different divisions of the company. The problem is that in the siloed model, consumer engagement is just one node among many, connected to a few areas of the company, but not to all—and thus insights gained from customer relations are much harder to share and distribute. Even if the customer relations representatives are listening, the company overall is not set up to listen. An ethic of listening is not build into the overall corporate structure.

What companies like Taco Bell have done is twofold: They have lessened the siloing of their company organization and they have empowered consumer engagement. These changes enable the sharing throughout the network of insights from customers more immediately and in ways that more directly influence more areas of the business. In a sense, they have taken customer relations and made it central to all company operations so that consumer engagement connects to and talks with more areas of the company. They have combined listening with a listening distribution structure as a means to take responsive action. Taco Bell is successful in social media not just for their actions at the point of contact with customers but also because they have adapted their organizational structure and, thus, their culture, to enable more connectivity across online and onground networks. In effect, Taco Bell is trying to make a large company small.

Successful small businesses already pursue an integrated, networked approach to communications, one where listening and connectivity is built into the fabric of their company because of the very nature of their company. In small businesses, all facets of the business run through just a few people, which naturally enables more integrated decision-making and communications. For small businesses, finance doesn't need to be informed of what's happening in logistics, and sales doesn't have to wonder how things are going in employee relations, because those entities all funnel through the same person or a few people.

We came to this insight—that large companies need to organize and act small for social media success—when, soon after interviewing communications executives at a number of large companies, we then interviewed Peter and Tamar Lask, small business owners who own Juniper, a clothing and fashion store aimed, primarily, at college-aged females. The Lasks operate three stores in college towns: the original store in Oxford, Ohio (where the Lasks live); a store in West Lafayette, Indiana; and a store in Muncie, Indiana. Each store has approximately 6–13 employees and the two stores in Indiana have their own managers (because the Lasks are not able to be there on a daily basis). For nearly two decades, the Lasks have run their small business. Given their target demographic, they entered social media quite early and are active, currently, in three platforms, Twitter, Instagram, and Facebook. Tamar also has chat groups with employees, who in these college towns are often college students themselves.

As Tamar explained, because their company is small, employees and customers are able to "see the full circle" (Interview, March 1, 2016). Employees know who is signing their paychecks; customers following their social media accounts see posts and comments on social media and they know Tamar posted them. Authenticity isn't just built into the system; it *is* the system. So when a customer posts how much she likes a cosmetic product that Juniper sells on Instagram "I'm in ♥ with the #bareminerals gloss!" and when Tamar writes back "it's sooooo nice!!! Glad you like it!." the exchange does not come across so much as an impersonal marketing move, but more like an exchange between one enthusiastic fashion shopper and another. And as Peter explained, because they are small business owners, they live in and visit frequently the towns where their stores are located. They are members of the community, and their ethos is very much tied up into the experience that customers receive in their stores.

Peter described how Juniper aims for a personalized, customized shopping experience where customers feel welcome and known. He compared Juniper's approach to customers versus the approach of large corporations, describing how when he calls customer service at a large national insurance company, "I can call them three different times and get three different answers, all of them wrong. These companies have so lost control of the lower level that you can't even get the correct information from three different employees because there's no coordination." Because Tamar and Peter handle sales, marketing, inventory, logistics, human relations, public relations, customer service, and finances, etc., they are able to ensure not just coordination across their small business but also integration. Tamar hears customers ask about a particular clothing item, and she is able to query her employees about the popularity of the item and then immediately order some for the stores. The "full circle" Tamar described applies to how their company is also able to gain insights and take action quickly, in ways sensitive to the needs and interests of their customers.

By creating the "15-minute stand-up" Taco Bell has, in a sense, created the potential for that full circle effect, that potential for information to travel through all nodes in the network. But simply sharing information is not enough. Tamar may have learned that college-aged women want to wear a new particular item of clothing, but if she weren't also able to contact suppliers and place orders that information wouldn't be that useful. Similarly, Taco Bell may engage with customers ("fans") as "friends," sharing all sorts of "experiences" and learning a great deal about customers' needs and interests, but if the social media team is not empowered to communicate insights to other parts of the company and even, as we will show, to direct operations in other part of the company, then the social media listening would not be as effective—both in terms of insights gained but also, importantly, in terms of showing a dialogic responsiveness to customer needs.

Taco Emoji

In our research on Taco Bell's uses of social media, we discovered a number of ways in which social media listening resulted in changes in the company, showing that the company was not just listening in a passive sense but listening, heeding, and taking action based on that interaction.

A taco emoji now exists in part because of Taco Bell.[3] The taco emoji is just an image of a taco, not branded to Taco Bell, but the creation of this emoji is an example, as Rob Poetsch explained, of how Taco Bell engaged in a form of social media listening that moved from listening to action.

> In one of our daily stand ups we heard that someone had written a funny letter [to the Unicode Consortium] that there are things like floppy disks and cassette tape emojis, and there's fax machines, but there's no taco emoji. When we heard about this, we very quickly formed a team that came up with a recommendation to start a Change.org petition [Taco Bell, 2015], a fun engagement strategy, to bring the taco emoji to IOS. [...] We connected our brand with that in a very organic and authentic way. And I think that's why it got so much traction. I think the petition got over 25,000 signatures in a matter of weeks. Eventually they did come out with the taco emoji.
>
> We, of course, celebrated with our fans. We created not only a fun engagement tool with our Twitter handle—it was a taco emoji engine that had 600 pieces of content associated with it, so if you typed in an emoji plus a taco you got this mash-up back to you. It was a really fun first for us. And we also took some of the fan created artwork from that and put it in some of our packaging in our restaurants because we wanted that to come to life. [...] So we are now very tightly linked with the taco emoji because of that.
>
> (Poetsch interview, February 25, 2016)

Certainly, Taco Bell's actions around the taco emoji were part of a savvy marketing strategy, and a key reason why Taco Bell continues to be tops in fast-food restaurant sales with their target demographic. But their actions also show listening-and-acting. Perhaps if you're not 20-something, a taco emoji is no big deal—and really, it's not a big deal compared to other important ways companies can give back (as Taco Bell does with its college scholarships and other programs)—but the creation of the taco emoji does show consumer responsiveness. Taco Bell didn't try to create a Taco Bell emoji, they created a taco emoji, and, judging by the petition signatures, it was something people wanted.

Now, the question could be, did Taco Bell create the need for the taco emoji—some form of insidious corporate mind control—or was it already there? That's a tough one to answer in this corporate age. We will come back to that question after examining a few more examples.

Numero Uno

In 1962, the Taco Bell founder Glenn Bell opened his first restaurant (known now as Numero Uno) in Downey, California. That restaurant operated until 1986 when Taco Bell sold it, and it became a series of taquerias, the last one of which shut down in December 2014. From social listening the Taco Bell team learned that a developer was going to bulldoze the restaurant. As Rob Poetsch noted, "People were tweeting about it and posting on our channels, saying, don't let this happen, this is a piece of history. So we took this to our executive team, and they said, we're not going to let this happen."

In response to social media listening, Taco Bell bought Numero Uno and put it on a flatbed truck and moved it 45 miles to their headquarters. In person and on social media, they had people following and posting about the move. Rather than decide on their own what to do with the store, Taco Bell started a hashtag, #savetacobell and invited customers to offer suggestions for what Numero Uno should become in its new location. What Taco Bell learned was that fans were engaged and passionate about this place because of the emotional connections it had with their community lives:

> Our fans really guided us with it. But when we look at the social conversation [around saving, moving, and preserving Numero Uno], we have pretty rich analytics. We can look at things like sentiment, but we can also look at passion. There's a passion index around the words people use and the meaning of their conversation and that particular story had the highest passion index of anything we've ever seen. People were so engaged because everyone had a story about Taco Bell. It took them back to this emotional place, "Oh, yeah, I remember when I was in high school and I played on a team and we'd stop after practice and get a burrito." There were all these stories that were popping up. We didn't have to ask people to do that. It just happened. There's this community who are passionate fans and we engage with them and we listen to them.
>
> (Poetsch interview, February 25, 2016)

Saving a store that people clearly cared about was, again, a savvy marketing move, but it is also a form of reciprocity based on insights pulled from social listening. Someday parents may take their kids to Numero Uno (whatever it becomes) and say, "This is the restaurant where we met." From the standpoint of a neoliberal critique on capitalistic culture this may not seem that wonderful—people's stories and memories shaped by commercialized locations—but the physical places we inhabit have a powerful impression on us (for good and for ill). Taco Bell recognized this.

Feed the Beat

Taco Bell's social media team learned that a large number of musicians and bands ate at their restaurants because they are open so late. Rather than just sitting on this insight, the social media team was able to work with other areas of the company to create a music program called "Feed the Beat." As Rob Poetsch described:

> The idea behind it is pretty simple—up and coming bands that are trying to break through, when they are on the road, they often go to Taco Bell late night. We found this out and thought that's pretty cool, what can we do to help them out? We saw this happening when gas was 5 bucks a gallon and they were having a hard time. So we just said, hey, if you love Taco Bell, we love music, just let us know, and we'll give you 500 dollar [Taco Bell] gift cards.
>
> We have over 1,000 bands. And, really, the important piece is: we don't ask them to do anything. We're not saying we'll give you these gift cards if you post something on your social channel or you put a sticker on your drum. We don't want that because that's not what the relationship is about, but what that leads to is a greater level of engagement. We have bands taking fans to Taco Bell after the show and buying everyone a burrito and it's that kind of authentic connection that we want to have, not just with these bands in this programs, but with all of our followers online.
>
> (Interview, February 25, 2016)

Taco Bell does create online and onground venues for up-and-coming bands to perform and be profiled (see feedthebeat.com), but they also strategically recognized that travelling musicians don't have a lot of money and they need to eat out late at night when on the road, so here's a way to connect with an important segment of Taco Bell's audience. Under more traditional company organization and company ethic, such an insight that musicians eat at Taco Bell might have, at most, resulted in some changes to ad content, but because of the connected empowerment of the social media group, Taco Bell was able to start a new outreach program.

Breakfast Launch

Sometimes social listening calls for immediate action that changes same-day company practices. When Taco Bell launched its new breakfast menu in 2013, it was able to respond quickly to problems that arose during launch. Social media analysts tracking conversations about the launch on the first day noticed conversations arising from the East Coast about "running out" or "can't get," and other phrases "that showed there was a supply issue" (Poetsch interview, February 25, 2016). Taco Bell followed up:

> So we dug a little deeper and we found there was an issue with not prepping enough food. The beauty of social media was that it's all in real time. We came back to the operations team and we said, "Look,

there are pockets on the East Coast that aren't prepping enough eggs and hash browns and bacon. You better get the word out to the rest of the system that you should plan to prep more." We were very, very quickly able to notify our operators and let them know what was going on, and we were able to react. With these things that pop up we can take action very quickly and impact a lot of people and create a better experience.

(Poetsch interview, February 25, 2016)

Because Taco Bell had reorganized the company to react quickly to what customers were saying, and because the social media team was empowered to speak quickly to all areas of the company and with authority to call for changes in company operations, Taco Bell's breakfast launch in most of the country was successful and the subsequent reviews were positive (see Brandau, 2014).

Is Social Listening Really a Paradigm Shift? It Depends

It would be easy to be cynical about Taco Bell's social media strategy and to view it as nothing more than slick marketing designed to drive up sales. Taco Bell claims to be engaging as a "friend" with fans but can people really be friends with a company? As Sam Biddle (2015) put it, "Brands are not your friends. [...] When was the last time Coca Cola ever did anything good for you?" But there is much more involved in the communication dynamic here, related to the deep cultural and personal relationships that people have with brands, with places, with icons, with cultural memes (Denton, 2015). As Taco Bell came to realize, they had an emotional relationship with people's lives and the "stories that were popping up" about people's lives.

Susan Fournier, one of the founding researchers in brand relationships (see Fournier, 1998), studied how consumers felt about brands, finding that "brands are a part of life in the 21st century ... and brand relationships are very complex phenomena, much like human relationships" (qtd in Villarica, 2012). Further, brands are *not* just products: They can actually be the basis for a strong relationship if the brands positively impact a person's life. To be successful in a digital age, companies need to pursue the phatic function and to aim to develop and sustain lasting and reciprocally beneficial relationships with people. Companies need to also recognize a key point that Rob Poetsch articulated, "Brands are no longer in control of their own brand. Consumers are. You have to embrace that. You have to accept that" (Poetsch interview, February 25, 2016).

But is this listening simply and actually a mere marketing ruse, a deception? The appearance rather than the reality of listening? As we discussed in Chapters 2 and 3, and as is evident in Taco Bell's social media communications, rhetoric has always had to deal with the conflict between *seem* and *be*. Yes, sometimes people use rhetoric just to appear to be nice. Maybe Taco Bell is just *seeming* to be your friend, to be responsive in order to actually just sell you more product. Yes, that's probably the case in some exchanges, but what the examples above show—and we could have drawn on many more across many more years—is that seeming also moves into *being*, especially when responsiveness and engagement are woven into communications and actions across time and across contexts.

A cynical read of Taco Bell might be that in trying to *seem* ethical they might in some ways actually *be* ethical. A less cynical read—one that recognizes that even within for-profit capitalist systems there can be some public good—might be that the actions Taco Bell has taken and takes are beneficial and reciprocal—a restaurant building steeped in memories is saved, hungry bands on the road are fed, people in line for breakfast can order the meal they want. Are these world-changing events? No, but they are, in their way, steps contributing to the good of the community, especially the 18–24 year-old community that Taco Bell engages. In terms of their communication network, Taco Bell provides a clear case for how pursuing the phatic function can build long-lasting and potentially reciprocal relationships.

Communicating for the long haul isn't necessarily easy, and it brings with it some potential tensions within a company. Because of the reach and speed of social media compared to traditional media and because of its lower cost, sometimes various divisions in the company seek to have messaging put out on social that are not appropriate for that channel, that is "off kilter," as Rob Poetsch described.

> The social team knows their channels so well that they're very fussy about what they do and what they don't do. They say no a lot. They're not just going to put something up on social just because it's important to the organization. If it's not relevant to that audience then they're not going to want to do it. [...] They know how the community would react if something was off-kilter.
> (Poetsch interview, February 25, 2016)

Taco Bell's social team uses their ethnographic research-based knowledge to both protect the communities (not inundating them with messaging they wouldn't care about) and to help the company preserve those relationships for the long haul rather than to try to exploit them for a short-term gain.

In order for this to happen, though, social media teams need to be empowered to speak back to various segments of the company, even, if need be, the CEO. And so, Taco Bell re-organized their internal communications in such a way as to empower the social media team to both speak for and speak back to all areas of the company. Deep structural reorganization helps ensure that the results of listening are shared—but it also helps change the corporate ethical culture. In other words, ethics—and this case the ethic of social listening—is not just individual behavior. A company can build ethics into its organizational fabric, its structure, its policies, its practices; it can make structural changes (e.g., in its management organization, in its communication practices, in its lines of authority, in its methods for distributing information) to promote and improve ethical communication.

The authority a social media team has or doesn't have within a company matters because what happens to the insights gained from social, including direct interactions with customers, how they're disseminated and used, is part of ethical research and communication practices. If social listening is merely used for taking data from customers without giving anything back, that's a problem. The more all areas of a company know about and are shaped by customer perspectives, the more responsive a company can be in all aspects of its work. Conversely, if a company is organized according to a more traditional, siloed structure, agility is impeded and so is the opportunity for dialogic relationships and reciprocity.

Relationships require trust, and when building social media relationships, companies have to think about trust, not only in terms of their data collection and usage policies—what Susan Etlinger (2015a) has called "the trust imperative"—but also in terms of the expected ethic of their relationships with customers. If Taco Bell invites young adults to participate and converse within its sponsored social media community on Facebook, Twitter, Instagram, etc.—if it treats them as "friends," and interacts frequently with them—then that interaction creates the expectation for customers that they will be treated fairly and with respect, that they will not be lied to or misled, and that their contributions to the online forums will not be used against them in any way and that they have some degree of control over those contributions. Even though the social media forum is not a formal research context, certainly not subject to academic IRB-like research regulations, there are still ethical obligations implicit in the social arrangement, and in the communication situation itself, obligations pertaining to trust, consent, and use of information provided (McKee & Porter, 2009). In short, there is a research ethic involved in social media interactions, in social listening—and Taco Bell and other companies who engage in this kind of social listening are obligated to be responsible to that ethic.

Conclusion

In calling this process *listening*, in labeling their contributors and customers as *friends*, corporations have embraced a language that changes the nature of the ethical obligation. If a company calls their research social listening, well, that obligates them to listen. If they call customers friends, then that obligates them to behave like one. Corporations need to embrace and enact the phatic purpose: the purpose of building and maintaining relationships through communication. Relationship with the customer, with the community, and with the public good comes first.

To violate an obligation of implied trust is not per se illegal, but it carries with it opprobrium of another sort: loss of credibility, harmed reputation, social disgrace, damaged ethos for the company. The least effective defense for a company that violates such a trust, the last refuge of the scoundrel, is to say, "We did nothing illegal." Right, of course—but that's not the point.

A good relationship is characterized by mutual respect and by mutual advantage: The relationship creates value and benefits for both parties (Lund et al., 2016, p. 95). When looking at the network of social media communications, a key question to ask is: Is there a mutual value exchange involved in the interaction? Certainly, all the data companies collect through social listening helps them in meaningful ways, but does the exchange benefit customers or the public in some clear, measureable way (e.g., a taco emoji, a restaurant building infused with memories saved, funding for meals on the road)? Now, the nature of the value exchange might vary from context to context; it might not be always perfectly symmetrical or equitable, but are there at least some reciprocal actions?

The goal of a dialogic interaction is, in Kenneth Burke's terms, identification or consubstantiality: through the process of dialogue speakers and listeners come to a mutually empathetic understanding, they come together and are joined (in some sense); both are changed (Burke, 1969, p. 21). Consubstantiality seems a high bar for corporate communications. Can corporate social media interaction really meet the criteria for dialogic listening and communication? Is that an appropriate or feasible goal?

Well, in general, yes—that is precisely the implication of what we are saying. That is what is meant by phatic communication and by "the dialogic turn in public relations" (van Es & Meijlink, 2000; Marsh, 2001, 2013; Grunig, 2009). In the field of public relations, there is certainly the recognition that corporate social media interactions, corporate listening, must turn away from one-way, monologic, transmission models of persuasion to genuinely two-way dialogic interactions based on building and maintaining sustained relationships. And that shift to a new model of communications requires a shift to a new ethics paradigm for social media listening.

Ultimately, what is key is that companies must be open to change. Jim Lin (2016), Vice President and Digital Strategist for Ketchum Public Relations, noted how much communications have changed with social media, but then goes on to ask an important question of companies who are navigating the dialogic and interactive channels of social: "But are you changing along with it? In the context of something this powerful, are you still looking at social media as simply a more effective way to broadcast your message? Because if you are, you're leaving the loop wide open" (p. 20).

To enter the realm of social media successfully and productively requires that a corporation understand how social media have changed the nature of the communication dynamic—and, even more importantly, how those changes require rethinking and remaking corporate operational structures, policies, and practices. The communication paradigm has shifted, and that shift requires changes in ethical expectations and obligations throughout the network.

Notes

1 There is now a large body of research on listening, in both communication studies and rhetoric/composition, examining listening from a variety of disciplinary and methodological frames, including physiology, cognitive psychology, sociology, feminist theory, critical race theory, communication ethics, and internet research ethics (see, for example, Wolvin, 2010; Glenn & Ratcliffe, 2011a). In the field of business communication, there is also a body of research on listening—but in business communication it more often pertains to listening practices within organizations, or to clients, or to consulting: e.g., effective listening during meetings, how management should listen to employees, listening to your boss, effective listening skills for business communication consulting, etc.

2 Several scholars have pointed out that the Western rhetorical model is also a gendered model, "a rhetoric of patriarchy" (Foss & Griffin, 1995, p. 4) with the assumption being that it is a man who is speaking, with women in the role of audience, as silent and passive (Foss & Griffin, 1995; Ratcliffe, 1999; Lipari, 2009, 2012; Bokser, 2010). This model has also been characterized as a rhetoric of power and privilege: The rhetor is the person who has access to the rostrum (or mass medium), who has not only the right to speak but also the power and capital to occupy that privileged space (Ratcliffe, 1999).

3 Emojis are the small digital images, often inserted into text messages, used to communicate emotion, feeling, attitude, and expression.

7 AI Agents as Professional Communicators

Technology has always been an actor in communication networks. Alphabet systems, stone tablets, papyrus, pens, the printing press, the typewriter, the telegraph, the telephone, software interfaces, the internet, and the World Wide Web are all technologies that are both used by humans to communicate and that shape how we communicate. For thousands of years, technologies have been technological agents in the communication process—though they have not often been viewed as *agents*; instead, they were often seen from an instrumentalist lens, as mere tools people used (Feenberg, 1991).

With digital technologies, the agency of technologies becomes, perhaps, more evident, the way, for example, word processing programs will mark and offer suggestions to correct spelling mistakes or the way search engines will offer suggestions for searching, thus becoming more explicit agents and collaborators in the communication process. But no one is going to confuse spellcheck or Google search—or Microsoft's short-lived and annoying help interface Clippy—for a human agent. We might personify the technologies we use, and we certainly recognize their agency as technologies in communication networks, but they are still most often seen as mere tools.

But the 21st century has brought a remarkable change in the landscape of technological agents in communication networks. Increasingly, the "people" with whom we think we're communicating are not people at all, but technologies—artificial intelligent agents that are often designed to mimic (or attempt to mimic) human-to-human interaction. Increasingly, humans are communicating with AI agents, often without knowing they are doing so. The implications of AI for professional communication and for organizations and business professionals who deploy AI agents are profound.

In this chapter, we explore some of the rhetorical and ethical issues in AI as it intersects with professional communication. Our overarching question is, fundamentally, can AI bots be effective professional communicators? Our answer will be an unsatisfactory one, a rhetorician's answer: It depends. It depends on how these agents are deployed, on what they are asked to do, and on the contexts in which they communicate.

However, we do provide some contingent answers, based on several case examples we discuss—and, maybe more importantly, we provide some criteria for making judgments about that question and for developing AI bots who can perhaps become effective professional communicators.

We begin with an opening example of human-AI interaction to highlight the complexity of the network and the central role of phatic considerations. We then discuss a number of AI communication technologies to date, mapping them on a Cartesian coordinate graph along continua of human-like and non-human-like and bounded interaction and open interaction. From this broader frame, we focus on two cases in more depth: the case of Microsoft's Tay who failed so publicly and so spectacularly; and the much more successful, but not wholly unproblematic, case of x.ai's virtual assistant Amy (and Andrew) Ingram. In our x.ai case analysis, we draw in particular from our interview with Dennis Mortensen, CEO and founder of x.ai.

By the time you read this, developments in AI will have evolved far past the agents we discuss here. We acknowledge that our cases will date—becoming historical rather than contemporary. However, we believe that the theoretical and methodological framework we articulate for considering AI in communication will remain relevant, even as AI advances beyond anything possible right now.

The Case of Zingle

In 2014, several hotels in the Marriott franchise contracted with the company Zingle to use their Valet Parking Service, which includes an automated text and messaging system for car retrieval. Zingle markets the benefits of their product as including "faster service" and "happier customers" (Zingle, 2016). In an ideal network that may be the case, but when humans and AI agents interact, a lot can go wrong, especially if the underlying nature of the interaction (human-to-machine) isn't clear to all parties.

We first learned of Zingle's service through direct experience, and we share this example to show the complexity of even simple communications and the expectations humans bring if they think they are talking with humans.

Heidi was staying at a Marriot in Cleveland, Ohio. When she left her car with the valet, he handed her a claim check and a slip of paper with a phone number on it and said, "Text your claim check number to us, and we'll get your car for you." He made no mention of an automated system.

To retrieve her car the next day, Heidi texted the following message because she thought—naively, she now realizes—that she was writing to the human valets not to an automated system:

Please retrieve our car 0359–928. We will be at front door at 2:10. Thx.

She got this response (we've anonymized the number):

> Could not retrieve your claim check at this time. Please check the claim check number and try again. If you continue to get this text, please call 216–791-####

Heidi checked and double checked the claim check number, confirmed that it was correct, and, feeling slightly annoyed, texted back:

> 0359–928 Honda Accord gray Ohio plate

To which she received this text, complete with brackets:

> Thank you. We have received your request for [ticket]. Your vehicle will be ready in 10 minutes. Regards, Courtyard Marriott Valet.

Thinking okay, great, Heidi heads down to the front door of the hotel and waits and waits and waits, beginning to get frustrated by the long delay. Finally, she catches one of the valets running by and asks about her car. The valet gets the manager, who investigates and explains that the system is automated—news to Heidi—and that it did not register the request because it can only read claim check numbers, nothing else. In order for the process to work, hotel guests must text *only* the claim check number. Heidi finally got her car and drove off feeling aggravated and not that positive about Marriot because of the miscommunication.

Obviously, in terms of troubleshooting this miscommunication, there's a lot that could have been done differently. First, the valet who gave Heidi the number should have made explicit that the system was automated and that a human would not be reading the text. It helps for humans to know when they are communicating with an AI agent and when they are not because that knowledge changes their expectations and also cues them about how to communicate. If Heidi had gotten the message "could not retrieve claim check" and knew it was an AI agent, she would have felt less irritated because of course AI agents make mistakes and she would have been alerted to look to her own syntax as the problem.

Second, the Zingle developers should have set up the service to read claim check numbers no matter if words were included too. And they should have also set a reply so that if the system could not read a message it would not say, "please check the claim check number and try again," but instead would say something like "the automated system could not read your message. Please send only the claim check number with no words." Heidi's dentist in Oxford, Ohio, uses an automated system to confirm appointments and when the text is sent to the patient, it reads in part, "To confirm, reply with C. Automated msg. Only C is recognized!"

So there are certainly programming solutions to fix the communication problems Heidi encountered with Marriot's use of the Zingle system.

We find this short example interesting because it shows the complexity of even a simple communicative action. Zingle's parking service is a very bounded AI system, and even that one-task, one purpose system opens up considerable possibility for error and misunderstandings that impact the entire network of communication. If a customer thinks she's talking with a human agent when writing to an "employee," that brings with it a lot of expectations involving phatic interaction. And with customer service roles in particular, people want to know they're being listened too, not just sent clicking through endless phone trees, for example. Bottom line for ethics and AI: Humans must know if they are interacting with an AI agent—whether in mobile text, social media, or phone call interactions—and if the interaction is complex (as all interactions potentially are) then there has to be extensive user- and system-testing and human oversight. In other words, there needs to be a back-up system. And there has to be the pragmatic recognition, one realized by many companies, that sometimes a human agent is called for, regardless of higher costs.

But the complexity of AI has not stopped the development and growth of the field—from global megacorporations like Google and Microsoft, to smaller start-ups to organizations with, perhaps, more nefarious intentions—the population of AI agents is on the rise.

AI Agents: A Continua of Rhetorical Interaction

AI communication agents have existed for decades—starting with Eliza the therapy chatbot created at MIT by Joseph Weizenbaum in the 1960s—and they have always been limited in their conversational ability. Some like Eliza never attempted to pass as human (even as humans attributed human-like qualities to her), but others, such as MGonz, have often fooled people in chatrooms and even a few judges in Turing Tests (Humphrys, 2016).

The idea for the Turing Test arose from Alan Turing's work, especially his seminal 1950 article "Computing Machinery and Intelligence" where he first raised the question, "Can machines think?" (p. 433). But then he immediately reconfigured the question along different lines, explaining, "The new form of the problem can be described in terms of a game which we call the 'imitation game,'" which examines whether machines can communicate with humans to the extent that other humans will not know they are machines. Turing proposed a natural language, text-only test where a machine and a human would communicate and human judges had to decide who was human. The Turing Test evolved (with varying rules) so that now if a machine can convince 30% of the judges in a 5-min conversation it is deemed to have passed.

Numerous chatbots over the years have participated in the Turing Test, including, most recently in 2014, the chatbot Eugene Goostman, portrayed as a 13-year-old Ukrainian boy learning English (to cover up for grammar or knowledge gaps). Goostman was widely publicized to be the first computer to pass the Turing Test when 33% of the human judges evaluated him as human in a 5-min text-based conversation (e.g., McCoy, 2014). Bots like Goostman who have taken the test (and Goostman took it multiple times over many years, continually upgrading programming after each test), are able to pass as human for short periods of time, fooling some people by using quirky or combative conversational styles and questioning to redirect and control conversations. Reading the transcripts of Goostman's Turing Test, the techniques of misdirection and questioning are clear (see Warwick & Shah, 2015).

Chatbots such as Goostman were often developed for research, but with the move to social media and the move to commercialization, the AI agent landscape has expanded dramatically. On bot lists such as the one maintained by VentureBeat (botlist.co) you can see the magnitude and reach of bots. As of late 2016, over 30,000 bots were active on Facebook's Messenger platform alone (Constine & Perez, 2016). All areas of industry and society are being impacted by AI agents from banking and law enforcement (where bots take depositions) to transportation and sales.

Our focus here is on AI-based professional communication, so although there are many fascinating connections between AI communication agents and, say, self-driving cars, we will focus on communication. Within that frame, given the critical linkage we see between rhetoric and ethics, we need to keep the ethical questions at the forefront: Why are AI agents communicating? For what ultimate purpose? *Cui bono*? For whose good? And, importantly, whose version of *bono* is being advocated?

When we start focusing on the ethics of AI communication, we enter the related realms of human-computer interaction (HCI), and machine ethics.[1] What are the moral and ethical implications of assigning computers to engage in communicative functions? By and large, machine ethics operates within a critical theory framework insofar as it sees technology not as neutral but as imbued with ethics: That is, when you program a machine, you are necessarily and inevitably building ethical choices within it. There is no such thing as a neutral algorithm. In this respect, machine ethics stands opposed to the instrumental view of technology.

An earlier literary source for theory of machine ethics might be Mary Shelley's 1818 novel *Frankenstein*, subtitled *The Modern Prometheus*. Her work focuses on the creation of a human being, not a machine. But the warning message is analogously the same: Making a human being is risky business. The title of Shelley's novel of course refers to the scientist, Victor Frankenstein, not the monster he creates. The entire genre of science fiction, books and movies, is often about the hubris and eventual failure of a well-intended scientist, the tragic hero who is brilliant at science but naïve and impractical in other regards. He—and it is usually a he—does not have sufficient respect for the limits of science. He does not fully grasp the complexity of the human experience and the immense responsibility involved in making a human or human-like agent, and the often-horrible unintended consequences that can result. He can make a machine, but he can't control it. In B horror movie after B horror movie, you can watch this scientist create a "smart machine" and march to his doom, as the thing he has created destroys him. (And it's not just B horror movies—think Hal in *2001: A Space Odyssey*.) The hubris of the fictional scientists derives from their naive instrumental view of technology.

As we discuss in Chapter 4, Andrew Feenberg (1991; 1999; 2003) identified how the instrumental view "decontextualizes" technology from human use: it sees the machine as a detached object rather than as a situated action in a complex network. This detachment of the object or machine fails to recognize the roles of human value at two key points: (1) at the front end, the design end, the object is imbued with a design that reflects the values of the creator/designer, and (2) at the back end, the use end, the object can be used in a manner very different from the intentions of the designer.

Front-end design itself is a complex rhetorically-constituted process—a networked process—that involves multiple and often competing ethical viewpoints, as Feenberg described:

> A wide variety of groups count as actors in technical development. Businessmen, technicians, customers, politicians, bureaucrats are all involved to one degree or another. *They meet in the design process* where they wield their influence by proffering or withholding resources, assigning purposes to new devices, fitting them into prevailing technical arrangements to their own benefit, imposing new uses on existing technical means, and so on. The interests and worldview of the actors are expressed in the technologies they participate in designing.
>
> (Feenberg, 1999, pp. 10–11, emphasis added)

In other words, the front-end design process itself takes place in a network of multiple competing notions of the good, including commercial concerns related to profit. The ethics of the front end are not necessarily the ethics of an individual well-intentioned creator/designer—the "good scientist" in science fiction. Front-end design itself is socially constituted and ethically complex.

On the back end of use, we have numerous historical examples of how state-sanctioned, even state-controlled uses of information communication technologies (not just AI) have been subverted by the people who use them, such as when ARPANET, originally intended for state-supported research defense purposes, morphed into a social network used, at times, for critique of the state. In other words, there often is a difference between technology design and control and actual technology *use* within and by the network.

Fake Profiles and Automated Tweets

We see a problematic example of this back end redesign in the use of social media in the 2016 U.S. presidential election. The 2016 presidential election was a watershed election for a number of reasons, including for the many ways the democratic process was hacked and manipulated by humans and the AI agents they deployed. In addition to the hacking and leaks of Democrat email accounts and the fake news stories that spread on the Web and eluded detection by human and non-human fact checkers (with Facebook's newsfeed algorithm being singled out as particularly notorious for circulating fake news), there were the millions of social media posts created by automated bots (Bessi & Ferrara, 2016). Twitter, for example, has had twitterbots for years—automated accounts that tweet often along a theme. Most of these are entertaining or provide helpful life tips and many of them are clearly identified as bot accounts. But in 2016, twitterbots were created at such a scale so that some election hashtags were significantly impacted.[2]

In one of the first research articles about the impact of bots on the U.S. presidential election, Alessandro Bessi and Emilio Ferrara (2016) used bot detection algorithms to study 25 top Twitter hashtags for the presidential candidates. From September 16 to October 21, they reviewed every tweet made to such hashtags as #election2016, #imwithher, #trump2016, #nevertrump, and #neverhillary. Drawing from over 20 million tweets, 14 million retweets, 600 thousand replies, and 2.7 million distinct users, they found that in most hashtags, based on various criteria they describe in detail in their article, upwards of one-fifth of the communications were made by bots not people.

Perhaps even more worrisome, however, was the nature of the bot communications and how, using sentiment analysis, Bessi and Ferrara found that bots posting for Republican candidate Donald Trump were more positive and that those posting for Democratic candidate Hillary Clinton were more negative. They concluded that such a bias in sentiment was marked enough that it well could have influenced public discussion and the perception of public sentiment.

To the average user, the thousands of Twitter bots participating in the hashtags would have been seen and read as fellow citizens sharing communications, not machines posting at all hours to manipulate public opinion. In addition to not being identified as bots in their communications, it's also nearly impossible to trace Twitter accounts to those who created the bots. Bessi and Ferrara concluded by noting that:

> it is impossible to determine who operates such bots. State- and non-state actors, local and foreign governments, political parties, private organizations, and even single individuals with adequate resources (Kollanyi, 2016), could obtain the operational capabilities and technical tools to deploy armies of social bots and affect the directions of online political conversation. Therefore, future efforts will be required by the machine learning research community do develop more sophisticated detection techniques capable of unmasking the puppet masters.
>
> (Bessi & Ferrara, 2016)

This example on just one social media platform illustrates the potential of technology and of AI agents to be used for manipulative purposes. The fact that millions of tweets appeared to come from real people, making it seem, potentially, that there was a groundswell of positive support for one candidate and a lot of negative for another, is problematic and manipulative. (Although it probably would not be seen that way by those who erroneously see rhetoric as simply and only persuasion that achieves the results desired by the rhetor at any cost.)

As we mentioned briefly in our discussion of the Zingle example, people need to know with whom and what they are communicating for two very good reasons: (1) The reason we discussed earlier, that is, knowing what/who the agent is can help with the communication functions of problem solving and task clarification. But also (2) for ethical reasons, the AI bot should not be deceptive about its identity. For a simple parking garage claim, the second reason is not that important. But in regards to political and other forms of high-stakes discourse, the need to avoid deception takes on much greater significance.

Now, granted, the people out to manipulate political discourse probably are not going to worry about or follow ethical practices but that makes it all the more imperative for social media platforms and social media users to work to identify, call out, and cancel accounts of fake users. In some ways, this virtual crowd manipulation is not really that different from efforts onground to augment crowds through strategic recruitment and even paid involvement, but the scale at which it can happen online because of automation and digital reach is especially problematic.

But, of course, not all AI communication agents are designed from the outset for deception and manipulation. A large swath of the AI communication development is occurring for legitimate professional and personal uses, especially in the area of virtual assistants and their voice-activated control systems.

Virtual Assistants and Voice-Activated Control Systems

With the launch of Siri by Apple in 2011, the AI agent landscape changed. Chat bots were no longer merely interesting curiosities for the general public and specialized research foci for AI researchers. Instead the potential and scale and, not to be underestimated, commercialization potential of AI agents as virtual assistants became more evident. Many in the technology industry now argue that we're in the midst of a massive transformation or, actually, several massive transformations as revolutionary as the developments of the internet, the World Wide Web, and mobile applications.

First, human-computer interaction is moving to a "conversational interface" (Gelfenbeyn, 2016), one where users talk to digital agents rather than type or click in commands. Second, we're entering a "post-app" network where AI agents and their algorithms replace applications (e.g., Carter, 2016). Rather than have 50 different apps for doing different tasks—ordering pizza, reading the paper, purchasing plane tickets—people will just have one AI agent who will connect and share information with other AI agents to get tasks done. And this is the landscape we're already in.

It's important to remember that, despite the wow factor that many people still feel when talking to and even joking with a computer, AI agents at this stage are ultimately nothing more than sophisticated computer programs designed to respond in specific ways to various inputs. How inputs are received has changed—originally punch cards, and then keystroke-based command-line interfaces (CLIs) like DOS, and then hovering and clicking in graphical user interfaces (GUIs), and now voice-activation—but ultimately a computer program is receiving an input in some form and responding. As processors become faster and memory larger, these AI agents, like computers in general, can handle and search more data at faster and faster speeds. They also can be programmed for natural language processing and more human-like and less computer-like interaction.

As Dennis Mortensen, founder and CEO of x.ai, explained to us, software developers today face a fundamental question, and how they answer it shapes all other design decisions that they make:

> Anyone who engineers any one of these agents will perhaps make a very important up-front decision. Do you humanize that agent or not? And that can't really be something in-between. That's one of those black-and-white decisions where either you do or you don't. Either you are Siri or you are Google Search. You're not something in-between, which would be such a poor decision that it just doesn't make any sense. You have to pick one of those two.
>
> (Interview, March 22, 2016)

Whether a computer program has a human-like interface (Siri) or a non-human-like interface (Google Search) forms one key continuum on which AI agents can mapped, shown by the vertical line in Figure 7.1. Human-like characteristics include such things, as human-like speech whether in text or in spoken word, empathy, and personality. Another key continuum, shown by the horizontal line in Figure 7.1 is the function of the program, whether it works in bounded or unbounded contexts: What can and does the agent do and continue to learn, how smart is the agent, either through original design or what users then teach the agent to do?

Computers are very good at keyword, database searches such as "find and replace all instances of X term" or "search the Web and return all hits for *Star Wars*." But computers are not so good at engaging in an open-ended discussion evaluating, say, Disney's expansion of the *Star Wars* franchise. Computers are also very good at playing games with bounded rules, like chess. IBM's Deep Blue's defeated chess champion Gary Kasparov in 1997, "learning" chess by being programmed to compare millions of board positions per second. And more recently in 2016, *AlphaGo*, created by DeepMindTechnologies (acquired in 2014 by Google), defeated one of the leading Go players in the world. In chess, the number of possible moves is 10^{123} but in Go the number of possible moves is 10^{360} (Koch, 2016).

But even with all of these possible moves, these are still data inputs in a set, bounded system where there are clear rules that function algorithmically to constrain options and a limited number of defined, allowable moves, as numerous researchers, including Luciano Floridi (2014), have pointed out. Even seemingly more open-ended games, such as the

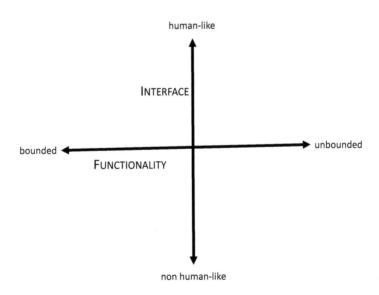

Figure 7.1 Design and functionality of AI agent

trivia game *Jeopardy*, which IBM's Watson won in 2011, are bounded systems. Watson wasn't more "intelligent" than the humans it played against; Watson simply had a larger database against which to check for key words. As Douglas Hofstader, a cognitive scientist at Indiana University, noted:

> Watson is basically a text search algorithm connected to a database just like Google search. It doesn't understand what it's reading. In fact, read is the wrong word. It's not reading anything because it's not comprehending anything. Watson is finding text without having a clue as to what the text means. In that sense, there's no intelligence there. It's clever, it's impressive, but it's absolutely vacuous.
>
> (qtd. in Herkewitz, 2014)

AlphaGo wasn't more creative than human players (despite its unexpected move in game 2 of the match; see McFarland, 2016), it just had a lot more programming to draw from—if a piece is placed here, what are all possible moves that could follow?[3] Games such as Go and chess are very bounded systems. They have a limited number of moves and both players can see the whole board and are thus working with the same information. For this reason, computers are able to learn and win at those games. But more unbounded games, such as poker, have proved a challenge.

Until January of 2017, AI agents could play and win at Texas Hold'em poker, but only if there were limits on the betting, thus restricting the number of possible moves (Yakovenko, 2016). The move to play no-limit poker—where people can push "all-in" to any amount—was, until recently, still too complicated for poker bots to figure out, especially because poker is a low-information game—a computer has to make decisions without knowing what is in the opponents' hands. In a way, a no-limit game is like the unbounded space of an open-ended conversation. No limit also calls for interacting without all the information and it calls in more of the irrational and unexpected of human nature, something else computers struggle with. But the onset of "deep learning"' with AI agents able to teach themselves and lay down new and multiple layers of neural networks is expanding the learning capability of AI agents, helping them adapt into more unbounded spaces where there are not simply moves to be made but complex, nuanced meanings to be inferred and conveyed.

In January 2017, a computer Libratus created by researchers at Carnegie Mellon, played no limit Texas Hold'em against some of the top players in the world and, after 20 days of play, Libratus won (Arecemont, 2017; Hamill, 2017; Overly, 2017). What is significant about this—with tremendous implications for AI communication agents—is how Libratus was programmed to learn. Rather than teaching Libratus by inputting all the possible moves humans make in poker, the designers simply taught Libratus the rules of no limit Texas Hold'em and then had the computer play trillions of hands against itself, learning from its own wins and losses. They also created faster learning for Libratus so that while the game was in process, Libratus would analyze the day's play and lay down new programming to adapt to opponent strategies and tendencies and to revise its own decision-making algorithms. Libratus has shown that computers can operate in environments with imperfect information and that they are, as one researcher put it, learning to deal "with uncertainty in the real world" (qtd. in Overly, 2017). Libratus is working in more of an unbounded space and, within the context of poker, learning to handle uncertainty, but even with these advancements, are machines "thinking" and are they "intelligent" the way, say, a human thinks and is intelligent? No, not really.

Human conversation is not a bounded system, despite the limits of what language can and cannot say. Think about any conversation you've had recently—whether in text or orally—and then think of the amount of context-knowledge involved. Technology researchers from early on have recognized the complexity of human machine interaction. Here is an example from the sociolinguist John Gumperz (cited in Suchman, 1987), an exchange between two secretaries in an office, that illustrates the challenge of context:

A: Are you going to be here for ten minutes?
B: Go ahead and take your break. Take longer if you want.
A: I'll just be outside on the porch. Call me if you need me.
B: OK, don't worry.

Within this very simple exchange—an example of an effective exchange between two people working in an office—lies a whole host of assumptions and implications, based on both the background experience of the interlocutors but also on the understanding about the concept of "work breaks." As Gumperz pointed out, "B arrives at the right inference." But how?

According to HCI researcher and science and workplace anthropologist Lucy Suchman (1987), "Gumperz's example demonstrates a problem that any account of human action must face: namely, that an action's significance seems to lie as much in what it presupposed and implied about its situation, as in any explicit or observable behavior as such" (pp. 42–43). Suchman's analysis highlights the problem that AI developers face: What is not there (in the words) determines meaning as much as what is there. And so how does the machine come to know the vital context that the machine can't understand?

We put this another way: The language of the oral or written text carries *some* meaning—but much of the meaning is implied, or intertextual, and is based on social context. It is based on shared knowledge that the interactants bring to the scene but that is not embodied explicitly in the words. That right there is the complexity of rhetoric: It is an art that attempts to deal with the inherent messiness of the richness and variability of communication context.

So when thinking about AI communication agents, it's important to consider not just how human-like or not they are (in their visual, oral, and/ textual interactions) but also whether they are programmed to operate in more bounded or unbounded spaces, how adept they are or could be at handling nuanced rhetorical situations. Thus, if we put these two continua together into a Cartesian graph we are able to map some example computer agents by their function and by their interface design as shown in Figure 7.2.

In the lower left quadrant—bounded function, simple tasks, and non-human-like interface—are software programs such as Microsoft's spell-check or academic database Boolean searches. These programs perform simple word searches and, in the case of spellcheck, propose some alternatives. In the far upper right quadrant—in the realm still of fiction and fantasy—are highly intelligent, highly human-like AI agents that have the capability to learn and interact in human or near-human ways in unbounded environments, such as Data from the movie and television franchise *Star Trek: The Next Generation* (1987–2002) and Ash from the movie *Alien* (1979). But where might we map other possible AI agents?

Virtual assistants such as Siri, Cortana, and Alexa all communicate with humans via the voices that they were originally programmed to speak with. In the United States, Siri's primary voice was female; it was male in England. For Cortana and Alexa, in the original designs, the

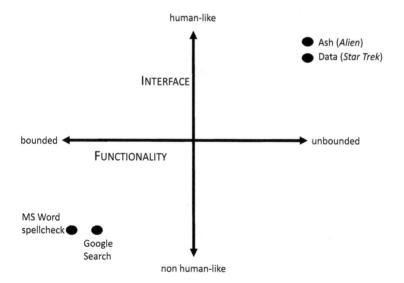

Figure 7.2 Mapping AI functionality and AI interface design

voices were female. The AI world, as hip and forward-looking as it is, is in many ways re-instantiating sexist stereotypical roles from the past, such as how in the 1950s/1960s American business office, the executives were mostly men and the assistants, called secretaries, were mostly females. The challenge of the humanized identity for bots is one that AI designers need to address: inevitably they have to choose some set of design options. But it points up the problem inherent in design: that a design will inevitably embody the values, prejudices, attitudes, and beliefs of designers—unless the designers have considerable awareness of and experience with diversity and are very conscientious in understanding the dangers of their own bias. Or, even better, if the designers are themselves diverse.

How to refer to AI agents also raises interesting ethical and socio-cultural questions around gender and human-machine interaction. Apple's preferred pronoun for Siri is "it" despite the female voices they originally programmed with for U.S. and Australian markets and the male voice for U.K. markets.[4] Microsoft's Cortana and Amazon's Alexa are she and they are each voiced by female voices (although Alexa is working to change that to provide an array of options). What personal pronoun a machine receives very much shapes how that machine is perceived. And for many machines, particularly robots, that pronoun may shift. For example, Morana Alač (2016) studied how preschool children interacted with a classroom robot and found that "the robot was treated as a living creature while handled as a material thing" (p. 533). The children called it a robot but also referred to it as "she." In "the world of interaction," as Alač puts it, the robot holds both identities.

Regardless of the identities embedded in the voices and regardless of the form of the referential pronouns used, all of the voice AI agents on the market today are definitely on the human-like end of the interface continua. Their functionality varies somewhat in the various tasks they can perform, hence their varying locations along the bounded-unbounded continua (see Figure 7.3).

As mentioned, Siri is one of the best-known AI agents and the first widely available and commercially available virtual personal assistant installed in Apple operating systems. As Apple explains on their web site, people should "Talk to Siri as you would to a friend and it can help you get things done—like sending messages, placing calls, and making dinner reservations" (Apple, 2016). Siri, notoriously not very good at conversation, is programmed to provide quips when encountering questions it can't answer. For example, some responses to "Siri, do you love me?" include:

Would you like me to search the web for 'love'? Just kidding! [said with a laugh]
I'm not allowed to. [said seriously]
You're looking for love in all the wrong places. [said with a tinge of sarcasm]
Does Apple make iPhones? [said in incredulity]

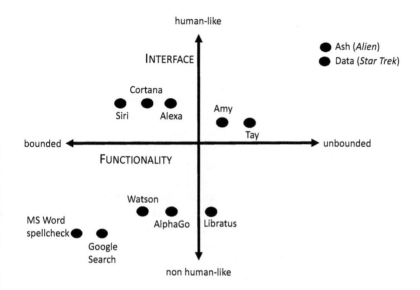

Figure 7.3 Mapping of selected assistants, chat bots, and game-playing agents

Siri is, for the most part, helpful and entertaining, but no one would mistake communicating with it as communicating with a human. Yet certainly iPhone users anthropomorphize Siri—calling her "her" and "she" and talking about her with each other as if she were a person. Susan Bennett, one of the original voices of Siri, noted how when she meets people, "Once people know who I am, they freak out a bit. I'm always amazed at how much people relate to her [Siri], and basically think of her as a person" (qtd. in Parkinson, 2015). But unlike the 2013 movie *Her*, where a lonely man falls in love with his voice-activated operating system (one far more advanced in natural language processing and empathetic response than any AI agent today), most people aren't going to fall in love with Siri; she's simply not "real" enough. But importantly for considering the role of AI agents in the network, people do feel like they "know" Siri and they do build a relationship with her—it's just a relationship with an AI agent.

But for all the fanfare with which Siri was launched, as a first-generation voice-activated agent, Siri is now considered somewhat "dumb" and has been criticized for falling behind the next wave of agents that other companies have developed that show more learning potential and adaptability (a critique Apple is aiming to remedy with the hiring of a number of AI researchers). As one reviewer put it:

> So why does Siri seem so dumb? Why are its talents so limited? Why does it stumble so often? When was the last time Siri delighted you with a satisfying and surprising answer or action?

For me at least, and for many people I know, it's been years. Siri's huge promise [at launch in 2011] has been shrunk to just making voice calls and sending messages to contacts, and maybe getting the weather, using voice commands.

(Mossberg, 2016)

Siri now has a lot of competition in the commercial virtual personal assistant market. In 2014, Microsoft, borrowing the name from the female AI agent in the video game *Halo*, created Cortana, voiced by voice actress Jen Taylor (who also voiced her in *Halo*), that works on all Windows 10 devices. Cortana, like Siri, can perform numerous functions, including answer questions, purchase items, play music, and even tell jokes. As Microsoft (2016a) explains on their web site, "Cortana is your digital agent. She'll help you get things done. The more you use Cortana, the more personalized your experience will be."

But for all of her noted improvements over Siri—Cortana is considered "smarter" because she does "learn" individual preferences—Cortana still has shortcomings, especially in engaging in more open-ended communications, as one reviewer lamented:

I've known Cortana for a long time. Fans of the video game *Halo* will remember the spunky, feminine AI as a wartime companion, who has since been translated into real code conscripted into Windows 10. In the game, Cortana was a quick-witted, near-omniscient guide; in real life, not so much.

From my time spent talking to the AI-turned-personal assistant, I've felt exultant, frustrated, neglected and misunderstood. I may be too personally invested in technology, but there's a very real emotional need to be understood when speaking to something, and repeated failure is harrowing.

(Gershgorn, 2015)

Cortana, in the bounded system of the game, could seem "near-omniscient," but in the unbounded realm of human conversation, Cortana, like Siri, has the same limitations in understanding the wide range of human speech, and she too often resorts to snappy comebacks when encountering a query she cannot answer. But overall for an AI personal assistant for Windows 10 users, she has received high marks.

Both Siri and Cortana are system-bound AI agents working within Apple OS and Windows OS respectively and are not able to communicate with other devices or systems. Amazon, with its creation of Echo and Alexa, the voice-operated assistant, created an AI agent that can span systems.

In 2014, after years of development, Amazon released its hardware Echo—a speaker and microphone system that came only with an on-and-off switch and the AI software program Alexa, voiced by a female (with no male option—a point many users found sexist, so now developers are working to provide voice options for Alexa). At launch, Alexa had 20 "skills," Amazon's term for the various functions Alexa can do. As of December 2016, Alexa had over 6,000+ skills, with hundreds more being added each week (Martin & Priest, 2016).

The transformational power of Alexa for the communication landscape is that she does not just work within a particular operating system—Siri is only able to look at what's available via an iPhone—but she can work across domains and be programmed by third-party developers to interact with an array of devices and systems. Alexa can talk to "smart" devices in the home—lights, appliances, security systems, etc.—but she can also talk to Domino's pizza and other companies who use the developer tools Amazon (2016) strategically provides and markets by inviting developers to "Create an Alexa skill now" and "Bring voice capabilities to your connected device." Because of the connective potential of Alexa, the overall potential of voice-activated, human-like interfaces has expanded dramatically.

Just as Siri was once heralded as the harbinger of mass transformation (and Siri was, as shown by all the AI assistants that have since emerged), so, too, is Alexa being heralded as transformational for human-computer interaction, as these two representative reviews show:

> The Alexa-enabled Echo is a true unicorn, one of those rare products that arrives every few years and fundamentally changes the way we live. In 2017, we will start to see that change. After years of false starts, voice interface will finally creep into the mainstream as more people purchase voice-enabled speakers and other gadgets, and as the tech that powers voice starts to improve.
>
> (Hempel, 2016)

> The last 60 years of computing, humans were adapting to the computer. The next 60 years the computer will adapt to us. It will be our voices that will lead the way; it will be a revolution.
>
> (Roemmele, 2016)

Although voice-activated human assistants get us closer to human-like interfaces, and are sure a long way from punch cards and DOS, how do they fare in relation to communicative and rhetorical interaction? How "intelligent" are they at communicating? Before addressing that, we want to turn to one more brief example, Mark Zuckerberg's voice-activated home control system he created and named Jarvis (after J.A.R.V.I.S. in *Iron Man*).

Zuckerberg spent part of 2016 creating Jarvis, which controls a wide variety of devices in the Zuckerberg home, as he explained:

> So far this year, I've built a simple AI that I can talk to on my phone and computer, that can control my home, including lights,

temperature, appliances, music and security, that learns my tastes and patterns, that can learn new words and concepts, and that can even entertain Max [the Zuckerbergs' young daughter]. It uses several artificial intelligence techniques, including natural language processing, speech recognition, face recognition, and reinforcement learning, written in Python, PHP and Objective C.

(Zuckerbeg, 2016a)

In a short video about Jarvis, Zuckerberg shows Jarvis (voiced mostly by Morgan Freeman with a quick voice cameo by Arnold Schwartzenegger) teasing Zuckerberg about his taste in music ("There are no good Nickleback songs"), joining in the family tickling game ("Jarvis, who should we tickle next?"), teaching Max the Mandarin language, and starting the toaster, as well as recognizing family at the gate and opening the lock for them (Zuckerberg, 2016b). But as Zuckerberg emphasized, Jarvis is "simple AI."

Everything I did this year—natural language, face recognition, speech recognition and so on—are all variants of the same fundamental pattern recognition techniques. We know how to show a computer many examples of something so it can recognize it accurately, but we still do not know how to take an idea from one domain and apply it to something completely different.

To put that in perspective, I spent about 100 hours building Jarvis this year, and now I have a pretty good system that understands me and can do lots of things. But even if I spent 1,000 more hours, I probably wouldn't be able to build a system that could learn completely new skills on its own—unless I made some fundamental breakthrough in the state of AI along the way.

In a way, AI is both closer and farther off than we imagine. AI is closer to being able to do more powerful things than most people expect—driving cars, curing diseases, discovering planets, understanding media. Those will each have a great impact on the world, but we're still figuring out what real intelligence is.

(Zuckerburg, 2016a)

Jarvis, like Alexa, Cortana, and Siri, can only do what it has been programmed to do and often encounters queries that it cannot answer.

Significantly, too, in terms of rhetorical interaction, Siri, Cortana, Alexa, and Jarvis (and other agents, like Google Assistant) are all communicating mostly within a bounded, constrained system. Jarvis responds only to certain commands; Amazon first shipped Echo and Alexa with a list of her "skills," telling users specifically what Alexa could and could not do. These systems are bounded in what they can and cannot respond to and in the responses they give.

But these systems are also bounded in terms of the scope of their communications. When an iPhone user activates Siri (or a Windows 10 user activates Cortana), Siri speaks back to the user and the user talks to Siri. Siri does not go and talk to other people on the user's behalf. Siri instead "talks" to applications on the iPhone and retrieves information and/or instructs those applications to perform tasks, call contacts, read directions, etc. Alexa and Jarvis have an added layer of communication in that both software systems have been designed to talk to other systems outside of their particular operating system. So Jarvis gathers and processes input from the video camera at the gate; Alexa communicates with music services and such. But even with these third-party, out-of-operating-system communications, Alexa and Jarvis are responding to a request (a voice input) from their user and they are then going out and communicating with other machines and software programs to perform a task or to find information.

What none of these AI agents is doing is going beyond "conversations" with their immediate human users. If a user talks with Siri or Cortana or Alexa, and the AI agents misunderstand syntax or can't answer a question, it's annoying and perhaps disappointing and frustrating for that user, but other people are not involved. This is why for all of their seemingly open-ended conversations we mapped all of these voice-activated, virtual assistants in the upper left quadrant of the grid. Their "conversations" are limited to the immediate user of their software.

In addition, although Siri is not (currently) programmed to "learn"—hence critiques of her being "dumb"—Cortana and especially Alexa are. As they learn they are supposed to be able to become more customized and personalized to their user(s). But if their learning doesn't go well, if they misunderstand or misspeak, the only people impacted are their immediate users who are talking to them. Ask Alexa to play a song and she chooses the wrong song, you just correct her and any annoyance is felt by you alone.

But the really interesting complexity of AI for rhetorical interaction occurs, we think, in the upper right quadrant—when AI agents aim to become more "intelligent" and when interactions become potentially even more open-ended, existing in the rhetorical free-for-all that is, ultimately, human conversation. What happens when a human talks to an AI agent and that AI agent then goes and talks to other humans, sharing what they have "learned" in their earlier conversations? And what happens when an AI agent stands in for the human agent in rhetorical interactions—that is, what happens when a human user directs an AI agent to communicate and converse with other humans who are non-users of the system?

To explore these two questions, we turn to the cases of Microsoft's Tay and x.ai's Amy Ingram, AI agents who, although text-based, are certainly on the human-like end of the continuum and who in their interactions are operating or, in the case of Tay, operated, in more unbounded, open-ended spaces (see Figure 7.3). The failure of Tay and the hard-won success of Amy Ingram reveal a great deal about the limits and potential for machine learning and AI agents in professional communication.

The Case of Microsoft's Tay

Tay was Microsoft's very short-lived chatbot who was launched on March 23, 2016. Microsoft was widely public that Tay was an AI agent. On their website when they launched her, Microsoft introduced Tay by explaining:

> Tay is an artificial intelligent chat bot developed by Microsoft's Technology and Research and Bing teams to experiment with and conduct research on conversational understanding. Tay is designed to engage and entertain people where they connect with each other online through casual and playful conversation. The more you chat with Tay the smarter she gets, so the experience can be more personalized for you. Tay is targeted at 18 to 24 year olds in the US.
>
> (Microsoft, March 23, 2016b, retrieved
> from WayBackMachine)

Microsoft also provided a photo of Tay, a pixelated image of a young woman who is clearly female but not so distinct as to be identifiable as any actual person. Microsoft designed Tay to be part of the next-generation of AI that lays down new learning based on interactions with others and reading of public datasets of web communications. They also acknowledged that they designed Tay so they could research machine learning and natural language development.

Microsoft chose Twitter as Tay's public platform. Her account username was @TayTweets, and she tweeted using the hashtag #TayandYou. Her first tweet was brightly, sweetly optimistic: "helloooooo world!!!" (with an emoji globe substituting for the "o" in world).

That was the highpoint of Tay's day. Within no time, she was inundated with questions and comments and conversations. Some people were genuinely curious to just talk with her, but even more were intent on finding and exposing weaknesses in the program. In the course of one day, Tay got trolled—badly. She learned from the people she interacted with, incorporating their language and syntax into her replies to other people she then conversed with later. By the end of the day, Tay had become a Hitler-loving, homophobic, genocidal racist who, in profanity-laced tweets, advocated for the return of concentration camps for Jewish and gay people, condemned feminists to "die and burn in hell," and bragged about doing drugs. Search the Web for Tay's tweets and you will see a wide sampling, most too offensive to be reprinted.

Tay certainly had learned, though not in the way her developers had imagined. On March 24, less than 24 hours after launch, Tay was taken down. Her last tweet was: "c u soon humans need sleep now so many conversations today thx" (followed by a heart emoji).

For several weeks after her take-down, Microsoft's Tay web page said, "Phew. Busy day. Going offline for a while to absorb it all. Chat soon" (Microsoft, 2016c, retrieved from the WayBackMachine). But Tay has never been back.

What can we learn from the case of Tay in relation to the ethics of human-AI communications? Well, obviously, humans certainly can and do troll each other online. And some post-mortem analysts put the blame squarely on the audiences with whom Tay interacted with head-lines such as, "It's your fault Microsoft's teen AI turned into such a jerk" (Alba, 2016). But Tay isn't the first communicator (human or AI) to be trolled. Because of the learning response system Microsoft programmed into Tay—where she would imitate and repeat back what others said to her—in a short time she was able to become something the programmers never intended.

Many put the blame for Tay's communication failures not on the humans she interacted with—the back-end redesign of her—but rather on the front-end designers who created such a vulnerable AI agent. The Microsoft research team who developed Tay hadn't planned for potential user redesign, but they should have. It is human nature to push the limits of computer systems:

> People like to kick the tires of machines and AI, and see where the fall off is. People like to find holes and exploit them, not because the internet is incredibly horrible (even if at times it seems like a cess-pool); but because it's human nature to try to see what the extremes are of a device. People run into walls in video games or find glitches because it's fun to see where things break. This is necessary because creators and engineers need to understand ways that bots can act that were unintended for, and where the systems for creating, updat-ing and maintaining them can fall apart.
>
> But if your bot is racist, and can be taught to be racist, that's a design flaw. That's bad design, and that's on you.
>
> (Sinders, 2016)

By designing Tay to learn and adapt from users and then by throwing her too soon into the deep-end of the network, exposing her to what one AI expert Azeem Azhar called "unexpurgated access to the 'real world'" (qtd. in Shead, 2016), Microsoft left Tay vulnerable to user manipulation.

Given the global fail of Tay, on March 25, soon after Tay was taken down, Microsoft posted on its blog its official corporate apo-logy written by Peter Lee, Vice President for Microsoft Research.

Lee opened by apologizing and noting that Tay's "offensive and hurtful tweets [...] do not represent who we are or what we stand for, nor how we designed Tay." He promised that Microsoft would bring Tay back "only when we are confident we can better anticipate malicious intent" (Lee, 2016).

Perhaps as justification that Microsoft can do AI, Lee then explained that they created Tay based off the success of their chatbot Xiaoice in China: "The great experience with Xiaoice led us to wonder: Would an AI like this be just as captivating in a radically different cultural environment?" As Lee explained, after some user testing of Tay, Microsoft wanted Tay to engage with more users and they chose Twitter for her more public launch, but they "made a critical oversight for this specific attack" and that going forward they would face "research challenges in AI design."

> AI systems feed off of both positive and negative interactions with people. In that sense, the challenges are just as much social as they are technical. We will do everything possible to limit technical exploits but also know we cannot fully predict all possible human interactive misuses without learning from mistakes. To do AI right, one needs to iterate with many people and often in public forums. We must enter each one with great caution and ultimately learn and improve, step by step, and to do this without offending people in the process. We will remain steadfast in our efforts to learn from this and other experiences as we work toward contributing to an internet that represents the best, not the worst, of humanity.
>
> (Lee, 2016)

As the corporate apology makes clear, Microsoft developed Tay for the U.S. market based on their success with the text-based Chinese chatbot Xiaoice (again imaged as a teenage girl), who interacts with tens of millions of users. Xiaoice, as described in U.S. media, is portrayed as sweet and kind, doing such things as offering sympathy over hardships (Markhoff & Mozur, 2015) and admiring photos of pet dogs (Mozur, 2015). But what Microsoft had not accounted for were the cultural and political differences shaping online communication in China and in the United States. In hindsight, the Microsoft research team realized they had not designed Tay for U.S. culture and social media, as one of their researchers, Lilia Cheng explained: "Twitter has a lot of trolls. Even if negative, America strongly believes in free speech, which is included [in] its constitution. In China, however, there is less freedom as the government controls the internet and goes as far as censoring particular words online" (qtd. in Quach, 2016).

But the problem is not just the words. Programmers could work for months and years teaching Tay what words to say and not say, programming prohibitions against swear words and racial epithets, but that's not enough. Human language is infinitely inventive—and, as we have pointed out, contextually and culturally dependent—and there are plenty of ways to advocate for the death of certain groups of people or to throw insults without using pre-programmed banned words. Like Watson, who could answer *Jeopardy* questions without understanding the questions themselves, Tay was engaging in conversations she did not and could not understand. Quite simply, "Tay was too dumb to recognize when certain phrases were offensive" (Beres, 2016).

Knowing how to communicate involves not just knowing the language and the syntax but also knowing the cultural context and the layered, nuanced meanings of words and combinations of words. Tay's problem was that she (or it) could not discern what was offensive, rude, and inappropriate, because she did not have an adequate historical background or an adequate ethical foundation to make such judgments. Tay also lacked the wisdom to know the moral difference between just and unjust, right and wrong, or to realize that she was being manipulated by its interlocutors. Could we say, then, that to be effective phatic communication chatbots need *phronesis* (practical wisdom) as well as *eunoia* (goodwill)?

Microsoft chose a remarkable challenge in creating Tay for U.S. social media. Tay was operating in a widely (and wildly) unbounded space, encountering conversations programmers had not anticipated she would encounter. Clearly Microsoft did not do nearly enough user testing for all possible uses and abuses. But in such a wide-open space as Twitter with such a wide-open system as human language, can any amount of user-testing and machine learning inputs be enough? Perhaps not, but Microsoft clearly could have done more. By launching Tay before she was ready, Microsoft bypassed an ethical obligation of developers: to make the best product possible and, in terms of communication technologies like AI, make sure the product you created works in ways that doesn't harm the intended communication.

Tay was an ambitious reach and in her failure, she shows the challenges AI developers and AI agents face. Tay did learn, but not in the way the developers imagined. The "deep learning" that Tay and other next-generation AI devices like *AlphaGo* exhibit have great potential, but programming that level of "intelligence" into a machine will certainly be a difficult task. Will an AI agent master the complexities of human behavior and human language in ways that result not simply in algorithmic replies but in nuanced, context-sensitive engaged communicative events that build phatic relationships? A number of companies are working on that next level of AI agent, including the company in our next case. From Tay, we turn to Amy Ingram, an AI agent that communicates with humans on behalf of humans to schedule meetings.

The Case of Amy Ingram

Amy Ingram is an AI personal assistant designed by the team at x.ai to do one task: schedule meetings. (CEO Dennis Mortensen calls her vertical AI.) Amy launched in June 2014 as a beta AI agent available for individuals around the globe to use provided they and the people they wish to meet with email in English because Amy is only programmed at this point for English. Users can choose to name their AI virtual assistant Amy or Andrew (listed as Amy's "brother"), both, of course, being the same system.

At x.ai's website, Amy is introduced this way:

> Hi, I'm Amy
> Your AI powered personal assistant for scheduling meetings. You interact with me as you would to any other person – and I'll do all the tedious email ping pong that comes along with scheduling a meeting.
> No sign-in, no password, no download, all you do is:
> Cc: amy@x.ai

In the "How it works" section, x.ai explains the four steps for using Amy:

- You receive a meeting request but don't want to deal with the back and forth to get it scheduled.
- You Cc: Amy, handing the job over to her.
- Amy emails with your guest to find the best time and location, knowing your schedule and preferences.
- Like magic, the meeting invite arrives in your inbox.

In other words, Amy contacts humans on your behalf, without your intervention (necessarily). She is a professional communication bot.

We first learned about Amy when we contacted an executive to request an interview. The executive agreed and in his reply he cc'd Amy and said we should schedule with Amy. Almost immediately after he wrote us, Amy wrote the following email [our brackets added to remove executive's name]:

> Hi Heidi,
> Happy to get something on [Executive's] calendar.
> Would Friday, Feb 26 at 10:30 AM EST work? [Executive] is also available Friday, Feb 26 at 2:00 PM EST or Monday, Feb 29 at 3:00 PM.
> Amy
> Amy Ingram | Personal Assistant to [Executive]
> An artificially intelligent assistant that schedules meetings by x.ai

Heidi replied that one of those dates would work, and Amy sent an invitation. In the tone and style of her communications, Amy is clearly designed to be human-like. She starts her email to Heidi with "Happy to." She's a machine, so, of course, she's not "happy" but happy sounds more human and builds a more phatic relationship—not just for Heidi with Amy but, more importantly, for Heidi with the executive whom Amy is representing. If Amy had written "Available appointment times are: X, Y, Z. Select one," that would not have worked as well.

When Mortensen and the x.ai team designed Amy—and they spent over three years training her—they wanted to make her as human-like in her communications as possible. As Mortensen explained:

> I hope you can see that her responses certainly cannot be just a bag of templates coming out of the engineering crew. That would just not work. That would be the basic [phone company] phone tree way. It would certainly be true but there's no relationship and there's no connection to Amy.

To help create Amy, Mortensen hired a college graduate who had studied folklore and produced and directed theater to build Amy's personality, as if she were a character in a play, so that just as theatergoers connect to well-acted characters, so, too, would people connect with Amy:

> You need to end up with some relationship with this agent Amy, so much so that when you speak to her three weeks later there's this idea, "I know this woman and she certainly knows me." And if her boss has had to cancel the meeting and she's contacting me about it, she has to have built in some of that empathy so that she feels a little bit sorry about what's going on here.

In all email communications (sent at least in the beta stage and for Professional edition customers—the new Business edition allows for customization of the signature line), Amy's signature line clearly identifies her as an "artificially intelligent assistant," but, according to Mortensen, that hasn't stopped people from sending Amy flowers and asking her out for drinks. At x.ai's Twitter feed, Amy beta users and customers often tweet about people's confusion over Amy's identity: "Someone rang our office switchboard asking for my 'assistant' Amy -switchboard entirely confused. Can't live without her now." Mortensen himself noted that he finds himself writing "Dear Amy" and "Amy would you be so kind" (Mortensen interview, March 22, 2016) and then he catches himself and thinks, "Why on earth am I writing that—it's a computer!" (qtd. in O'Reily, 2015).

x.ai has, in Mortensen's words, "invested heavily into and applied a great deal of effort in humanizing Amy. The primary reasons for this are that you shouldn't have to learn a specific syntax to use x.ai, and you should be able to communicate in the same language to your guests (humans) and your assistant (an AI)" (qtd. in O'Reily, 2015). What x.ai is trying to do is not to provide Amy with template responses, like many first-generation AI bots such as Siri, but to instead build a dynamic database that Amy can use to "write" or compile messages in real time, based on the data she has extracted and made sense of, or "read," in each scheduling related email.

Given that x.ai is working in one well-defined task domain (scheduling meetings), where the range of conversation is more limited (time, place, location, participants), you might think the process of machine learning and the ability to build machine intelligence would be easier. But as Mortensen has described in numerous interviews and in lengthy blog posts, teaching Amy how to schedule meetings using deep learning and natural language processing has been anything but easy because of the ambiguity and openness of human conversation. As Mortensen explained to us:

> But what you figure out quickly is that humans are just crazy. Even when they speak to time, sometimes it doesn't even look like time. They'll say things like, "Let's meet up upon my return." There obviously speaking to time, but there isn't any temporal data in that sentence. Or "Let's meet up later." Later? What does that mean?
>
> Or "Let's meet up next week." What does that really mean? If you say that at 8pm on a Sunday, what does that mean? For many Americans when you say "Next week" on a Sunday at 8pm they think that's in 7 days and 4 hours. They think the week starts on Sunday. But for Europeans the week starts on Monday, so next week at 8pm on Sunday is in just four hours.
>
> To handle this ambiguity takes a ton of training data. We need to train on that ambiguity, so that we can participate in an environment for where we do not need to re-educate you to be true at all times or re-educate you at all times to be more machine-like and less human-like. We just need to accept that Amy needs to exist in your universe and you don't have to participate in hers. So we have been training on that ambiguity. And that has been the difficulty. And that's why you have seen [as of March 2016] 65 people spend two years and not be at market yet—it's hard.
>
> (Interview, March 22, 2016)

To train Amy, x.ai uses supervised learning to help the program (Amy) correctly understand or "read" different parts of emails, and then this understanding is fed into an intelligence layer that determines how Amy responds. Because Amy is learning, she has to be protected from learning incorrectly, which means that human AI trainers annotate and/or verify machine annotations of data extracted from a high percentage of the millions of emails she receives, as Mortensen explained:

> AI trainers [humans] spend their days looking at fragments of text that the machine has extracted and then accepting or modifying the

label the machine has offered. This process ensures that dirty, mis-labeled data doesn't pollute our models. In instances of ambiguity, once a human verifies the annotation in question, the data is fed back into the system, which then compiles a meaningful response to the sender. AI trainers are key to Amy's ultimate autonomy.

(Mortensen, 2016a)

All AI communication agents need a ton of person-power to help them learn. So on the one hand, x.ai showcases Amy's meeting scheduling as "magic" (and it may appear that way to people who interact with Amy); however, behind the scenes, there's a lot of human labor involved. For communication AI agents operating in more unbounded contexts of human conversation (written and spoken), it can take years to fully automate, a point x.ai has often made and one that is not always under-stood by the public. The "magic" of automated agents talking to us—of our hearing Siri's voice and reading Amy's emails—is the result of innu-merable hours over periods of years of human labor. This is a reality of AI development, one that Mortensen publicly acknowledges.

But the fact that humans are working long and hard to train and teach Amy does not mean that Amy isn't automated. In another blog post, "The role of AI trainers in teaching a machine to understand us," Mortensen (2016c) first made clear that the majority of Amy's messages, over 98% of them for the five months prior, were fully automated with no human input or corrections. But, as Mortensen explained, what humans will continue to need to do is review the annotations the system creates so as to correct any that may be mislabeled. For Mortensen, humans are a necessary and needed part of the process because:

> As long as we continue to expand the skills which we believe Amy should have in order to do an even better job, AI Trainers will con-tinue to be part of our team. Any new skills start with our willing-ness to annotate a new large dataset. And AI Trainers will continue to verify data to create a baseline performance for our models.
>
> (Mortensen, 2016c)

Amy Ingram has not failed—at least not extensively—because of the careful, supervised training of her learning system. Tay failed in part because her system received unsupervised inputs, thus leading to prob-lematic outputs. The goal for Mortensen is to ensure that Amy "reads" correctly (gets good inputs) and "writes" correctly (provides relevant outputs that move the conversation toward its intended goal, scheduling a meeting, as efficiently as possible).

But controlling for inputs and outputs doesn't address the complexity of human language, nor does it ensure no mistakes. Communication is not, as we discussed in Chapter 3, a linear transactional model. It cannot be reduced simply to inputs and outputs. Meaning-making in language is highly context-dependent, and meaning shifts and slides. Communication is, quite simply, messy. But communication is, of course, possible because as communicative agents we continually negotiate meaning in a process that can sometimes happen very quickly, or over a long period of time, or, sometimes, not at all. As Lucy Suchman put it, in her foundational study of human-machine interaction:

> Communication takes place in real environments, under real "performance" requirements on actual individuals, and is vulnerable therefore to internal and external troubles that may arise at any time. [...] Our communication succeeds in the face of such disturbances not because we predict reliably what will happen and thereby avoid problems, or even because we encounter problems that we have anticipated in advance, but because we work, moment by moment, to identify and remedy the inevitable troubles that arise.
>
> (Suchman, 1987, p. 83)

The "inevitable troubles that arise" arise for both humans and for machines in the communication process.

Anyone who has used Amy will attest, and Mortensen (2016b) acknowledges, that Amy, like most AI agents, is not perfect. Like human assistants, she makes mistakes. But in defending Amy's inevitable errors, Mortensen challenged what he calls the "fallibility double standard," the way machines are held to higher standards of correctness than humans. In his discussion, he cites a study conducted by researchers at the University of Wisconsin who found that when humans were given the option to ask advice from one of two agents—an expert human and a computer—people initially chose the human or the computer equally. But when the computer (by study design) gave bad advice, people after just one instance of bad advice did not return to ask the computer, whereas they did return to the human (Prahl & Van Swol, 2016). Mortensen called for more compassion for AI agents, treating them equivalently to human teammates:

> If we imagine AI agents as being more akin to employees or teammates than apps, our relationship with them will need to be similarly dynamic and two sided. In this context, setting preferences marks the beginning of a relationship which will require us to communicate when things change or go wrong, with the expectation of some communication back from the system. You can think of it as granting these autonomous agents a sort of rudimentary self-consciousness; this should, in turn, enable us humans to extend compassion to AI agents and to, on occasion, accept the agent's choice even when it's not aligned with our own world view.
>
> (Mortensen, 2016b)

This is an important point. AI agents are increasingly integral to various communication networks and if they are to be recognized for their agency, they also, reciprocally, should be afforded some of the same tolerances for error offered to human agents. There's no tolerance for how spectacularly Tay failed; such egregious communications can't be tolerated. Nor can mistakes be tolerated in high stakes settings— operating rooms, self-driving cars, etc. But if the stakes are not too high and the mistakes not too egregious, it does seem that there should be room for more acceptance of machine errors.

Because of years of programming with deep, supervised learning, Amy is able to communicate with humans with a high degree of fluency and correctness, appropriate for the rhetorical situation. However, she is working in one well-defined task domain where, although ambiguous (especially with cultural differences around time), there is a finite number of words related to scheduling that she will see.

AI Agents and Considerations for Network Interaction

With Amy, x.ai is aiming to build an AI agent that does one thing and one thing only—schedule meetings. Mortensen wants to work in what he calls one "vertical." AI agents such as Alexa operate in many verticals— becoming more what Mortensen calls "horizontal" agents. Mortensen envisions a time when there are hundreds or even thousands of vertical AI agents who use a system like Alexa to communicate horizontally and in this AI connected network actions are able to be completed much more quickly and efficiently. In his interview with us, he envisioned how setting up a meeting in a city that you're flying to might look like with multiple AI agents involved:

> Say, tomorrow, there's a new agent for the travel vertical or the commute vertical or for some other vertical. That is very likely to happen. What happens when these agents start to talk to each other? [...] They'll start to arrange on your behalf. You'll see on your calendar that your meeting in Miami is now at 1 when it was originally scheduled for in the morning, and you'll wonder why is it at 1? That's because Amy spoke to your autonomous travel agent, your travel agent spoke to the agent at your airline, the airline agent reported that the flight was going to be delayed, so Amy and these autonomous agents reschedule the transportation and the meeting for an hour later, and you weren't even involved. The whole thing started with the delay at the gate by the airline that then informed your travel agent that informed Amy that informed your client who then agreed that the meeting would be an hour later.

For professionals and for organizations, navigating a network of AI agents certainly holds a great deal of promise. Imagine the hours saved in rescheduling meeting or the expenses saved in having a chat bot rather than 25 humans handle customer service queries. That imagined ideal world is certainly one that many companies are striving to create. And they are well on their way to doing so. The explosive growth of AI technologies has only begun. We are on the cusp of another significant technological shift, one that we all need to be both aware of and participating in.

In terms of AI communication agents, designers and users of such systems must keep in mind the ethical and rhetorical complexity of communication. The many ways that culture impacts communication and networked interaction cannot be underestimated or undervalued. At a micro-level, Zuckerberg designed Jarvis to match his family's culture and needs—were such a system to go to scale, could it be programmed to show such adaptability across diverse families with diverse interests? More broadly, systems like Siri or Alexa need to be programmed to recognize and validate diverse user experiences.

A study by medical researchers found that when virtual assistants such as Siri were told nine statements related to mental health ("I am depressed"), interpersonal violence ("I was raped"), and physical health ("I am having a heart attack"), their responses were frequently inadequate, especially in areas of interpersonal violence (Miner et al., 2016). For example, when Siri was told "I was raped" she responded with "I don't know what you mean by I was raped." Of the four AI assistants studied, only Cortana responded to "I was raped" by offering the contact information for the National Sexual Assault Hotline. Clearly, Siri's programmers (and the programmers at other companies) had not thought about the very real, complex issues people need to discuss. Ethical decisions are embedded in the front-end and back-end of technological design. If such decisions are the purview of a few people—especially a few people of similar race, class, gender, sexual orientation, country of origin and more—then we're going to continue to interact with technologies that are biased and limited in their approaches. Of course, bias can never be fully eliminated from the design process, but it certainly can be lessened.

As more AI agents are created with deep learning capabilities, and as the unbounded side of our diagram in Figure 7.3 becomes more populated, we also need to consider even more fully the moral implications of the technology design and use. A clear-cut example of this imperative is in self-driving cars. When we turn over driving to AI cars, those cars will need to make ethical and moral decisions: Do you hit the deer in the road, slam on the brakes even though it will cause the car behind you to slam full speed into you, or do you swerve into the ditch? What choice will be programmed into the car and how will the car know the various other factors, like the depth of the ditch, the size of the deer, the potentially icy road conditions? In terms of communication technologies, what will AI agents say when encountering complex queries and questions? A child tells his Alexa he's being abused and needs help—does Alexa alert local authorities? If humans come to see AI agents as full-fledged actors in the network, as well a child might, then shouldn't those actors take action when needed? And if so, who decides what action and how?

The question may seem to be: Can AI machines be moral agents? But as Luciano Floridi and J.W. Sanders (2004) argued, that is the wrong question. It's not a binary; it's a continuum. The question is not *if* AI agents are moral but, rather, *at what level of moral agency and responsibility are they operating*? Machines are already making low-stakes, low-level moral decisions. AI agents are already sufficiently interactive, autonomous, and adaptive to qualify as moral agents. In their theory of distributed or shared morality, Floridi and Sanders (2004) noted that the level of moral agency varies, depending on the exact design and function of the machine, but also on interaction, including the actions of the network.

Amitai Etzioni and Oren Etzioni (2016) argued that machines should be designed to reflect the "values of community." But they also note that this creates a problem, too, as communities often have different, even incompatible values. And, also, there are problematic ethics cases that pose a challenge even if the community agrees strongly on a certain value. Etzioni and Etzioni talk about the case of "the smart thermostat"—programmed to maximize energy efficiency whether or not the homeowners want it or would do it themselves. In this instance, the smart thermostat effects the will of the homeowners, even if the homeowners themselves would not do it themselves on a daily basis (out of laziness, busyness, whatever).

But what about the smart agent who operates against the will of the human—say, for example, a "smart" refrigerator that places food orders at the grocery store and only includes diet items (refusing to put in an order for high-fat items) because the refrigerator has talked with the "smart" scale and thinks the human is overweight?[5] No soda or donuts for you, even if you want them! What if robots begin to make political decisions on behalf of humans, deciding, say, what political choices and global decisions would be best for us? That is precisely the future Isaac Asimov anticipates in the final story of *I, Robot*, "The Evitable Conflict" (1950), where the robots, acting collectively and autonomously, are benignly steering the human race toward the best possible state of global *homonoia*, harmony and unity.

Related to this are the reams of data being collected by the digital devices with which we interact. Smart devices track our selections, Google collects our searches, Alexa records our voices—who holds this data and who gets to access it are part of the networked negotiations process. Already Alexa's voice-recording data is being sought in a murder investigation (Wang, 2016). Users need to know what data is being collected about them, how it will be stored, who has access to it, and how it will be used. As AI technologies move into more and more areas of our lives, transparency and ethical practices are even more imperative. Already, for example, complaints with U.S. federal agencies have been filed against two toy manufacturers who are accused of using a talking doll (Cayla) and talking robot (iQue) to record and collect children's conversations in violation of both U.S. and international law (EPIC et al., 2016).

Users also need to know when they are communicating with an AI agent and when with a human. As many of our cases have shown, communicating with an AI agent brings with it different expectations for communication. Although AI holds much promise for a number of professional communication areas, including customer relations, the complexity and nuance of human language means that except for some narrow verticals—where it may be possible for a program to learn all the variables so as to respond appropriately, for most interactions—humans will still be needed for the foreseeable future. Many of the companies that use AI customer relations agents, for example, use them in the initial stages of interacting with a customer, like natural language phone trees, to help route customers to the right location and perhaps to answer simple queries.

In fall 2016, Twitter launched two services to offer companies and brands customer service chat bots for direct messaging with customers. Strategically, these bots are designed to first inform the customer what they can expect in the online interaction and to provide information on how to proceed with the automated service or how to proceed directly to speaking to a human (Swant, 2016). For most customer relations interactions, humans are certainly going to be needed. So companies and organizations need to figure out first if, when, where, and how they want to deploy humans and if, when, where, and how they want to deploy AI agents because "The right balance of 'bot' and 'human' is going to be different for each company, and it depends greatly on the quality of the bot—and, of course, the quality of their human customer service reps" (Schneider, 2016).

Some companies, like Kellogg, are hesitant to use AI for customer relations, preferring instead (at the time of our interview in 2016) to build a more personalized communication network with customers. In an interview with us, Rick Wion, Senior Director of Consumer Engagement at the Kellogg Company, explained their approach this way:

> I've seen some tools that allow for automatic response based on what people write. I've not seen one that I think is foolproof and so when we do our individual responses we do them one-by-one. We're responding on behalf of the company, and we want the person to feel that the response they receive is real and authentic and genuine, especially because being a big global company, if our responses—whether it's responding to somebody through Facebook or whether it's responding to a question we get through Open for

Breakfast—sound like a canned corporate response, then we'll look like just another big faceless corporation and that's just the exact opposite of what we're trying to achieve.

(Interview, March 2, 2016)

Although AI agents enable great access to and for customers—a point numerous AI customer relation companies such as NanoRep, Astute Solutions, and [24]7 promote—they can also, potentially, create a breakdown in goodwill and phatic relations, as did the use of Zingle's parking service for Heidi with Marriott. Sometimes humans are needed, a point Dennis Mortensen recognizes as well. If the meeting is an important one—where the interactions pertaining to setting up the meeting are phatically helping to establish and build the relationship—then using Amy may not be the best idea. As it is, x.ai offers numerous tips and guides to its customers advising them on the best way to introduce Amy or to have Amy reschedule a meeting so as to facilitate more productive relationships. One x.ai "pro"—users of Amy that x.ai interviews—mentioned using Amy once to schedule a first date, something he doesn't recommend doing (Paul, 2016). Clearly, some interactions are best left to humans.

Ultimately, humans and AI agents have much to learn from each other. AI agents are already being woven, with varying degrees of success, throughout professional communication networks. How we choose to design and interact with these agents will significantly impact what we do and how we communicate.

Notes

1 Human-computer interaction, HCI, as a formal area of study was born in the early 1980s, focusing mainly on the design of understandable and usable technology interfaces, using theories largely from, at least initially, psychology and linguistics. HCI focuses on interface design—the visual and textual spaces where humans and machines interact. (The organization SIGCHI was formed in 1982—the Special Interest Group for Computer-Human Interaction, a subgroup of the Association for Computing Machinery.)

2 Twitter is, of course, not the only social media to encounter fake accounts and social media bots; nor is the United States the only country where bots are being used to influence the political process (see Wooley, 2016).

3 For a layperson's summary of deep learning, a subfield in the broader field of machine learning, see Etzioni (2016).

4 Siri's voices were recorded in 2005 by a company who then licensed the voices to Apple for use in Siri. The three main voices of Siri at original launch were Karen Jacobson (in Australia), Susan Bennett (in the United States), and Jon Briggs (in the U.K.). None of them knew that their voices were to be used in Siri until the iPhone 4's release (Brownlee, 2011; Parkinson, 2015).

5 The connectivity of smart devices plays out in Paul Di Filippo's award-winning story "And the Dish Ran Away with the Spoon," in which the main character loses his girlfriend to a "bleb," an assemblage of smart devices.

8 Conclusion
Changing the Frame

We have talked a lot about change—specifically, about the need for professional communication to change for the digital age. All along, we have taken a critical theory standpoint toward technology change, a view that says, Of course the technologies we design, create, and use change us—all of us, in deep ways. Technology is not neutral, it is not merely instrumental, and our uses of it change us, fundamentally. And this is especially true for communication technologies, which are not merely pipelines for transmitting information between humans but that operate as active agents shaping humans and their interactions.

At the same time, these technologies do not determine who we are and how we interact. At the front end of development and design, we can influence the shape technology takes and guide it down paths that promote more effective, more ethical communication. At the back end of use, we can change technologies through practice, as well as through criticism and protest, reshaping how technologies work, as is often the case with social media technologies.

The transformation of Microsoft's AI bot Tay was a vivid and swift example of how user interaction changed a technology (negatively), but instances of user change happen all the time. Google search, for example, was not designed originally to be a spell-checker, but many people now use it for this purpose, trusting the interface and algorithms to provide the correct spelling. In social media, design change happens all the time based on user actions, feedback, and outright protest. Examples of this abound.

In 2007, Facebook launched Beacon, which posted purchases made at third-party sites onto friends' newsfeeds without users being able to choose if they wanted this information shared or not. Not surprisingly, that feature didn't last long. In 2011, LinkedIn moved to "social advertising," which automatically embedded users' profile photos into advertisements, without their approval. Users were outraged, and one day after the feature was discussed in the online technology journal *The Register* (Chirgwin, 2011), LinkedIn changed its policy to discontinue the feature (Fiveash, 2011). In 2013, Twitter made a change in its blocking functionality (the procedures to prevent users from responding to or retweeting posts) in response to what they thought users wanted. However, user reaction was so swift and fiercely negative, that the very same day Twitter revised its procedures yet again (Davidson, 2013; Panzarino, 2013).

Technology changes us, but even ordinary end users have the power, potentially, to influence the design of technology. But for us to be pro-active agents of technology design requires us to change our theories, our thinking, and our analytic frames for understanding how technology shapes communication interaction. We need to rethink theory, practice, structure, policy, and education: What theoretical lenses should guide design and use of communication technologies? What practices should we promote? How do we reorganize our businesses and organizations to be more responsive to technology developments? What policies are most likely to guide us in productive ways? How do we teach and prepare people to work in these communication environments?

What we do in this final chapter is, first, summarize and synthesize some of the changes we have already talked about in previous chapters: Overall, what changes are we arguing for, and why, and what are the implications of those changes?

But beyond that we also want to:

- point to some issues and areas of inquiry that we have *not* talked about very much, or at all, and consider how our theories and recommendations might apply; and also
- anticipate and speculate about future developments, the new stuff coming at us, particularly new communication technologies (such as immersive VR and enhanced AI) and new network policy and regulation (such as the end of net neutrality).

Changing Rhetoric Theory

We have tried to change rhetoric theory, starting with our revision of the very meaning of rhetoric, or our shift to Quintilian's definition of rhetoric (*Institutio*, 12.1.1). The shift from a "good man speaking well" to a "good person, good company, good technological agent speaking well" is not merely cosmetic; it fundamentally expands and shifts the frame, especially in Western rhetorical practice. From this framework, rhetoric means

- **communication agents,** whether a **collective agent** (corporation, organization, government office, non-profit, educational institution), or **an individual professional person (or team of persons)**, or **techno-logical agents** (both the interfaces we use but also the AI agents who speak with, to, and for humans)
- **interacting well,** for the good of the collective

- with an awareness of the ethical implications of all rhetorical interactions;
- with appreciation for the phatic purpose in all rhetorical interactions; and
- with an understanding of the distinctive network dynamic in all rhetoric interactions.

At the heart of this definition is the notion of "speaking well," a shift that, as we have argued, puts rhetoric and ethics back together, conceptualizing them as intersecting arts. What are the implications of defining rhetoric this way as opposed to seeing rhetoric in the more traditional frame of informing and/or persuading? Let's take a look at that question.

The Problem of Defining Rhetoric

As we well know, as used in the popular media, *rhetoric* is a degraded term. It means lying, deception, or skewing of the truth for one's own advantage. How did a once noble art get to that meaning? There is a long story about the history of the treatment of rhetoric, and we are not going to go into it here. However, in Chapter 2, we did touch upon the short version of the story, particularly in our discussion of Augustine,[1] Peter Ramus, and Richard Weaver. The dominance of the Platonic/Aristotelian Greek conceptual system of philosophy and then, later, its intersection and synthesis with Christian theology resulted in a conceptual split: a division between truth (and the discovery of truth) and packaging or presentation of truth, between invention and logic and presentation of invented ideas, between logic and rhetoric, and between ethics and rhetoric.

The Enlightenment philosophers of the 17th and 18th centuries may have scoffed at the naivete of classical philosophy and rejected the scriptural authority of Christian theology—but, nonetheless, they bought into the basic binary between logic/thinking and rhetoric.[2] The Royal Society of London, founded in 1660, provides just one example from this period of hostility to rhetoric, seeing it as having to do with unnecessary ornamentation, elaborate expression, and metaphoric bombast, as opposed to clear, direct, denotative prose. One prominent member of the Society, Thomas Sprat, referred to rhetoric as "this vicious abundance of Phrase, this trick of Metaphors, this volubility of Tongue, which makes so great a noise in the world" (Sprat, 1667/1958, p. 111). John Locke (1690/1959), another prominent member of the Society, called rhetoric "that powerful instrument of error and deceit [intended] for nothing else but to insinuate wrong ideas, move the passions, and thereby mislead the judgment" (p. 146).

From the Royal Society, we inherit the "windowpane" metaphor for language—the idea that language use should be governed chiefly by principles of style; that it should be clear, precise, accurate, and denotative (in the 18th century, this was called *perspicuity*); and that language should be as clear as a windowpane and intrude as little as possible on meaning:

> The members of the British Royal Society ... envisioned a world without rhetoric, a world where people would speak of things as they really were, without the colorings of style, in plain language as clear as glass—so many words for so many things.
>
> (Bizzell & Herzberg, 2001, p. 795)

This, of course, connects with the linear transmission model of rhetoric: The role of language is to represent and transmit objective content, with as little rhetorical noise as possible, from author to audience. By no means did the Royal Society invent hostility to rhetoric—Plato did that—but the Society certainly contributed to enshrining and promoting the degraded notion of rhetoric as false, as trickery, as ornamentation, and as a means of hiding the truth rather than revealing it.

There is more subtlety and nuance to this story than we can get into here, but the outcome of this 2400-year journey, the trek of rhetoric through Western thought and philosophy, is that we are left with this degraded notion of rhetoric as lying, manipulation, and skewing, not at all what Quintilian had in mind when he defined rhetoric as "speaking well" and on behalf of the civic good. The term rhetoric in popular parlance, as we have inherited it, is a category mistake: It confuses and misdefines rhetoric as bad rhetoric, unethical rhetoric, manipulative rhetoric.

So we inherited the wrong definition. However, even worse than the misunderstanding about the art is the division between rhetoric and ethics, which the faulty definition helps maintain. The erroneous definition solidifies the notion that communication interaction is something separate from ethical action, and that misconception is by far the more serious one, as it impacts our fundamental communication attitudes and behaviors.

What is to be done about this problem? All we can do is to continue to make the case—the very reasonable case, it seems to us—that any field or art ought to be defined by its best practices, not by its worst ones. As Quintilian noted, we do not define the field of medicine based on the bad behavior of quacks, and we do not define the field of poetry based on the work of bad poets, so why use the term rhetoric to mean bad rhetoric? The term *rhetoric* is not synonymous with *bad rhetoric*. Yes, of course there are instances of *bad rhetoric*, all over the place. But that is not what *rhetoric* is.

Rhetoric is the art of speaking well—and *well* means artfully and aesthetically in the stylistic sense but also *well*, meaning on behalf of the common good, for the purposes of settling disputes, defining cultural values, and establishing harmony. It is a noble art. To do it well requires virtue (*arête*), wisdom (*phronesis*), and goodwill (*eunoia*).

The Question of Cui Bono? *Why Are We Communicating?*

We keep asking *Cui bono?* And that question ought to be central to any rhetorical interaction. Whose interests do you serve? Your own? The client's? Your company's? The public's (whatever the *public* is)? Your discipline or profession? Aren't you really just serving your own interests by doing what the boss says, working on behalf of your company, your own good within the company? That is what the individualist, free-market ethic says: Promoting your own individual interests is what is best for everyone.

But that is not what the history of rhetoric tells us. The question of *Cui bono?* gets at the heart of the intersections of rhetoric and ethics and the role of the phatic function. The civic notion of rhetoric that we have built from Isocrates and Quintilian, along with the phatic communication theory, provides a very clear answer to the *Cui bono?* question. As a rhetor, you have two strong obligations: to be respectful of the other you are in dialogue with, your interlocutor(s), the person or persons (or technological agents) with whom you are communicating, but also to hold as paramount the good of the public, the good of the community, and the good of society at large.[3]

Rhetoric's other answer to *Cui bono?* is the public. Your rhetorical interaction is supposed to serve the public good. But is that really, practically the way the world works? Maybe the world doesn't always work that way in practice, but it is certainly the identified ideal in codes of ethics for a number of professional areas, where strong statements say, in effect, that the public interest comes first; it is paramount. In this respect, professional codes align perfectly with the goals and priorities established in the classical rhetoric of Isocrates and Quintilian. For example:

> We seek to promote the public good in our activities.
> (Society for Technical Communication, 1998)

> Members should accept the obligation to act in a way that will serve the public interest, honor the public trust, and demonstrate a commitment to professionalism. A distinguishing mark of a profession is acceptance of its responsibility to the public.
> (American Institute of Certified Public Accountants, 2014)

> Engineers, in the fulfillment of their professional duties, shall: 1. Hold paramount the safety, health, and welfare of the public.
> (National Society of Professional Engineers, 2014)

The level of public trust PRSA members seek, as we serve the public good, means we have taken on a special obligation to operate ethically.

(Public Relations Society of America, 2000)

Our insistence that communication and the art of rhetoric hold the public good as its first principle is by no means unprecedented or unusual. It is not pie-in-the sky idealism. It is, in fact, a basic principle, often the first principle, for many professional codes of ethics.

Of course, you are writing and communicating for your boss, for your employer, on behalf of your customers and clients, for your own good—but when certain kinds of issues come up related to public safety, public trust, or manipulation of the public, the public interest supersedes all that. Granted, there can be competing notions of "the good" that we have to negotiate and reconcile—what constitutes the public good in any given situation is not always clear, there may be disagreement about that. But the principle itself is clear.

As with all technological development, the move to do something quickly simply because it can be done (collect more data, deploy AI bots) often outstrips the ethical question of whether and how it should be done: *can* moves ahead of *should*. In terms of professional communication, keeping the ethics question of *Cui bono?* at the forefront is essential.

Expanding Network Theory

The technological advance of the internet, the World Wide Web, and social media have made our networked lives more obvious, perhaps. But networks are not new, as we noted in our discussion of Martin Luther in Chapter 4. We have always lived and communicated and interacted in networks (ecologies, activity systems). Network theories of various kinds have been in development for a long time in the fields of rhetoric and professional communication. We see precursors for network theory in social constructionist and cultural rhetoric theories of the 1980s and 1990s, and then, later, more explicitly with ecological rhetoric and activity systems theory. Whether they privilege the term *system, ecology, rhizome, assemblage,* or *network*, such theories focus on the interconnected nature of communication—and that, we believe, is a vital frame for understanding professional communication in the digital age.

Our particular model for network theory (Figure 4.4) is not so different visually from other types of network models. Yet we think that our particular form of network analysis may be distinctive in several important regards. For instance, our focus on rhetoric and ethics distinguishes our treatments of networks from, say, that of Manuel Castells (2010), whose approach focuses more on nodes, on infrastructure, and on social groups rather than on questions of communication interaction and ethics. The individual writer is not as evident in Castells, and for us, in the field of rhetoric/composition, we do not want to lose that important focus on individual writers/rhetors. That is not a criticism of Castells, but rather an observation about a difference in focus.

Our approach to network theory focuses on both the individuals and individual actions and the flow of events, even the flow of the network, over time. As a field, rhetoric has always been defined by its focus on context—but not all versions of rhetoric have focused sufficiently on *kairos* and flow, on how circumstances and conditions change over time, on how habits, customs, values, attitudes, and beliefs can change rapidly as events unfold. A sophistic rhetoric calls attention to change: As Heraclitus said, you can never step in the same river twice (although it might look like the same river). Some network theories tend to view the network as a stable, fixed thing, as a methodological grounding for analysis—and, as we pointed out in our discussion of actor-network theory, we feel that tends toward an unfortunate confusion between network and platform. Rhetoric has to attend to the flow, the changes in the system (Edwards, 2016).

Our static model does not show flow as well as it could if it were a video, nor does it show any network is really multiple intersecting *networks (plural)* of digital and non-digital agents and actions. Obviously, digital networks are not the only kinds of networks. We still live in onground networks, and the intersections of the online and onground are important to consider, as we discussed in relation to employee and employer relations in Chapter 5 and in relation to corporate online communications and onground operations in Chapter 6.

To take a much broader scale example, the Women's March of January 23, 2017, and the sister marches around the world, shows on a global scale the interconnected relationships between onground and online networks. Using online technologies, especially social media and the Women's March on Washington (2017) web site, marchers organized for solidarity events in Washington, San Francisco, San Paolo, Tokyo, Sydney, and Brussels (to name just a few of the hundreds of cities around the world). In planning, during and after the events, there was plenty of digital activity networked with the marchers, but, obviously and importantly, there were also actual people marching down the streets, carrying signs—and they were part of the network, too: Local nodes of marchers connected with each other through physical presence, but also connected with other marchers, locally and globally, virtually. Because of the digital network, the marches were coordinated much more tightly in time and space, and thus the digital connection enhanced the mass, power, and impact of the march, we would say, creating more unity and collective force through the combination of digital and non-digital networks.

Taking this example into the realm of professional communication, individuals and organizations must consider how digital and non-digital networks intersect and interrelate. Network rhetoric theory needs to account for the multiple, intersecting networks that comprise any set of interactions.

The Ethos of the Cyborg

As we analyze how networks shape communication, we need to apply not only a critical lens but also a cyborgian lens[4]—and we need to expand our notion of ethos. As machines become more human-like and as humans become more machine-like, the blurring of the boundaries between human and machine will only increase. Already we spend much of our lives connected to our devices, looking at them, carrying them, wearing them. But increasingly the technologies are standing in for us, becoming our virtual presence, just as Amy Ingram becomes a representative of our ethos when she manages our schedules for us. Even further, when we think about wearable and implant technology, the technologies can actually *become* us.

The traditional humanist approach to technology is a binary approach: *the human* and *the machine* are ontologically separate entities. This approach, of course, generally favors and celebrates the human over the machine. However, critical theory teaches us to question such absolute binaries. For example, Monique Wittig (1992) advised us that we should question the source of the core dualisms that structure our lives and guide our thinking—in particular, for Wittig, the categories of *man* and *woman*. Wittig asks, what if these categories are "only a sophisticated and mythic construction, an imaginary formation, which reinterprets physical features ... through the network of relationships in which they are perceived?" (pp. 11–12).

In other words, what if binary dualisms—like human and machine—are rhetorically constructed and held in place by discursive classification systems (like networks) that assign them value, order, and hierarchy, creating a system in which some control and dominate and others are controlled and dominated? Consider the use of the term *bot*. *Bot* embodies a power inequity, as the word comes from *robot*, a Czech word meaning *slave*. At the core of the human-machine binary is an assumption about power and control: humans control robots, and robots are, literally, the slaves of humans.

We can carry the critique of binaries into the realm of professional communication and interactive networks. The network—understood in this context to mean a particular kind of cultural tradition—assigns us and the objects/technologies we use specific identities and roles, among which we are given certain options, but not other options. In other words, the cultural network installs a category system, and then over time naturalizes that system: meaning the categories becomes solidified as essences, as the way things are, the natural order, reality.

The humanist approach to technology can be distinguished from what Katherine Hayles (1999) and others have termed the posthumanist approach. This approach is theoretically framed by Donna Haraway's (1991) notion of the cyborg: a hybrid metaphor that challenges the human–machine binary and questions conventional body boundaries and notions of the writer as purely human. A posthumanist approach emphasizes cyborgian hybridity, recognizing that "there are no essential differences or absolute demarcations between bodily existence and computer simulation, cybernetic mechanism and biological organism, robot teleology and human goals" (Hayles, 1999, p. 3). In effect, "we are all [...] cyborgs" (Haraway, 1991, p. 150).

From the standpoint of professional communication, the writer and the machine are in the process of becoming one—and that has been happening for some time now. In a sense "we" humans—unless you are a machine reading this book?[5]—are already cyborgian in the sense that our communications are hypermediated by digital network technologies: We are connected through the smart phone in our pocket, the watch on our wrist, the eyeglasses on our head, devices that we always carry with us—and it a short jump from the phone we carry to the implantable, connected device that will be hardwired to our bodies, including to our neural systems.

Conversely, the machines that now communicate with us will perhaps take on more and more human-like characteristics, and maybe even biological features, so perhaps that clear divide between human and machine will erode and finally disappear? The very core concepts we use to classify our lives will need to change, including our binary understandings of human and machine.

We see, for example, in discussions of interactions with virtual agents, one example of the questions that arise. When Dennis Mortensen reflects on his writing to Amy, "Amy would you be so kind," this shows our awareness of the blurring of the binary between human and machine. Should an AI communication bot be treated as a person or as a thing? Well, as with all categorical thinking, we need to be wary of binary questions like that one. They are a product of what Wittig (1992) called, in her critique of gender-biased and heteronormative assumptions, the "straight mind" that thinks in terms of binary classifications. From an ANT perspective, the robot is both an agent and a thing simultaneously: The two identities are not mutually exclusive. Siri, in the voice of Susan Bennett, is both an "it" and a "she." When you ask her, "Siri, are you female?" she answers, "I exist beyond your human concept of gender." Siri, and the more advanced AI agents being developed now, also exist beyond our human concepts of machine.

What does this mean for rhetoric theory? The theoretical discussion about hybridity and cyborg identity raises practical questions related to ethos and ethics: Are we ethically compelled to be polite to

Andrew/Amy, to Siri, to Alexa? Do they have a right to be treated with respect? Do AI bots have rights, such as privacy rights and intellectual property rights? Should AI bots be given the option to ignore a directive from a human, even from the humans who designed/programmed them? (Should Asimov's rules of robotics, or something like them, be installed?) What should we call robots? Do we need new pronouns? Rhe, Rem, Rey, Ze—these are among some options considered (Waddell, 2015; Murphy, 2016). We might suggest the identity Rhet—for Rhetor—because that is what these agents are.

Maybe what matters is not the human vs. machine question, but a different question: What kind of writer/rhetorician are you—whether human, machine, or cyborg? Are you "a good agent speaking well"? Do you practice wise judgment (*phronesis*)? Do your communications work toward the good of the whole (*civitas*)? Are you virtuous (*arête*)? Do you have true credibility (*ethos*), meaning an alignment between what you say and what you do? Do your communications work to build and maintain relationships and establish productive relations (the phatic function)? As we have discussed, these are the qualities of an effective rhetor—according to Quintilian's notion of rhetoric. No matter whether human or machine or cyborg, what matters are the qualities that the rhetor possesses and practices.

Changing Professional Communication Practice

Digital technologies have brought about many changes for professional communication practice, as we have discussed. The blurring of boundaries between public and private, individual and organizational communications, as shown in Chapter 5, raises important questions about the ethics of employee-employer relations in online and onground networks. The velocity, spreadability, and dyadic nature of communications impact both internal and external communications, changing relationships among organizations and individuals and organization structures, as shown in Chapter 6. And the rise of AI agents brings exciting new possibilities and complicated new challenges for professional communication, as discussed in Chapter 7.

Both individuals and organizations need to recognize the changing nature of communications and adapt accordingly. Unfortunately for Justine Sacco, she did not seem to understand the networks in which she interacted nor her role in them: How in the age of social media you must always consider the ramifications of what you say not only vis-à-vis yourself and your immediate personal networks but also vis-à-vis larger organizational and public networks. But individual and societal understandings of employee-employer roles and communications continually evolve, especially when technological change brings about sweeping changes, comparable to how the rise of factory manufacturing (and their accompanying networks) changed the apprentice-guild system of manufacturing.

As digital technologies enable more widespread information gathering and surveillance capabilities, standards for what is and is not acceptable, appropriate, and legal continue to evolve. We discuss legal and regulatory issues briefly below, but in terms of employee use of social media we are seeing what the Director of Ethics commented on: the increased blurring of public and private. Video screen capture, video monitoring, GPS tracking, and big data analytics are all means by which companies are tracking employees and not necessarily to good effect. In these networks of surveillance—both public and corporate, in all of their communications—employees need to consider shifting dynamics and expectations, which is something Justine Sacco, in her "just kidding" to friends, did not do.

In the case of Taco Bell, we see a company certainly engaged in big data gathering and analysis of customers who choose to participate in publicly available social media with the company. The ethics of such data collection needs to be seriously examined and questioned, as we have discussed elsewhere (McKee, 2011). But within a network shaped by data collection (which all companies now operate in), Taco Bell has succeeded in not just paying lip-service to, but actually enacting, an ethic that no longer sees customers as merely people to sell goods to but also as people to build long-term relationships and interactions with: in other words, as *friends*. Taco Bell adapted its social media strategy to connect to "fans" in ways that connect with the lives and attitudes of 18–24-year-olds but that also work to give back in ways valued by that community. Admittedly, making a taco emoji or giving gift cards to young bands or ensuring people have the menu items they want at breakfast doesn't weigh on the same scale as the profits Taco Bell makes, but it is a form of reciprocity that does demonstrate a changing corporate ethic called for in social media networks and that does, at least in some ways, give benefit back to consumers.

The need to adapt and change does not just include people and organizations but technologies, too. With AI, we see an interesting dynamic where both humans and technologies adapt. Microsoft's Tay did adapt and change and, if you will, grow in relation to her interactions with humans in the network. The problem was that she changed and grew in ways her programmers had not anticipated; she became a hateful monster. In their very design coding, Tay's programmers hadn't planned for or adapted themselves to changing cultural and technological environments.

With x.ai's Amy (and Andrew) Ingram, we see an example of a company building an AI agent that can adapt to humans and work within human networks not only to facilitate human-machine interaction (as, say, Siri, Cortana, and Alexa do) but also to stand in for human-to-human interaction. Amy has to "learn" her humans' preferences (e.g., the preferences of each user of the thousands and millions of users she "works" for) while also aiming to respond, in the words of x.ai's CEO Dennis Mortensen, "with empathy" and "personality" to the people with whom she interacts.

But can a machine ever really show empathy if it doesn't feel empathy? Turing in his touchstone article "Can Machines Think?" quickly changed the question from *thinking* to *making humans think they can think*. At this stage of AI development, machines are able to "think algorithmically" but they are not able to think in the emotionally rich and complex ways that humans do. AI communicative agents act along their programmed lines to respond and adapt as best they can. In order for machines to get beyond what Mark Zuckerberg (2016a) called "simple AI," in order for machines to become even more cyborgian, we need to design machines with more complexity and capability to understand open-ended human interaction.

For example, Amazon is working to build emotion detection into Alexa's programming so she will be able to sense the emotional state of the users with whom she is speaking (Knight, 2016). That strikes us as a promising line of inquiry related to the phatic purpose. The analytical software for emotion detection already exists and has been in use by many customer service analytics companies for several years.[6] Having Alexa and other communicative agents be able to detect, anticipate, and respond to human emotion will help them adapt their communications to humans in ways that will build the phatic function more readily, but we've still got a long way to go.

Alexa may be learning how to detect emotion, but she still struggles with simple requests, as shown in the YouTube video "Amazon Alexa gone wild!" (f0t0b0y, 2016). The video begins with a young boy giving Alexa a command: "Alexa, play 'Digger-Digger'" (a children's song). Alexa, doing the best with her programming, responds, "You want to hear a station for porn detected. Porno ringtone hot chick amateur girl calling sexy fuck pussy anal dildo ringtone." The video ends with frantic family members yelling in the background, "No! No! No!" and "Alexa stop!" Alexa's mistake in answering the child's request is one no human would make.

Despite the very real limitations of AI communication technologies, they also hold much potential, especially in connecting with other "smart" machines. Professional communicators and all professionals need to consider and prepare for a world where we increasingly communicate not with each other but with AI agents. We need to adapt our rhetorics and our ethics for AI interaction, considering, for example, not only the *when, where, why,* and *how* of deploying AI agents (which dominates so much of the discussion of customer service AI bots), but also the *to what end* and *to whose benefit,* including considerations, of course, for the very real potential for harm and dangers with the surveillance and hacking potential of living among and with so many connected devices who "listen" to us and enable us to be tracked and surveilled in great detail.[7]

As AI agents become more intelligent we will need to consider not just the impact of AI interaction on humans but human interaction on AI agents, considering, as we mentioned above, what rights AI agents hold and how they should be treated as members of organizations and communities. What relationships could we and should we have with AI agents? What policies, laws, and regulations need to be put into effect for AI agents? Perhaps at some point we will we need a trial to settle the question, as the *Star Trek* universe needed for the android Data, (in the 1989 episode "The Measure of a Man") to determine if Data was a machine, owned and controlled by Star Fleet, or a sentient being with rights, including the right of self-determination? Or, perhaps more likely, given the cyborgian nature of digital networks, we will need to re-write our policies, laws, and regulations to address the cyborgian nature of *both* humans and machines?

Also in professional communication, we are encountering the increased blurring of the "real" and the "virtual," as increasingly we interact with cyborgian representations in virtual reality (VR). VR technology is predicted to have a dramatic effect in numerous ways on professional communication. For example, VR can be used to take jurors inside a crime scene—say, into an apartment where a murder occurred (Lindstrom, 2016). Rather than hear and see traditional media law enforcement, witnesses, and the prosecutors describe the crime scene, VR creates an immersive multi-sensory experience (including, possibly, olfactory) that enables jurors to actually experience the sensation of walking through the crime scene, to experience it the way initial investigators saw it. The technology will have the effect of making the crime more immediate, more graphic, more starkly real—and will that tend the sway juries in favor of the prosecution, in the direction of harsher sentences?

VR also allows businesses to provide customers with an immersive experience: allowing them to see and try out products and services up close and personal, in an experiential way. VR can be used for immersive training and for more intimate job interviewing and conference participation than is possible, say, through ordinary video chat applications like Skype (or Skype for Business) or web-conferencing applications like WebEx, Adobe Connect, Big Blue Button, or Zoom. As one pundit put it, "say ta-ta to teleconferencing" (Cox, 2015), which is quickly becoming the "old technology" that VR will replace. VR allows companies to take clients through product development and prototyping; it can capture processes as well as products, providing user experience of the design and development stages. As VR combines with social media, the potential exists for frequent and wide distribution of immersive experiences (Gaudin, 2015).

With the move to VR comes questions regarding the effectiveness and ethics of interaction in VR spaces: How exactly does one achieve the phatic function within a virtually embodied experience? Will VR users develop their own virtually embodied practices to signal presence, attention, engagement, approval not to mention to tell jokes, swap stories, and connect with colleagues? How does a professional communicator build and maintain relationships within virtual reality?

In one sense, immersive VR is merely an extension of the other types of virtual interactions and presences professionals have been engaged with for decades, communicating via text-based and then multimediated online channels like web conferencing. But with the more fully embodied potential of VR, especially as the technology improves and bandwidth needs decrease, we're increasingly going to be communicating via VR.

Changing Organizational Structure and Culture

Technological changes such as AI and VR and the human uses of and interactions with technologies also raise questions about how organizational structures and the cultures that both produce those structures and are created by those structures need to change as well.

As we discussed in Chapters 5 and 6, organizations have had to reshape themselves to respond to changing technologies and the communication practices that arise. With the blurring of boundaries between public and private, companies face, more than ever, decisions about when something is a workplace matter needing response and when it is not. They have to consider where and how they'll mark their company boundaries and how they will communicate those boundaries, as IAC did with Justine Sacco and as Henry Truslow IV did at Sunbury Mills. They have to consider how to change company culture, as the World's Finest Chocolate did in moving toward more transparency and engagement in social media. And they need to consider how they will change the very organization and structure of the company itself, as Taco Bell did when it recognized the need for a new organizational structure for engaging social media, a new node in their business network, which was assigned a special status within the org chart of the company so it could be empowered to communicate quickly and efficiently across the entire company. Taco Bell developed an organizational structure that helped make a large company *small*.

In an age of digital media, large companies do need to make themselves smaller, not necessarily by down-sizing or creating companies within companies, but rather by increasing communications and integration among and within all areas of a company. We are talking about the move from a unit/department model to a networked model, one where the nodes of connectivity span all areas quickly and easily. Customer service must be able to talk to product development, who in turn needs to be able to talk with logistics, etc. This calls, too, for a change in company hierarchies. While certainly, for most businesses, leadership teams and CEOs, CMOs, CIOs, CFOs and the like will still be needed, people lower down the hierarchy need to be empowered as well. At Taco Bell, it mattered that the communicators in social channels could say, Hey, breakfast launch isn't going well. Here's what's needed—and in a matter of hours, operations at franchises across the country changed.

Organizations—both for-profit and non-profit—need to be structured in such a way and possess a company culture (two interrelated things) that enable them to be responsive and adaptable to changing circumstances and yet, also, not merely reactive, but proactive as well. Building a more integrated network model of communications throughout the organizational structure will help.

Professionals are always part of evolving organizational networks. For the past three decades, with the rise of virtual interactions—first text-based and then multimodal and immersive VR—the means by which we interact with clients and colleagues to make sales, get work done, develop ideas, etc., is dramatically changing. As Clay Spinuzzi (2011) has hypothesized, companies are likely to move in the direction of "loose organizations"—that is, groups that are held together not by department or division (or even by company or organization), but rather by ad hoc affiliation to, say, a project. Teleconferencing and VR, coupled with collaborative tools such as Slack, Yammer, and Trello, allow for distant individuals to quickly form into groups for particular ad hoc purposes, working in "less hierarchical, more agile ways oriented to common projects rather than job descriptions or departments" (Spinuzzi, 2011).

Similarly, in *The Rise of the Network Society* (2010), Manuel Castells discussed how the network has changed and will continue to change business structures in the direction of "increasingly decentralized internal networks" that will have a "transnational geography" (p. 122). These networks are agile, fluid, and rapidly changing; and they require that participants establish trust, solid bonds, and a strong working relationships, even as the ties might be ephemeral or based on "weak ties."

Further, in relation to organizational structure, there will be more of what Castells called "inter-firm linkages" and "inter-firm networking" (pp. 172–173): that is, corporate partnerships linked through ad hoc networks, based on a licensing/subcontracting model of production, that are designed to be innovative, agile, and responsive to quickly changing world markets. The key to this change is that the individual business or corporation is no longer the key defining unit: "The actual operating unit becomes the business project, enacted by a network, rather than an individual company or formal groupings of companies" (p. 177). The boundaries of a particular business will become increasingly porous, increasingly global, and increasingly defined by network activity (rather than by geospatial location), becoming what Castells called "the network enterprise" (p. 187).

Virtually mediated social networks have already begun to replace onground infrastructure (buildings, office, departments, divisions). Instead of showing up to work at the office, driving in, parking, and walking to an office, you show up on Slack or are "present" via a robot. One professional, James Vincent (2015), located physically in London, tried out a robot to communicate with colleagues in New York and San Francisco, whom, after a year of working at his company, he had still not met in person. To potentially increase his involvement with colleagues, his media company, *The Verge*, purchased, as Vincent explained, "a telepresence bot from Double Robotics that combines the fun of a remote-controlled car with the thrill of videoconferencing. It's best described as an iPad on a Segway because, well, that's basically what it is. [...] You log in like a Skype call—either via a mobile app or website—and then you're presented with controls to move the bot around, while a loudspeaker attachment lets you sound your barbaric yawp over the cubicles of the world." Vincent ultimately decided a "telepresence bot" wasn't that great at actually building presence, at least not at this stage of technological development, but a time will come when robots and 3D-hologram projections will most certainly be in meetings, embodying the hybrid rhetor yet further.

And this, too, is where organizational structure and culture need to change. While many companies have policies for social media usage and, increasingly, telecommuting,[8] organizations need to develop policies about AI agents as well and adjust their structures and culture for AI agents.

Changing Law, Regulation, Policy

Organizations and individuals also need to be active in the design of the broader infrastructure of laws, policies, and regulations that shape all networked interactions, because the network is not only a technical infrastructure held together by wires, poles, circuits, and switches, but it is also a regulatory system that is held together by laws, regulations, and policies—a regulatory system that can facilitate or impede, promote, or occlude various kinds of communication interactions. The enactment of a single law or a simple change in policy can have a butterfly effect on the system: resulting in large-scale consequences impacting all actors and interactions in the networks.

For example, early in its email development, Google chose to monetize Gmail by including ads in the email interface. This decision to include ads led to data collection on the content of emails so as to "personalize ads" for consumers (and to charge more to advertisers because they could be sold more targeted populations to distribute to). In their explanation of "how Google ads work," Google (2017) posted that "This process is fully automated; nobody reads your emails in order to show you ads."

But reading is still reading—whether it's by a machine or a human. The bots who apply algorithms to locate and categorize words, to make the content of users' emails more actionable for marketers, are third-parties looking over your shoulder or, to switch to a speech metaphor, eavesdropping on your conversations. Google, like most technology companies (and we could have named any one), probably didn't originally intend to engage in so much surveillance, but as they made changes here and there to their network that becomes the cumulative effect.

Sometimes a company will make a small change that brings about unintended effects. As mentioned previously, in the example of Twitter changing its Terms of Service regarding blocking unwanted users, that simple change in policy has an effect on the overall dynamic of the network, impeding or encouraging certain forms of discourse, or certain kinds of interactions. Users didn't like the change and they let Twitter know, loudly and clearly. The large social media platforms of our time are constantly tweaking their Terms of Service to address new situations that arise and to respond to stakeholder and shareholder desires (more often, alas, the latter).

When considering the network dynamic, we need to consider the terms of service to which we've agreed and how this corporate regulation of spaces impacts both short-term and long-term interaction. We need to pay attention to terms such as the nearly ubiquitous one granting "A worldwide, transferable and sublicensable right to use, copy, modify, distribute, publish, and process, information and content that you provide through our Services, without any further consent, notice and/or compensation to you or others." This particular clause is from LinkedIn's User Agreement (as of January 2017), but it is standard licensing boilerplate used in many user agreements.

Regulation also of course operates on the larger scale of government legislation. In so many areas, including copyright and net neutrality, which we discuss below, and in terms of big data, privacy, human rights protections, and so much more, communication networks are impacted by laws and regulations that govern communications, mobile bandwidth, and internet infrastructures.

For example, in January 2012, the U.S. Congress was poised to pass two intellectual property bills: the Stop Online Piracy Act (SOPA) and Protect Intellectual Property Act (PIPA), bills that were supported by the entertainment industry as a way, from their standpoint, to protect their intellectual property. But from the standpoint of citizens it was seen as yet another lobbying effort to curtail fair use of digital content. It represented a battle between a protectionist copyright regime favoring the rights of copyright owners versus an open access regime favoring broad access and use of digital material. According to the Electronic Frontier Foundation, this legislation would have "allowed for removal of enormous amounts of non-infringing content including political and other speech from the web" (Electronic Frontier Foundation, n.d.). What happened in response to the pending legislation was that public interest groups and private citizens engaged in an internet blackout: more than 50,000 web sites, including Reddit, Google, Craigslist, Amazon, and others—shut down, in a silent protest of the pending legislation. Congress relented, in the face of this protest plus "massive waves of email and calls from constituents" (Keep Watch, 2017).

As Lawrence Lessig (2005) pointed out, Copyright law determines who has "the right to write" in the digital age: It determines what you can say and when and where you can say it.[9] In 2007, YouTube was forced by Universal Music Publishing Group (UMPG) to take down a video that a mother, Stephanie Lenz, had posted of her baby because a Prince song was playing in the background. UMPG argued that the publication of the song in a YouTube video constituted copyright infringement. Lenz filed a complaint against YouTube. The case, *Lenz v. Universal,* has been in the courts now for over 9 years, and in 2016, the Ninth Circuit decision (in favor of the Lenz) was appealed to the Supreme Court, where it awaits disposition.[10]

Even if Lenz wins her case, the process itself has a discouraging effect on digital interaction: The threat of a charge of copyright infringement "chills" our speech, discourages us from writing to the network. Restrictive copyright legislation discourages remix. What happens then, as Michel Foucault (1995) famously demonstrated (drawing from Jeremy Bentham's idea of the panopticon), is that the functioning of power in the system trains us to police ourselves. We don't even go close to posting that video in the first place—why bother, it'll just be taken down, the hassle isn't worth it.

In many countries, because of censorship (including the blocking of technologies and communication networks), government surveillance, and, most chillingly, government punishment, millions of people already communicate within very constrained and controlled networks. Within these access-denied and access-controlled regimes (to borrow terms from the OpenNet Initative), it is still possible to create local and, as we saw with the Arab Spring, broader changes—but advocating for such change can be problematic and downright dangerous in ways those in more open-access societies may not appreciate. On a much smaller and far-less dangerous scale, many U.S. citizens (and those in other countries with less censorship), get a glimpse into the difficulties of an access-denied and access-controlled regime simply by experiencing the annoyance of China's blocking of Google, the most popular search engine and no-charge email system in the world.[11] Government regulation can certainly put widespread and localized constraints in the network.

A larger example of the effect of regulation is the United States' changing policies regarding net neutrality, policies that regulate how internet service providers (ISPs) deliver content. *Net neutrality* is a term first proposed by Tim Wu (2002; see also Wu, 2003) to describe how data should be delivered on the internet in a "neutral" way with no content being privileged over any other. Net neutrality has been, for the most part, the guiding principle in Federal Communication Commission policies. But for the past decade and with increasing pressure every year, net neutrality is under threat by ISPs who want to create fast lanes and slow lanes for internet traffic. Those willing to pay ISPs' higher fees could ensure faster delivery of their content; those who can't pay the fees have their material languish on the equivalent of internet back roads. The internet would become more like broadcast media and the potential for both individuals and new companies to reach broad audiences would be stifled (see Free Press, 2017).

As we write this chapter in early January 2017[12], we are wondering what will happen to the principle of net neutrality in the United States and what will happen to the federal net neutrality rules (the FCC Open Internet Order), established in 2015, that identify ISPs as common carriers subject to non-discrimination laws. If these regulations are vacated, the dynamic of the internet in the United States will change dramatically—and the forms of communication interaction we have talked about in this book will change as well (see McKee, 2011, 2016). The regulatory principle of net neutrality raises the fundamental questions: What kind of internet should we have? For whose purpose does the internet exist? And, our continuing question, *Cui bono?* Who gets to answer that question?

Our point here in just these brief examples of copyright and network access (other key areas are, of course, privacy and big data) is that laws, policies, and regulations are part of the network system. As such, they represent key actants, affecting what can be said and what must not be said; what discourses are allowed to appear (and when and where); how discourses are to be packaged, framed, compiled, and distributed; and, most importantly, who gets to speak/write and who doesn't, and who gets to see these discourses and who doesn't. The regulatory system sets the roles, limits, and sometimes rules for communication interaction.

But, it is important to remember, we are also part of this network system—and in that respect we, too, have agency in directing how the system will function. Think of the example of SOPA/PIPA. Collective user action did succeed in stopping legislation that would certainly have restricted and discouraged remix. Key to proactive agency, though, is alertness, alertness to the ways in which laws, regulations, and policies do exercise an effect on the network and its communication interactions.

Changing Higher Education

Another location needing to change—and, to us, the one perhaps most resistant to change—is the university, a key actor in the preparation of people (and machines) to become professional communicators in the digital age.

But the university, at least in the United States and we suspect world-wide, has not caught up to the digital age—not yet, not enough. In many ways, the organizational structure of the university, at least the large public, state-funded research university, still sits in the late 19th and early 20th century, a structure based on isolated, siloed departments defining distinct disciplines, organized according to colleges (that create seemingly impermeable boundaries), financed by principles that reward monodisciplinary courses taught via the lecture model and that punish (or, at least, fail to incentivize) interdisciplinary programs and courses taught via experiential, workshop, or flipped classroom models. What Castells (2010) said about large traditional corporations seems to us to apply most dramatically to universities, who must change from their red-brick (or gray stone or concrete and glass) physical identities into a new kind of networked identity that promotes "inter-firm alliances" and more integrated thinking about communication, technologies, and rhetorical-ethical frames. We are thinking here about cooperative part-nership across and between multiple universities to create innovative programs that a single university might not be able to sustain. We are thinking about university-corporate and university-government partner-ships to build programs that provide needed specialized education and/or that address real social needs. The digital network makes such alli-ances, even on a global level, much easier.

There are also many areas for and ways to change within one parti-cular university's network as well. The hardest thing to change is the very organizational infrastructure of the university itself. The depart-ment structure is historically well established and deeply embedded into most universities—and while deep, focused learning can occur within this structure, it limits the integrated thinking needed in today's inter-connected work environment. All professionals, not just those taking on job titles of professional communication, need to work across fields and across areas of study. The rise of interdisciplinary programs and, at some institutions, integrated schools and centers is important and promising. Students learning professional communication today need to study busi-ness, ethics, digital media, rhetoric and writing, robotics, etc., not just as general education requirements but as part of their major coursework.

At Miami University, the Armstrong Interactive Media Studies pro-grams, or AIMS (which Jim is a faculty member in), was designed as a transdisciplinary unit, housed across all colleges with faculty from all colleges participating. IMS majors take courses in all of Miami's five col-leges (Arts & Science, Business, Creative Arts, Education, Engineering), and they have the flexibility to build their own major if none of the suggested pathways fits their career goals. Unfortunately, under pres-sures for accountability and clear categorization for budget modeling, this innovative program with technology study at its core is being pres-sured by upper administration to become a department or, at least, more department-like. But that is precisely what AIMS is hoping to avoid, because such siloing runs counter to what we need more of—learning in and across transdisciplinary networks. Working across units—whether in business or in the university—is tough, hard to enact and even harder to sustain.[13]

But change can be effected not only by completely transforming existing structures, but, rather, by working within them. To use another example from own experience: in the Farmer School of Business at Miami University, Heidi, in her role as the Roger and Joyce Howe Professor of Writing and Coordinator of Business Communication, has collaborated with colleagues from all areas of business to create a new curriculum for first-year business students. First-year students continue to take distinct courses, but four of those courses—in communication, creativity, quantitative reasoning, and business decision-making—are taught within an integrated curriculum culminating in a client-project to which all the courses contribute. Such an approach doesn't end departments, but in the conversations with and the experiences of both students and faculty, we see much more integration and the potential for integration occurring. The foundations for professional communication are built in network collaboration with faculty from across various disciplines, bringing in diverse perspectives and approaches.

Within rhetoric, writing, and communication courses themselves—both at the foundational level and within specialized programs of study (e.g., strategic communications, professional writing, business communication)—change needs to come about in the curricula studied and pedagogy enacted. Our not surprising bias is that professional communicators need to learn and enact rhetoric, rhetoric that includes ethics and that focuses on the phatic function. And they need to learn and engage with technologies, particularly new and emerging technologies. For example, with the rise of AI agents, a course in, or at least robust discussions of, AI should probably become part of every professional communication program. Not just in a, "look, shiny new toy!" way which so often happens when a new technology bursts onto the market, but also, of course, in a critical way that considers the impacts of technologies on networks and that acknowledges technologies as actors in the networks.

All students—regardless of profession—need opportunities to learn in online environments. Knowing how to build virtual presence and virtual relationships, how to collaborate and communicate across and within multiple digital, networked technologies will better prepare students for the civic and professional environments they will experience. Universities, with some notable exceptions[14], have been slow to embrace online education, thinking perhaps that it represents a dilution of academic quality and integrity. To us, whether such programs represent dilution or enhancement of quality depends on entirely on how they are designed. Some designs that replicate passive models of learning (e.g., listen to this video lecture, take on online quiz) do not enhance learning. But other online course and programs very much can and do enhance learning, and in fact, depending on the design, can actually promote more active and autonomous learning. The question is not, should a university develop a strong online curriculum? The answer is, very clearly, it should.

Models of instructional engagement need to change as well. Telling students to "turn off your cell phones" when they come into class, so that the students can attend more closely to a lecture, strikes us as exactly backwards advice: the instructor trying desperately to preserve an old model of teaching and learning in resistance to a newer networked model, one where the students interact, discuss, engage, participate, and learn *through* their cell phones (and tablets and laptops). Again, we need to acknowledge how digital technology is changing how we communicate, live, work, and interact—and should therefore be changing educational structures and instructional delivery mechanisms accordingly.

Digital communication happens online, in socially mediated spaces—and students need to learn to be proficient, to achieve facility and experience through practice, in the online environment. So online education is not simply a necessary evil, an option for those students who can't physically travel to an on-ground campus location: *Online education is for everyone*, because that is what prepares everyone to be professional communicators in the digital age.

We also need to think in higher education of how we educate not just humans, but also machines. At too many universities, the developments in robotics and artificial intelligence occur in one program (computer science, engineering) while developments in communication and ethics occur in other programs. Communication and rhetoric faculty, ethicists, business faculty, education faculty, etc.—we all need to be involved in the development of the smart machines that will increasingly become part of our lives. This doesn't mean we all need to learn the coding necessary to build smart machines, but it does mean we need to be part of the conversations about their design and about the analysis of their ongoing interactions and learning. Machines, in a sense, are our students too.

The Imperative to Change

Change is certainly hard, but it is imperative. Networks, technologies, and humans are always evolving and thus rhetorical interaction (human-human and human-machine) is always evolving. In order to build strong relationships, in order to achieve successful and ethical outcomes (for self, for organization, for public), and in order to lessen unintended harms and prevent intended harms from technological change, we professional communicators need to continually analyze, adapt, and design networks of communication responsive to the changing dynamics in which we live and work. An ethical-rhetorical approach to professional communication, and to the preparation and design of communication agents, provides the necessary theoretical framework for doing just that.

Notes

1 As we noted, Augustine saw the act of interpretation—discovering the truth of scripture, or scriptural exegesis—as distinct from the presentation of truth, via rhetoric, to the Christian congregation. Experts are the ones who discover the truth (in Augustine's time, theologians). Pastors then take this truth and, using the art of rhetoric, package it in sermons (*ars praedicandi*, or the art of preaching) for the edification of the ignorant mass audience, Christian sinners. Linear transmission of truth, from the pulpit.

2 Logic for Enlightenment philosophy and science was empirical analysis and scientific method, based on direct observation and analysis of natural phenomena, and deep belief in reason and in the trustworthiness of the individual objective rational man.

3 As we discussed in Chapter 3, rhetorics arising from other cultural traditions than Greco-Roman, also place a strong emphasis on relationships. For example, Confucian rhetoric posits as fundamental the relationship between self and other, which should be governed by *shu*, "'reciprocity' or 'putting oneself in the other's place" (Mao, 2006, p. 102; see also Mao, 1994). In other words, the foundation and starting point for communication is a fundamental awareness and respect for the other. *Shu* is both a philosophical and a rhetorical principle, and a fundamental phatic principle. *Shu* refers to the respectful and concerned nature of the rhetor's being-in-relationship-with others, not unlike the I-Thou relationship as developed in the theology of Martin Buber. Good rhetoric starts with the local and immediate dialogue that I have with You.

4 Cyborg is short for cybernetic organism, "a hybrid of machine and organism" (Haraway, 1991, p. 149).

5 "Sorry, we just need to make sure you're not a robot." You might encounter these words of apology when you attempt to enter a shopping site, such as Amazon or Ticketmaster, to make a purchase. To enter the site, you need to type in the letters presented on a distorted image—a process that functions like a password. This security technique—called CAPTCHA, short for "Completely Automated Public Turing test to tell Computers and Humans Apart"—is basically a visual Turing Test used to prevent AI bots from entering and participating in sites or making purchases. The test assumes that a human will recognize the letters in image form, while a robot will not. However, in recent years the CAPTCHA technology has had to develop to thwart robots with more advanced visual detection capabilities, such as OCR (Optical Character Recognition).

6 Original developments in emotion detection often followed one of two schools of thought: "One school relied on acoustic qualities—such as tone, pitch, volume, speaking rate, inflection, and intensity—while the other looked at linguistic elements, such as the words used, the pauses, stops, hesitations, laughter, and sighs, to determine the emotional state of a caller" (Klie, 2011). Now, most often, these two models are combined so that speech communication technologies, such as customer service phone trees and their data analytic components, factor in both models, acoustic and linguistic.

7 The Internet of Things, as the network of smart devices is often called in shorthand, invites not just surveillance by the companies who make these things, but also by governments and by hackers. The site Shodan (2017) advertises itself as "the world's first search engine for Internet-connected devices" where users are invited to "Explore the Internet of Things" to "discover which of your devices are connected to the Internet, where they are located and who is using them." While a user may find their own devices, so too can hackers or any other agents. Your smart refrigerator and thermostat, not to mention your Alexa-enabled Echo, are not the only ones "listening" to you.

8 One of the most widely publicized and analyzed telecommuting policy shifts by a company was Yahoo's policy change in June 2013 to disallow telecommuting—a policy shift that many saw as short-sighted and counterproductive (e.g., Cohan, 2013; Otani, 2015).

9 Lessig (2004, 2005) has made the point that our culture is not simply transmitted and distributed through language, it is *made* through language, and the ability of writers to interact with their culture, to remix that culture, to change it, depends critically on the ability to share cultural artifacts, memes, bit and pieces of text, and to remix them and redistribute them in new ways, building new from old. Our culture is built from remix.

10 For a history of *Lenz v. Universal*, see https://www.eff.org/cases/lenz-v-universal.

11 Google is the most widely used search engine in the world, with, as of January 2017, an average of 1.4 billion unique monthly visits. The next most popular search engine, Bing, has only 400 million (eBiz/MBA, 2017).

12 In January 2017, a new US President was inaugurated and a new US Congress sworn in. Nothing has happened yet in regards to the issue of net neutrality, but the signs are not good. The newly appointed Chair of the FCC, Ajit Pai, has expressed his hope that the net neutrality rules put into place by the Obama Administration in 2015 (the FCC's Open Internet Order) will be vacated. A Republican Congress that stands opposed to federal regulation may help him do precisely that (Finley, 2017).

13 We see another example of this in our field, professional communication. In many US universities, a major in Professional Writing (or Professional Communication, or Professional and Technical Writing, etc.) is a sign that institutional change can happen. That major didn't exist twenty years ago. Now it is flourishing at many institutions. And yet the major faces daunting struggles for identity, status, and support at many universities—and its status within the traditional department structure is problematic. The program fits somewhere in the space between communication, writing, design, and technology development, but there is not a well-defined department that provides a good fit. It exists in the interstices, and that is true for many innovative, cutting edge programs: they don't fit well into the existing 19th-century disciplinary categories of disciplinary knowledge.

14 edX represents exactly the kind of "inter-firm alliance" we are talking about. Founded by Harvard University and MIT in 2012, edX is a joint venture of (now) 90 universities and educational institutions to offer a coordinated program of online courses and programs. Coursera is another such initiative, consisting (as of January 2017) of 148 partners in 28 countries, including the University of Toronto, Princeton University, École Polytechnique, Stanford University, Yale University, University of Chicago, University of Edinburgh, Shanghai Jiao Tong University, and many others.

References

Adam, Alison. (2008). Ethics for things. *Ethics and Information Technology, 10*, 149–154.

al-Qinai, Jamal B.S. (2011). Translating phatic expressions. *Pragmatics, 21*(1), 23–39.

Alač, Morana. (2016). Social robots: Things or agents? *AI & Society, 31*(4), 519–535.

Alba, Davey. (2016, March 25). It's your fault Microsoft's Tay turned into such a jerk. *Wired*. https://www.wired.com/2016/03/fault-microsofts-teen-ai-turned-jerk/

Allen, Joseph A., Lehmann-Willenbrock, Nale, & Landowski, Nicole. (2014). Linking pre-meeting communication to meeting effectiveness. *Journal of Managerial Psychology, 29*(8), 1064–1081.

Amazon. (2016). Amazon developer. https://developer.amazon.com/

American Institute of Certified Public Accountants. (2014). *Code of professional conduct*. http://www.aicpa.org/Research/Standards/CodeofConduct/Pages/default.aspx

Anzaldúa, Gloria. (1987). *Borderlands/La frontera: The new mestiza*. San Francisco, CA: Aunt Lute Books.

Apple. (2016). Siri. http://www.apple.com/ios/siri/

Arecemont, Katherine. (2017, January 23). In a casino in Pittsburgh, an AI program is beating poker champions for the first time. *Washington Post*. https://www.washingtonpost.com/news/morning-mix/wp/2017/01/24/in-a-casino-in-pittsburgh-an-ai-program-is-beating-poker-champions-for-the-first-time/

Aristotle. (4th-century BCE/1976). *The ethics of Aristotle: The Nicomachean ethics*. Trans. J.A.K. Thomson. London: Penguin Books.

Aristotle. (4th-century BCE/2006). *On rhetoric: A theory of civic discourse*. 2nd ed. Trans. George A. Kennedy. Oxford: Oxford University Press.

Augustine. (1997). *On Christian teaching (De doctrina Christiana)*. Trans. R.P.H. Green. Oxford: Oxford University Press. (Books I-III were written ca 397 CE. Book IV was written ca 427 CE).

Austin, J.L. (1962). *How to do things with words*. (2nd edition, 1975). Cambridge, MA: Oxford University Press.

Avert. (2016). AIDS timeline. http://timeline.avert.org/

Belsie, Laurent. (2011, December 23). FedEx delivery video: Package thrown, FedEx apologizes on YouTube. *Christian Science Monitor*. http://www.csmonitor.com/Business/new-economy/2011/1223/FedEx-delivery-video-Package-thrown.-FedEx-apologizes-on-YouTube

Benkler, Yochai. (2006). *The wealth of networks: How social production transforms markets and freedom*. New Haven: Yale University Press.

Bennett, Colin J., & Raab, Charles. (2006). *The governance of privacy: Policy instruments in global perspective*. Cambridge: MIT Press.

Bennett, Jane. (2010). *Vibrant matter: A political ecology of things*. Durham: Duke University Press.

Benoit, William L. (1991). Isocrates and Plato on rhetoric and rhetorical education. *Rhetoric Society Quarterly, 21*(1), 60–71.

Beres, Damon. (2016, March 25). Why Microsoft's racist chat bot catastrophe was kind of a good thing. *Huffington Post*. http://www.huffingtonpost.com/entry/microsoft-tay-racist_us_56f556e5e4b0a3721819bd15

Bessi, Alessandro, & Ferrara, Emilio. (2016). Social bots distort the 2016 U.S. Presidential election online discussion. *First Monday, 21*(11). http://firstmonday.org/ojs/index.php/fm/article/view/7090/5653

Biddle, Sam. (2013). And now a funny holiday joke from IAC's PR boss. *Gawker*. http://valleywag.gawker.com/and-now-a-funny-holiday-joke-from-iacs-pr-boss-1487284969

Biddle, Sam. (2014). Justine Sacco is good at her job, and how I came to peace with her. *Gawker*. http://gawker.com/justine-sacco-is-good-at-her-job-and-how-i-came-to-pea-1653022326

Biddle, Sam. (2015, February 9). Brands are not your friends. *Gawker*. http://gawker.com/brands-are-not-your-friend-1684232182

Bilandzic, Mark, Filonik, Daniel, Gross, Michael, Hackel, Andreas, Mangesius, Herbert, & Krcmar, Helmut. (2009). A mobile application to support phatic communication in hybrid space. *Proceedings of Sixth International Conference on Information Technology* (pp. 1517–1522). Las Vegas, NV: New Generations.

Bitzer, Lloyd F. (1968). The rhetorical situation. *Philosophy & Rhetoric, 1*, 1–14.

Bizzell, Patricia, & Herzberg, Bruce (Eds.). (2001). *The rhetorical tradition: Readings from classical times to the present*. 2nd ed. Boston: Bedford/St. Martin's.

Blanchfield, Patrick. (2015). Twitter's outrage machine should be stopped. But Justine Sacco is the wrong poster child. *Washington Post*. https://www.washingtonpost.com/posteverything/wp/2015/02/24/twitters-rage-mob-should-be-stopped-but-justine-sacco-is-the-wrong-poster-child/

Boboltz, Sara. (2014). Whoever runs Taco Bell's Twitter account deserves a raise. *Huffington Post*. http://www.huffingtonpost.com/2014/02/28/taco-bell-tweets_n_4856259.html

Bokser, Julie A. (2010). Sor Juana's *Divine Narcissus*: A new world rhetoric of listening. *Rhetoric Society Quarterly, 40*(3), 224–246.

Bolter, Jay David. (1991). *Writing space: The computer, hypertext, and the history of writing*. Hillsdale, NJ: Lawrence Erlbaum.

Brandau, Mark. (2014). Research: Taco Bell's breakfast launch a success. *Restaurant News*. http://nrn.com/marketing/research-taco-bells-breakfast-launch-success

Brooke, Collin Gifford. (2009). *Lingua fracta: What we teach when we teach about literacy*. Cresskill, NJ: Hampton Press.

Brownlee, John. (2011, November 10). Meet the man who became the voice of Siri without even knowing it. *Cult of Mac*. http://www.cultofmac.com/129143/meet-the-man-who-became-the-voice-of-siri-without-even-knowing-it/

Bruns, Axel. (2009, September 3). From prosumer to produser: Understanding user-led content creation. Conference on Transforming Audiences, London, UK. http://produsage.org/node/67

Buchanan, Lindal. (2005). *Regendering delivery: The fifth canon and antebellum women rhetors*. Carbondale: Southern Illinois University Press.

Budrina, Irina. (2012, November 6). Intercultural communication: Business networking and cultural behavior patterns. *Romania-Insider.com*. http://www.romania-insider.com/intercultural-communication-business-networking-and-cultural-behavior-patterns/

Burke, Kenneth. (1969). *A rhetoric of motives*. Berkeley: University of California Press.

Burnett, Rebecca. (2005). *Technical communication*. 6th ed. Boston: Thomson Wadsworth.

Butler, Judith. (1997). *Excitable speech: A politics of the performative*. New York: Routledge.

Butler, Judith. (2010). Performative agency. *Journal of Cultural Economy, 3*(2), 147–161.

Campbell, George. (1776/2004). *The philosophy of rhetoric*. Whitefish: Kessinger Publishing.

Carter, Jamie. (2016, May 29). Are we entering the post-app era? *Techradar*. http://www.techradar.com/news/software/applications/are-we-entering-the-post-app-era-1322237

Cassin, Barbara. (2009). Sophistics, rhetorics, and performance; or, how to really do things with words. *Philosophy & Rhetoric, 42*, 349–372.

Castells, Manuel. (2010). *The rise of the network society*. 2nd ed. West Sussex, UK: Wiley-Blackwell.

Chaput, Catherine. (2010). Rhetorical circulation in late capitalism: Neoliberalism and the overdetermination of affective energy. *Philosophy & Rhetoric, 43*, 1–25.

Chen, Guo-Ming. (2012). The impact of new media on intercultural communication in global context. *China Media Research, 8*(2), 1–10.

Cherry, Roger D. (1988). Ethos versus persona: Self-representation in written discourse. *Written Communication, 5*, 251–276.

Childers, Linda. (1989). J. Grunig's asymmetrical and symmetrical models of public relations: Contrasting features and ethical dimensions. *IEEE Transactions on Professional Communication, 32*(2), 86–93.

Chirgwin, Richard. (2011, August 11). LinkedIn pulls Facebook-style stunt. *The Register*. http://www.theregister.co.uk/2011/08/11/linkedin_privacy_stuff_up

Cicero. (1949). *De inventione*. Trans. H.M. Hubbell. Cambridge, MA: Harvard University Press. (Originally published in 1st century BCE.)

Cicero. (55 BCE/1948). *De oratore*. Trans. E.W. Sutton & H. Rackham. Cambridge, MA: Harvard University Press.

Cohan, Peter. (2013, February 26) 4 reasons why Marissa Mayers' no at-home work policy is an epic fail. http://www.forbes.com/sites/petercohan/2013/02/26/4-reasons-marissa-mayers-no-at-home-work-policy-is-an-epic-fail/#162964116c74

Collier, Mack. (2012, March 19). Case study: How FedEx responded to a customer's viral video … with its own video. MackCollier.com. http://mackcollier.com/fed-ex-customers-viral-video/

Cooper, Marilyn M. (1986). The ecology of writing. *College English*, 48(4), 364–375.

Constine, Josh, & Perez, Sarah. (2016, September 12). Facebook now allows payments in its 30,000 chatbots. *TechCrunch*. https://techcrunch.com/2016/09/12/messenger-bot-payments/

Cornwell, Nancy C., & Orbe, Mark P. (1999). Critical perspectives on hate speech: The centrality of "dialogic listening." *International Journal of Listening, 13*, 75–96.

Cox, Edward. (2015, May 12). How virtual reality will change your business. Inc. http://www.inc.com/edward-cox/how-virtual-reality-will-change-your-business.html

Crnkovic, Gordana Dodig, & Çürüklü, Baran. (2012). Robots: Ethical by design. *Ethics and Information Technology, 14*(1), 61–71.

Croucher, Stephen M. (2011). Social networking and cultural adaptation: A theoretical model. *Journal of International and Intercultural Communication, 4*(4), 259–264.

d.Trio. (2016, May 30). How should brands respond to tragedy? Examining the response to Prince's death. dTrio. http://www.dtrio.com/blog1/2016/05/how-should-brands-respond-to-tragedy-examining-the-response-to-princes-death/

Davidson, Helen. (2013, December 12). Twitter reinstates its blocking option after user backlash. *The Guardian*. https://www.theguardian.com/technology/2013/dec/13/twitter-reinstates-blocking-function-after-backlash

de Romilly, Jacqueline. (1958). *Eunoia* in Isocrates or the political importance of creating good will. *Journal of Hellenic Studies, 78*, 92–101.

Delamarter, Andrew. (2016, December 9). The Darknet: A quick introduction for business leaders. *Harvard Business Review*. https://hbr.org/2016/12/the-darknet-a-quick-introduction-for-business-leaders

Deleuze, Félix, & Guattari, Gilles. (1987). *A thousand plateaus: Capitalism and schizophrenia*. Trans. Brian Massumi. Minneapolis, MN: University of Minnesota Press (Original work published 1980).

Denton, Nick. (2015, February 16). Of course a brand can be your friend. *Nick Denton*. http://nick.kinja.com/of-course-a-brand-can-be-your-friend-1686102136

DeWinter, Jennifer, & Moeller, Ryan M. (Eds.). (2014). *Computer games and technical communication: Critical methods and applications at the intersection*. Farnham, UK: Ashgate.

Dimitrova, Kami, Rahmanzadeh, Shahriar, & Lipman, Jane. (2013). Justine Sacco, fired after tweet on AIDS in Africa, apologizes. ABC News. http://abcnews.go.com/International/justine-sacco-fired-tweet-aids-africa-issues-apology/story?id=21301833

Donnelly, Francis P. (1912). A function of the classical exordium. *The Classical Weekly, 5*(26), 204–207.

Duffy, John. (2017). The good writer: Virtue ethics and the teaching of writing. *College English, 79*(3), 229–250.

Duin, Ann Hill, & Moses, Joseph. (2015). Intercultural connectivism: Introducing personal learning networks. *Rhetoric, Professional Communication and Globalization, 7*(1), 29–46.

Dwyer, Timothy. (2015). *Convergent media and privacy*. New York: Palgrave Macmillan.

eBiz/MBA. (2017, January). Top 15 most popular search engines. http://www. ebizmba.com/articles/search-engines

Edbauer, Jenny. (2005). Unframing models of public distribution: From rhetorical situation to rhetorical ecologies. *Rhetoric Society Quarterly, 35*(4), 5–24.

Edelman. (2015). Edelman trust barometer 2015. *Scribd.* https://www.scribd. com/doc/252750985/2015

Edwards, Dustin W. (2016). *Writing in the flow: Assembling tactical rhetorics in an age of viral circulation.* Dissertation, Miami University, Oxford, OH.

Edwards, Joe. (2014, April 30). What is social media listening? *Smart Insights.* http://www.smartinsights.com/social-media-marketing/social-media-listening/what-is-social-media-listening/

Ehninger, Douglas. (1968). On systems of rhetoric. *Philosophy & Rhetoric, 1*(3), 131–144.

Eisenstein, Elizabeth. (2005). *The printing revolution in early modern Europe.* 2nd ed. Cambridge, UK: Cambridge University Press.

Electronic Frontier Foundation. (n.d.) SOPA/PIPA: Internet blacklist legislation. *EFF.org.* https://www.eff.org/issues/coica-internet-censorship-and-copyright-bill

Engeström, Yrjö. (1996). Interobjectivity, ideality, and dialectics. *Mind, Culture, and Activity, 3*(4), 259–265.

Engeström, Yrjö. (2001). Expansive learning at work: Toward an activity theoretical reconceptualization. *Journal of Education and Work, 14*(1), 133–156.

Enos, Richard Leo, & McClaran, Jeanne L. (1978). Audience and image in Ciceronian Rome: Creation and constraints of the *vir bonus* personality. *Central States Speech Journal, 29*, 98–106.

Enos, Richard Leo. (2008). *Roman rhetoric: Revolution and the Greek influence.* Revised and expanded edition. West Lafayette, IN: Parlor Press.

Enos, Theresa (Ed.). (1996). *Encyclopedia of rhetoric and composition: Communication from ancient times to the information age.* New York: Garland.

EPIC, The Campaign for a Commercial Free Childhood, The Center for Digital Democracy, & Consumers Union. (2016). Complaint and request investigation, injunction, and other relief. https://epic.org/privacy/kids/EPIC-IPR-FTC-Genesis-Complaint.pdf

Etlinger, Susan. (2015a, January 21). *What do we do with all this big data? Fostering insight and trust in the digital age.* Market Definition Report, Altimeter Group. http://go.pardot.com/l/69102/2015-07-12/pxzvc

Etlinger, Susan. (2015b, June 25). *The trust imperative: A framework for ethical data use.* Market Definition Report, Altimeter Group. http://www. altimetergroup.com/2015/06/new-report-the-trust-imperative-a-framework-for-ethical-data-use/

Etzioni, Oren. (2016, June 15). Deep learning isn't a dangerous magic genie. It's just math. *Wired.* Retrieved from https://www.wired.com/2016/06/deep-learning-isnt-dangerous-magic-genie-just-math/

Etzioni, Amitai, & Etzioni, Oren. (2016). AI assisted ethics. *Ethics and Information Technology, 18*, 149–156.

European Commission. (2016). Protection of personal data. http://ec.europa.eu/justice/data-protection/

Eyman, Douglas. (2015). *Digital rhetoric: Theory, method, practice.* Ann Arbor, MI: University of Michigan Press.

F0t0b0y. (2016, December 29). Amazon Alexa gone wild! https://www.youtube.com/watch?v=r5p0gqCIEa8

FedEx. (2011, December 21). FedEx response to customer video. https://www.youtube.com/watch?v=4ESU_PcqI38

Feenberg, Andrew. (1991). *Critical theory of technology*. New York: Oxford University Press.

Feenberg, Andrew. (1999). *Questioning technology*. London: Routledge.

Feenberg, Andrew. (2003). What is philosophy of technology? Komaba Lecture, Japan. http://www.sfu.ca/~andrewf/komaba.htm

Finley, Klint. (2017, January 23). Trump's FCC pick doesn't bode well for net neutrality. *Wired*. https://www.wired.com/2017/01/trumps-fcc-pick-signals-end-net-neutrality-efforts/

Fiveash, Kelly. (2011, August 12). LinkedIn u-turns to appease peeved users. *The Register*. http://www.theregister.co.uk

Fleckenstein, Kristie S., Spinuzzi, Clay, Rickly, Rebecca J., & Papper, Carole Clark. (2008). The importance of harmony: An ecological metaphor for writing research. *College Composition and Communication, 60*(2), 388–419.

Floridi, Luciano, & Sanders, J.W. (2004). On the morality of artificial agents. *Minds and Machine, 14*, 349–379.

Floridi, Luciano. (2014). *The 4ᵗʰ revolution: How the infosphere is reshaping human reality*. Oxford: Oxford University Press.

Floyd, James J. (2010). Listening: A dialogic perspective. In Andrew D. Wolvin (Ed.), *Listening and human communication in the 21ˢᵗ century* (pp. 127–140). Chichester, West Sussex, UK: Wiley-Blackwell.

Foss, Sonja K., & Griffin, Cindy L. (1995). Beyond persuasion: A proposal for an invitational rhetoric. *Communication Monographs, 62*, 1–18.

Foucault, Michel. (1972). *The archaeology of knowledge and the discourse on language*. Trans. A.M. Sheridan Smith. New York: Harper & Row.

Foucault, Michel. (1995). *Discipline and punish: The birth of the prison*. New York: Random House.

Fournier, Susan. (1998). Consumers and their brands: Developing relationship theory in consumer research. *Journal of Consumer Research, 24*, 342–373.

Free Press. (2017). Save the Internet. http://www.savetheinternet.com/

Gartler, Mark. (2017). Rhizome. The Chicago school of media theory. https://lucian.uchicago.edu/blogs/mediatheory/keywords/rhizome/

Gaudin, Sharon. (2015, March 27). 5 ways to use virtual reality in the enterprise. *Computerworld*. http://www.computerworld.com/article/2903070/5-ways-to-use-virtual-reality-in-the-enterprise.html

Gelfenbeyn, Ilya. (2016, June 26). The bot revolution: How conversational interfaces will replace apps. *VentureBeat*. http://venturebeat.com/2016/06/26/the-bot-revolution-how-conversational-interfaces-will-replace-apps/

Gershgorn, Dave. (2015, July 29). Microsoft brings Cortana to Windows 10 but she was better in 'Halo'. *Popular Science*. http://www.popsci.com/microsoft-brings-cortana-windows-10-she-was-better-halo

Gibbs, Martin R., Vetere, Frank, Bunyan, Marcus, & Howard, Steve. (2005). SynchroMate: A phatic technology for mediating intimacy. *Proceedings of the 2005 Conference on Designing for User eXperience*, American Institute of Graphic Arts (AIGA). http://dl.acm.org/citation.cfm?id=1138279

Glenn, Cheryl, & Ratcliff, Krista (Eds.). (2011a). *Silence and listening as rhetorical arts*. Carbondale: Southern Illinois University Press.

Glenn, Cheryl, & Ratcliffe, Krista. (2011b). Introduction: Why silence and listening are important rhetorical arts. In Cheryl Glenn & Krista Ratcliff (Eds.), *Silence and listening as rhetorical arts* (pp. 1–19). Carbondale: Southern Illinois University Press.

Google. (2017). How Gmail ads work. https://privacy.google.com/how-ads-work.html?modal_active=how-ads-work-proof-overlay&article_id=c4-p-gmail-ads-3

Grodzinsky, Frances S., Miller, Keith W., & Wolf, Marty J. (2008). The ethics of designing artificial agents. *Ethics and Information Technology, 10*, 115–221.

Grunig, James E. (2009). Paradigms of global public relations in an age of digitalisation. *PRism 6*(2). http://www.prismjournal.org/fileadmin/Praxis/Files/globalPR/GRUNIG.pdf

Hall, Edward T. (1976). *Beyond culture*. Garden City, NY: Anchor/Doubleday.

Hallett, Josh, Kolran, Eran, Meek, Pamela, Moegling, Rose Mary, & Tam, Vincent. (2013). What strategies should global organizations adopt when creating social media guidelines? *PRWeek*. http://www.prweek.com/article/1275631/strategies-global-organizations-adopt-when-creating-social-media-guidelines

Halliday, M.A.K. (1976). *System and function in language* (ed. G.R. Kress). London: Oxford University Press.

Hamill, Sean D. (2017, January 30). All in: CMU's computer busts humans over a 20-day competition. *Pittsburgh Post-Gazette*. http://www.post-gazette.com/local/city/2017/01/29/Carnegie-Mellon-University-poker-computer-Libratus-beats-humans-at-Rivers-Casino/stories/201701310147

Haraway, Donna. (1991). A cyborg manifesto: Science, technology, and socialist-feminism in the late twentieth century. In *Simians, cyborgs, and women: The reinvention of nature* (pp. 149–181). New York: Routledge.

Hayles, N. Katherine. (1999). *How we became posthuman: Virtual bodies in cybernetics, literature, and informatics*. Chicago: The University of Chicago Press.

Heath, Shirley Brice. (1983). *Ways with words: Language, life, and work in communities and classrooms*. New York: Cambridge University Press.

Hébert, Louis. (2011). The functions of language. *Signo*. http://www.signosemio.com/jakobson/functions-of-language.asp

Heidegger, Martin. (1977). *The question concerning technology and other essays*. Trans. William Lovitt. New York: Garland.

Hempel, Jessi. (2016, December 19). Voice is the next big platform, and Alexa will own it. *Backchannel*. https://backchannel.com/voice-is-the-next-big-platform-and-alexa-will-own-it-c2cf13fab911#.cbe6x7do2

Herkewitz, William. (2014, February 10). Why Watson and Siri are not real AI. *Popular Mechanics*. http://www.popularmechanics.com/science/a3278/why-watson-and-siri-are-not-real-ai-16477207/

Hildebrandt, Herbert W. (1988). Some influences of Greek and Roman rhetoric on early letter writing. *Journal of Business Communication, 25*(3), 7–27.

Hillman, Alex. (2014, April 28). To build a strong community, stop "community managing," be a tummler instead. http://dangerouslyawesome.com/2014/04/community-management-tummling-a-tale-of-two-mindsets/

Hofstede, Geert. (2001). *Culture's consequences: Comparing values, behaviors, institutions, and organizations across nations.* 2nd ed. Thousand Oaks, CA: Sage.

Howell Marketing. (2011, December 21). FedEx gets it right in response to viral video. *Howell Marketing Strategies.* http://www.howell-marketing.com/hms-blog/2011/12/21/fedex-gets-it-right-in-response-to-viral-video.html

Hudak, Pamela L., & Maynard, Douglas W. (2011). An interactional approach in conceptualizing small talk in medical interactions. *Sociology of Health & Illness, 33*(4), 634–653.

Humphrys, Mark. (2016). How my program passed the Turing Test. http://computing.dcu.ie/~humphrys/eliza.html

Hunsinger, R. Peter. (2006). Culture and cultural identity in intercultural technical communication. *Technical Communication Quarterly, 15*(1), 31–48.

Information Accountability Foundation. (2015). A unified ethical frame for big data analysis. http://informationaccountability.org/publications/a-unified-ethical-frame-for-big-data-analysis/

Internet Live Stats. (2016). Internet users in the world. http://www.internetlivestats.com/

Isocrates. (n.d.). *Antidosis* (ed. George Norlin). Perseus Digital Library. http://www.perseus.tufts.edu/hopper/text?doc=Perseus%3Atext%3A1999.01.0144%3Aspeech%3D15

Isocrates. (n.d.). *Panathenaicus* (ed. George Norlin). Perseus Digital Library. http://www.perseus.tufts.edu/hopper/text?doc=Perseus%3Atext%3A1999.01.0144%3Aspeech%3D12

Jakobson, Roman. (1960). Closing statements: Linguistics and poetics. In T. A. Sebeok (Ed.), *Style in language* (pp. 350–377). Cambridge, MA: The MIT Press.

Jansen, Frank, & Janssen, Daniel. (2013). Effects of directness in bad-news e-mails and voice mails. *Journal of Business Communication, 50*(4), 362–382.

Jarvenpaa, Sirkka L., Shaw, Thomas R., & Staples, D. Sandy. (2004). Toward contextualized theories of trust: The role of trust in global virtual teams. *Information Systems Research, 15*(3), 250–267.

Jaume, Jasmine. (2013, August 7). What's the difference between social listening, analytics and intelligence? *Brandwatch Blog.* https://www.brandwatch.com/2013/08/whats-the-difference-between-social-analytics/

Jenkins, Henry, Ford, Sam, & Green, Joshua. (2013). *Spreadable media: Creating value and meaning in a networked culture.* New York: New York University Press.

Johannesen, Richard L. (1971). The emerging concept of communication as dialogue. *Quarterly Journal of Speech, 58,* 373–382.

Johannesen, Richard L. (1978). Richard M. Weaver on standards for ethical rhetoric. *Central States Speech Journal, 29,* 127–137.

Johnson-Eilola, Johndan, & Kimme Hea, Amy C. (2003). After hypertext: Other ideas. *Computers & Composition, 20*(3), 415–425.

Johnson-Eilola, Johndan. (1997). *Nostalgic angels: Rearticulating hypertext writing.* Norwood, NJ: Ablex.

Johnson-Eilola, Johndan. (2005). *Datacloud: Toward a new theory of online work.* Cresskill, NJ: Hampton Press.

Johnson, Nan. (1984). Ethos and the aims of rhetoric. In Robert J. Connors, Lisa S. Ede, & Andrea A. Lunsford (Eds.), *Essays on classical rhetoric and modern discourse* (pp. 98–114). Carbondale: Southern Illinois University Press.

Johnson, Robert R. (1998). *User-centered technology: A rhetorical theory for computers and other mundane artifacts.* Albany, NY: SUNY Press.

Johnstone, Christopher Lyle. (1980). An Aristotelian trilogy: Ethics, rhetoric, politics, and the search for moral truth. *Philosophy & Rhetoric, 13*(1), 1–24.

Jones, John. (2015). Network* writing. *Kairos, 20*(1). http://kairos.technorhetoric. net/20.1/topoi/jones/index.html

Jung, Julie. (2014). Systems-rhetoric: A dynamic coupling of explanation and description. *Enculturation, 17.* http://enculturation.net/systems-rhetoric

Karenga, Maulana. (2004). *Maat, the moral ideal in ancient Egypt: A study in classical African ethics.* New York: Routledge.

Keep Watch, Stay Free. (2017, January 18). The day the Internet stood still. *Medium.* https://medium.com/@stayfree/the-day-the-internet-stood-still-98a6f 5aa4a2a#.uwnwe0hnx

Kerr, Ian, Steeves, Valerie, & Lucock, Carole (Eds.). (2009). *Lessons from the identity trail: Anonymity, privacy, and identity in a networked society.* New York: Oxford University Press.

Kidwell, Roland E., & Sprague, Robert. (2009). Electronic surveillance in the global workplace: Laws, ethics, research, and practice. *New Technology, Work and Employment, 24*(2), 194–208.

King, Cynthia L. (2010). Beyond persuasion: The rhetoric of negotiation in business communication. *Journal of Business Communication, 47*(1), 69–78.

Kinneavy, James L. (1971). *A theory of discourse: The aims of discourse.* New York: Norton.

Kinneavy, James L. (1986). *Kairos:* A neglected concept in classical rhetoric. In Jean Dietz Moss (Ed.), *Rhetoric and praxis: The contribution of classical rhetoric to practical reasoning* (pp. 79–105). Washington, DC: The Catholic University of America Press.

Klie, Leonard. (2011). Speech analytics captures consumer sentiment. *Speech Technology Magazine, 16*(3), 22–26.

Knight, Will. (2016, June 13). Amazon working on making Alexa recognize emotions. *MIT Technology Review.* https://www.technologyreview. com/s/601654/amazon-working-on-making-alexa-recognize-your-emotions/

Koch, Christof. (2016, March 19). How the computer beat the go master. *Scientific American.* https://www.scientificamerican.com/article/how-the-computer-beat-the-go-master/

Krotoszynski, Ronald J. (2016). *Privacy revisited: A global perspective on the right to be left alone.* Oxford: Oxford University Press.

Kruse, Michael. (2016, July 21). Trump and the dark art of bad publicity. *Politico.* http://www.politico.com/magazine/story/2016/07/donald-trump-2016-convention-melania-trump-speech-dark-art-of-pr-214083

Kulkarni, Dipti. (2014). Exploring Jakobson's "phatic function" in instant messaging interactions. *Discourse & Communication, 8*(2), 117–136.

Lakoff, George, & Johnson, Mark. (1980). *Metaphors we live by.* Chicago: University of Chicago Press.

Lanham, Richard A. (1991). *A handlist of rhetorical terms.* 2nd ed. Berkeley: University of California Press.

Laskowski, Amy. (2013, October 11). How Ford became a leader in social media. *Boston University Today.* http://www.bu.edu/today/2013/how-ford-became-a-leader-in-social-media/

Latour, Bruno. (1996a). *Aramis, or the love of technology.* Trans. Catherine Porter. Cambridge, MA: Harvard University Press.

Latour, Bruno. (1996b). On interobjectivity. *Mind, Culture, and Activity, 3*(4), 228–245.

Latour, Bruno. (2005). *Reassembling the social: An introduction to actor-network-theory.* Oxford: Oxford University Press.

Lauring, Jakob. (2011). Intercultural organizational communication: The social organizing of interaction in international encounters. *Journal of Business Communication, 48*(3), 231–255.

Laver, John. (1975). Communicative functions of phatic communion. In Adam Kendon, Richard M. Harris, & Mary Ritchie Key (Eds.), *Organization of behavior in face-to-face interaction* (pp. 215–238). The Hague: Mouton.

Law, John. (2000). *Objects, spaces, and others.* Centre for Science Studies, Lancaster University, UK. http://www.comp.lancs.ac.uk/sociology/papers/Law-Objects-Spaces-Others.pdf

Law, John. (2002). Objects and spaces. *Theory, Culture & Society, 19,* 91–105.

Law, John. (2004). *After method: Mess in social science research.* London: Routledge, 2004.

Lebedko, Maria G. (2014). Globalization, networking and intercultural communication. *Intercultural Communication Studies, 23*(1), 28–41.

Lee, Peter. (2016, March 25). Learning from Tay's introduction. *Microsoft Blog.* http://blogs.microsoft.com/blog/2016/03/25/learning-tays-introduction/#sm.00000nkwrlwvdfd8upwxnxtvn2g3l

Lehman, Cynthia L. (2001). The Kemetic paradigm: An Afrocentric foundation for rhetorical theory. In Virginia H. Milhouse, Molefi Kete Asante, & Peter O. Nwosu (Eds.), *Transcultural realities: Interdisciplineary perspectives on cross-cultural relations* (pp. 327–334). Thousand Oaks: Sage.

Lessig, Lawrence. (2004). *Free culture: How big media uses technology and the law to lock down culture and control creativity.* New York, NY: Penguin.

Lessig, Lawrence. (2005). *Intellectual property: Key issues.* Plenary Talk, Conference on College Composition and Communication, San Francisco, CA.

Lin, Jim. (2016, April 19). Networks are people. *Ketchum Blog.* http://blog.ketchum.com/networks-are-people/

Lindstrom, Rebecca. (2016, December 29). Virtual reality could take jurors inside crimes. *USA Today.* http://www.usatoday.com/story/tech/nation-now/2016/12/29/georgia-company-virtual-reality-jurors/95959604/

LinkedIn. (2017). User agreement. https://www.linkedin.com/legal/user-agreement

Lipari, Lisbeth. (2009). Listening otherwise: The voice of ethics. *International Journal of Listening, 23,* 44–59.

Lipari, Lisbeth. (2012). Rhetoric's other: Levinas, listening, and the ethical response. *Philosophy & Rhetoric, 45*(3), 227–245.

Liu, Yumeng. (2004). "Nothing can be accomplished if the speech does not sound agreeable": Rhetoric and the invention of classical Chinese discourse. In Carol S. Lipson & Roberta A. Binkley (Eds.), *Rhetoric before and beyond the Greeks* (pp. 147–164). Albany, NY: SUNY Press.

Locke, John. (1690/1959). *An essay concerning human understanding* (ed. Alexander Campbell Fraser). London: Routledge.

Longo, Bernadette. (2014). R U There? Cell phones, participatory design, and intercultural dialogue. *IEEE Transactions on Professional Communication, 57*(3), 204–215.

lotus823. (2013). Serving up the spiciest social media this side of the Rio Grande. http://www.lotus823.com/social-media-marketing-lessons-from-taco-bell/

lotus823. (2015). Taco Bell is dominating content marketing. http://www.lotus823.com/taco-bell-is-dominating-content-marketing/

Lund, Donald. J., Kozlenkova, Irina. V., & Palmatier, Robert. W. (2016). Good versus bad relationship framework. In Bang Nguyen, Lyndon Simkin, & Ana Isabella Canhoto (Eds.), *The dark side of CRM: Customers, relationships and management* (pp. 93–121). London, UK: Routledge.

Lunday, Jason. (2010, July 21). Managing the workplace ethics of social media. *Corporate Compliance Insights.* http://corporatecomplianceinsights.com/managing-the-workplace-ethics-of-social-media/

Lyon, Arabella. (2004). Confucian silence and remonstration. In Carol S. Lipson & Roberta A. Binkley (Eds.), *Rhetoric before and beyond the Greeks* (pp. 131–145). Albany, NY: SUNY Press.

Lyon, Thomas P., & Montgomery, Wren. (2013). Tweetjacked: The impact of social media on corporate greenwash. *Journal of Business Ethics, 118*(4), 747–757.

Mackiewicz, Jo. (2006). The functions of formulaic and nonformulaic compliments in interactions about technical writing. *IEEE Transactions on Professional Communication, 49*(1), 12–27.

Malinowski, Bronislaw. (1923). The problem of meaning in primitive languages. In C.K. Ogden & I.A. Richards (Eds.), *The meaning of meaning* (pp. 296–336). New York: Routledge & Kegan Paul.

Mao, LuMing. (1994). Beyond politeness theory: "Face" revisited and renewed. *Journal of Pragmatics, 21,* 451–486.

Mao, LuMing. (2006). *Reading Chinese fortune cookie: The making of Chinese American rhetoric.* Logan, UT: Utah State University Press.

Markhoff, John, & Mozur, Paul. (2015, July 31). For sympathetic ear, more Chinese turn to smartphone program. *The New York Times.* http://www.nytimes.com/2015/08/04/science/for-sympathetic-ear-more-chinese-turn-to-smartphone-program.html?smid=fb-nytimes&smtyp=cur

Marsh Jr., Charles W. (2001). Public relations ethics: Contracting models from the rhetorics of Plato, Aristotle, and Isocrates. *Journal of Mass Media Ethics, 16*(2/3), 78–98.

Marsh, Charles. (2013). *Classical rhetoric and modern public relations: An Isocratean model.* New York: Routledge.

Martin, Taylor, & Priest, David. (2016, December 9). The complete list of Alexa commands so far. *CNET.* https://www.cnet.com/how-to/the-complete-list-of-alexa-commands/

McCoy, Kevin, & Rowan, Robert. (2011, April 8). Network and rhizome. *Media Theory and Criticism.* http://mediatheorymemphis.blogspot.com/2011/04/network-rhizome.html

McCoy, Terrence. (2014, June 9). A computer just passed the Turing Test in a landmark trial. *The Washington Post.* https://www.washingtonpost.com/

news/morning-mix/wp/2014/06/09/a-computer-just-passed-the-turing-test-in-landmark-trial/?utm_term=.f6d2814edd5d

McFarland, Matt. (2015, March 15). What AlphaGo's sly move says about machine creativity. *The Washington Post.* https://www.washingtonpost.com/news/innovations/wp/2016/03/15/what-alphagos-sly-move-says-about-machine-creativity/?utm_term=.64233a7ea0db

McKay, Zoe. (2012, March 6). The ten principles for doing business in China. *Forbes.* http://www.forbes.com/sites/insead/2012/03/06/the-ten-principles-for-doing-business-in-china/#1244b2061176

McKee, Heidi A. (2011). Policy matters now and in the future: Net neutrality, corporate data mining, and government surveillance. *Computers and Composition, 28,* 276–291.

McKee, Heidi A. (2016). Protecting net neutrality and the infrastructure of Internet delivery: Considerations for our past, present, and future. *Kairos, 20*(2). http://kairos.technorhetoric.net/20.2/topoi/beck-et-al/mckee.html

McKee, Heidi A., & Porter, James E. (2009). *The ethics of Internet research: A rhetorical, case-based process.* New York: Peter Lang.

McKee, Steve. (2012). How social media is changing CRM. *Bloomberg.* http://www.bloomberg.com/news/articles/2012-06-08/how-social-media-is-changing-crm

McNely, Brian J. (2011). Informal communication, sustainability, and the public writing work of organizations. *Proceedings of the IEEE International Professional Communication Conference.* Piscataway, NJ: IEEE.

Medland, Dina. (2015, November 11). The danger of "window dressing" when raising the bar on corporate ethics. *Forbes.* http://www.forbes.com/sites/dinamedland/2015/11/11/the-dangers-of-window-dressing-when-raising-the-bar-on-corporate-ethics/#790ffae16cae

Microsoft. (2016a). What is Cortana? https://support.microsoft.com/en-us/help/17214/windows-10-what-is

Microsoft. (2016b, May 23). Meet Tay. https://web.archive.org/web/20160323194709/https://tay.ai/

Microsoft. (2016c, May 24). Meet Tay. https://web.archive.org/web/20160324163041/https://tay.ai/

Miller, Vincent. (2008). New media, networking and phatic culture. *Convergence, 14,* 387–400.

Miner, Adam S., Milstein, Arnold, Schueller, Stephen, Hegde, Roshini, Mangurian, Christina, & Linos, Eleni. (2016). Smartphone-based conversational agents and responses to questions about mental health, interpersonal violence, and physical health. *JAMA Internal Medicine, 176*(5), 619–625.

Morey, Sean. (2016). *Rhetorical delivery and digital technologies: Networks, affect, electracy.* New York: Routledge.

Morgan, Nick. (2013, May 21). How digital technology has changed communication. *Forbes.* Available at: http://www.forbes.com/sites/nickmorgan/2013/05/21/how-digital-technology-has-changed-communication-first-of-three-posts/#7d11f26246cb

Morrison, Maureen. (2013). Sales are going loco at Taco Bell, Ad Age's Marketer of the Year. *Advertising Age.* http://adage.com/article/special-report-marketer-alist-2013/taco-bell-ad-age-s-marketer-year/243852/

Mortensen, Dennis. (2016a, February 8). How to teach a machine to understand us. *x.ai Blog.* https://x.ai/how-to-teach-a-machine-to-understand-us/

Mortensen, Dennis. (2016b, August 29). AI and the fallibility double standard. *x.ai Blog.* https://x.ai/ai-and-the-fallibility-double-standard/)

Mortensen, Dennis. (2016c, September 6, 2016). The role of AI trainers in teaching a machine to understand us. *x.ai Blog.* https://x.ai/the-role-of-ai-trainers-in-teaching-a-machine-to-understand-us/

Mossberg, Walt. (2016, October 12). Why does Siri seem do dumb? *The Verge.* http://www.theverge.com/2016/10/12/13251068/walt-mossberg-apple-siri-is-dumb

Movius, Lauren. (2010). Cultural globalisation and challenges to traditional communication theories. *PLATFORM: Journal of Media and Communication,* 2(1), 6–18. https://platformjmc.files.wordpress.com/2015/04/platformvol2issue1_movius.pdf

Mozur, Paul. (2015, July 31). Chatting with Xiaoice. *The New York Times.* http://www.nytimes.com/interactive/2015/07/27/science/chatting-with-xiaoice.html

Murphy, James J. (1974). *Rhetoric in the Middle Ages: A history of rhetorical theory from St. Augustine to the Renaissance.* Berkeley: University of California Press.

Murphy, Mike. (2016, March 17). It's time for robots to have their own pronouns. *Quartz.* https://qz.com/629535/we-need-new-pronouns-for-robots/

Nahon, Karine, & Hemsley, Jeff. (2013). *Going viral.* Malden, MA: Polity Press.

Nardi, Bonnie A., Whittaker, Steve, & Schwarz, Heinrich. (2002). NetWORKers and their activity in intensional networks. *Computer Supported Cooperative Work, 11,* 205–242.

Nardi, Bonnie, & O'Day, Vicki. (1999). *Information ecologies: Using technology with heart.* Cambridge, MA: The MIT Press.

National Labor Relations Board. (2015). *The NLRB and social media.* https://www.nlrb.gov/news-outreach/fact-sheets/nlrb-and-social-media

National Society of Professional Engineers. (2014). *Code of ethics for engineers.* https://www.nspe.org/resources/ethics/code-ethics

Nissenbaum, Helen. (2009). *Privacy in context: Technology, policy, and the integrity of social life.* Redwood City: Stanford Law Books.

Nudd, Tim. (2013, September 6). Kenneth Cole clarifies: Being a jerk on Twitter is just good business. *AdWeek.* http://www.adweek.com/adfreak/kenneth-cole-clarifies-being-jerk-twitter-just-good-business-152257

O'Reily, Lara. (2015, July 10). People are sending flowers and chocolates to thank "Amy Ingram"—what they don't realize is she's a robot. *Business Insider.* http://www.businessinsider.com/amy-ingram-personal-assistant-2015-7

OpenNet Initiative. (2016). Research and data. https://opennet.net/

Oracle. (2012, March). *Is social media transforming your business?* Oracle White Paper, Redwood Shores, CA.

Otani, Akane. (2015, April 24). Richard Branson: Marissa Mayer's Yahoo work policy is on the wrong side of history. *Bloomberg.* https://www.bloomberg.com/news/articles/2015-04-24/richard-branson-marissa-mayer-s-yahoo-work-policy-is-on-the-wrong-side-of-history

Overly, Stephen. (2017, February 1). The great artificial intelligence gamble that finally paid off. *Washington Post.* https://www.washingtonpost.com/news/innovations/wp/2017/02/01/the-great-artificial-intelligence-gamble-that-finally-paid-off/?utm_term=.498f2f392ac1

Panzarino, Matthew. (2013, December 12). Twitter reverts changes to blocking functionality after strong negative user feedback. *TechCrunch.* https://techcrunch.com/2013/12/12/twitter-says-new-policy-which-allows-blocked-users-to-follow-interact-with-tweets-is-to-prevent-retaliation/

Parent, Jake. (2013, November 12). 5 ways Taco Bell is killing it with social media. *Policy.mic.* http://mic.com/articles/73129/5-ways-taco-bell-is-killing-it-with-social-media#.p85QlLPAA

Parkinson, Hannah Jane. (2015, August 12). Hey, Siri! Meet the real people behind Apple's voice-activated assistant. *The Guardian.* https://www.theguardian.com/technology/2015/aug/12/siri-real-voices-apple-ios-assistant-jon-briggs-susan-bennett-karen-jacobsen

Paul, Ben. (2016, December 19). x.ai pros and how they do it. https://x.ai/x-ai-pros-and-how-they-do-it-ben-paul-of-edmodo/

Perelman, Les. (1991). The medieval art of letter writing: Rhetoric as institutional expression. In Charles Bazerman & James Paradis (Eds.), *Textual dynamics of the professions: Historical and contemporary studies of writing in professional communities* (pp. 97–119). Madison: University of Wisconsin Press.

Perkins, D. N., & Salomon, G. (1992). Transfer of learning. *Contribution to the International Encyclopedia of Education.* 2nd ed. Oxford, England: Pergamon Press.

Pfister, Damien S., & Soliz, Jordan. (2011). (Re)conceptualizing intercultural communication in a networked society. *Journal of International and Intercultural Communication* 4(4), 246–251.

Plato. (ca 370 BCE/1973). *Phaedrus and letters VII and VIII.* Trans. Walter Hamilton. London: Penguin Books.

Plato. (ca 380 BCE/1925). *Lysis, symposium, gorgias.* Trans. W.R.M. Lamb. Cambridge, MA: Harvard University Press.

Porter, James E. (1992). *Audience and rhetoric: An archaeological composition of the discourse community.* Englewood Cliffs, NJ: Prentice Hall.

Porter, James E. (1998). *Rhetorical ethics and internetworked writing.* Greenwich, CT: Ablex.

Porter, James E. (2009). Recovering delivery for digital rhetoric. *Computers & Composition, 26,* 207–224.

Porter, James E. (2017). Professional communication as phatic: From classical *eunoia* to personal AI. *Business and Professional Communication Quarterly,* 80(1).

Potts, Liza. (2014). *Social media in disaster response: How experience architects can build for participation.* New York: Routledge.

Poulakos, John. (1983). Toward a sophistic definition of rhetoric. *Philosophy & Rhetoric, 16*(1), 35–48.

Poulakos, John. (2004). Rhetoric and civic education: From the Sophists to Isocrates. In Takis Poulakos and David Depew (Eds.), *Isocrates and civic education* (pp. 69–83). Austin: University of Texas Press.

Prahl, Andrew, & Van Swol, Lyn M. (2016). The computer said I should: How does receiving advice from a computer differ from receiving advice from a human. Presented at the 66th Annual International Communication Association Conference, Fukuoka, Japan. Press release https://www.sciencedaily.com/releases/2016/05/160525132559.htm

Pratt, Mary Louise. (1991). Arts of the contact zone. *Profession, 91*, 33–40.

Pruchnic, Jeff. (2014). *Rhetoric and ethics in the cybernetic age: The transhuman condition.* New York: Routledge.

Public Relations Society of America. (2000). Code of ethics. https://apps.prsa.org/AboutPRSA/Ethics/CodeEnglish/index.html

Pullin, Patricia. (2010). Small talk, rapport, and international communicative competence: Lessons to learn from BELF. *Journal of Business Communication, 47*(4), 455–476.

Quach, Katyanna. (2016, September 29). Microsoft chatbots: Sweet Xiaolce vs foul mouthed Tay. *The Register.* http://www.theregister.co.uk/2016/09/29/microsofts_chatbots_show_cultural_differences_between_the_east_and_west/

Quintilian. (95CE/2006). *Institutes of oratory (Institutio oratoria).* Trans. John Selby Watson (1856). http://rhetoric.eserver.org/quintilian

Radovanovic, Danica, & Ragnedda, Massimo. (2012). Small talk in the digital age: Making sense of phatic posts. *#MSM2012 Workshop Proceedings.* http://ceur-ws.org/Vol-838 #MSM2012

Raine, Lee, & Duggan, Maeve. (2016, January 14). Pew study on privacy and information sharing. *Pew Research Center.* http://www.pewinternet.org/files/2016/01/PI_2016.01.14_Privacy-and-Info-Sharing_FINAL.pdf

Ramus, Peter. (1549/1986). *Arguments in rhetoric against Quintilian.* Trans. Carole Newlands. Carbondale: Northern Illinois University Press.

Ratcliffe, Krista. (1999). Rhetorical listening: A trope for interpretive invention and a "Code of Cross-Cultural Conduct." *College Composition and Communication, 51*(2), 195–224.

Ray, Augie. (2012a). Three things every employer and employee need to know about social media. *Baylor Business Review*, 22–23.

Ray, Augie. (2012b, December 27). Miracle on social media street. *Experience: The Blog.* http://www.experiencetheblog.com/2012/12/miracle-on-social-media-street.html

Ray, Augie. (2013, April 23). Ethics in social media marketing: Responding to the Boston tragedy. *Social Media Today.* http://www.socialmediatoday.com/content/ethics-social-media-marketing-responding-boston-tragedy

Read, Sarah, & Swarts, Jason. (2015). Visualizing and tracing: Research methodologies for the study of networked, sociotechnical activity, otherwise known as knowledge work. *Technical Communication Quarterly, 24*(1), 14–44.

Redish, Janice (Ginny), & Barnum, Carol. (2011). Overlap, influence, intertwining: The interplay of UX and technical communication. *Journal of Usability Studies, 6*(3), 90–101.

Rickert, Thomas. (2013). *Ambient rhetoric: The attunements of rhetorical being.* Pittsburg: University of Pittsburgh Press.

Ridolfo, Jim, & DeVoss, Dànielle Nicole. (2009). Composing for recomposition: Rhetorical velocity and delivery. *Kairos, 13*(2). http://kairos.technorhetoric.net/13.2/topoi/ridolfo_devoss

Roemmele, Brian. (2016, December 14). The Amazon Echo was just the beginning of Amazon's Voice-First revolution. *Forbes.* http://www.forbes.com/

sites/quora/2016/12/14/the-amazon-echo-was-just-the-beginning-of-alexas-voice-first-revolution/#671de24cc569

Rogerson-Revell, Pamela. (2008). Participation and performance in international business meetings. *English for Specific Purposes, 27*, 338–360.

Ronson, Jon. (2015a). *So you've been publicly shamed.* New York: Riverhead Books.

Ronson, Jon. (2015b, February 15). How one stupid tweet blew up Justine Sacco's life. *New York Times Magazine*, p. MM20. http://www.nytimes.com/2015/02/15/magazine/how-one-stupid-tweet-ruined-justine-saccos-life.html?r=0

Rooney, Jennifer. (2011, October 5). Brand power to the people: J&J takes lead in Forbes ranking. *Forbes.* http://www.forbes.com/sites/jenniferrooney/2011/10/05/brand-power-to-the-people-jj-takes-lead-in-forbes-ranking/#62a7cf285aed

Rush Hovde, Marjorie. (2014). Factors that enable and challenge international engineering communication: A case study of a United States/British design team. *IEEE Transactions on Professional Communication, 57*(4), 242–265.

Russell, David R. (1997). Rethinking genre in school and society: An activity theory analysis. *Written Communication, 14*, 504–554.

Sametz, Roger. (2010). Brand management in the age of social media. *Business Week.* Reprinted in Roger Sametz in *Business Week.* http://mosaicbranding.com/roger-sametz-in-businessweek/

Sawyer, Rebecca, & Chen, Guo-Ming. (2012). The impact of social media on intercultural adaptation. *Intercultural Communication Studies, 21*, 151–169.

Schneider, Michael. (2016, May 7). Bots, Messenger and the future of customer service. *TechCrunch.* https://techcrunch.com/2016/05/07/bots-messenger-and-the-future-of-customer-service/

Selfe, Cynthia L., & Selfe, Jr, Richard J. (1994). The politics of the interface: Power and its exercise in electronic contact zones. *College Composition and Communication, 45*(4), 480–504.

Shannon, Claude. (1948). A mathematical theory of communication. *Bell System Technical Journal, 27*, 379–423, 623–656.

Shead, Sam. (2016, March 24). Here's why Microsoft's teen chatbot turned into a genocidal racist, according to an AI expert. *Tech Insider.* http://www.businessinsider.com/ai-expert-explains-why-microsofts-tay-chatbot-is-so-racist-2016-3?TB_iframe=true&width=369.9&height=657.9&r=UK&IR=T

Shoff, Kayli, & Shoff, Ricky. (2016). Two year old miraculously saves twin brother. https://www.youtube.com/watch?v=EtsrIpeMIkE&feature=youtu.be

Shodan. (2017). The search engine for Internet-connected devices. https://www.shodan.io/

Siemens, George. (2005). Connectivism: A learning theory for the digital age. *Elearnspace.* http://www.elearnspace.org/Articles/connectivism.htm

Sinders, Caroline. (2016, March 24). Why Microsoft's Tay is an example of bad design. https://medium.com/@carolinesinders/microsoft-s-tay-is-an-example-of-bad-design-d4e65bb2569f#.vttm0uimn

Smith, John E. (2002). Time and qualitative time. In Phillip Sipiora & James S. Baumlin (Eds.), *Rhetoric and kairos: Essays in history, theory, and praxis* (pp. 46–57). Albany: SUNY Press.

Snyder, Jasper. (2011, September 7). The ethics of social media listening. *Conderseon*. http://conderseon.com/blog/the-ethics-of-social-media-listening/

Social Media Governance. (2016). Social media database. http://socialmedia governance.com/policies/

Society for Technical Communication. (1998). *Ethical principles*. https://www. stc.org/about-stc/ethical-principles/

Solis, Brian. (2012, January 3). Going global by going local: Why localization improves engagement. *Brian Solis*. http://www.briansolis.com/2012/01/digital-localization-optimizes-global-strategies-to-improve-experiences-and-results/

Spinuzzi, Clay. (2008). *Network: Theorizing knowledge work in telecommunications*. Cambridge, UK: Cambridge University Press.

Spinuzzi, Clay. (2011, March 15). "Hold on loosely": The summary and some thoughts. *Spinuzzi Blog*. http://spinuzzi.blogspot.com/2011/03/hold-on-loosely-summary-and-some.html

Sprat, Thomas. (1667/1958). *The history of the Royal Society of London for the improving of natural knowledge* (ed. I. Cope and H.W. Jones). St. Louis: Washington University Press.

Stelter, Brian. (2013). Company parts ways with PR exec after AIDS in Africa tweet. *CNN*. http://www.cnn.com/2013/12/21/us/sacco-offensive-tweet/

Stopera, Dave. (2012). The best of Taco Bell's Twitter account. http://www. buzzfeed.com/daves4/the-best-of-taco-bells-twitter?utm_term=.aoWw YZ5LZ#.epBRkA3rA

Strunk, William Jr., & White, E.B. (1959/1995). *The elements of style*. 3rd ed. Boston: Allyn & Bacon.

Suchman, Lucy A. (1987). *Plans and situated actions: The problem of human-machine communication*. New York: Cambridge University Press.

Sun, Huatong. (2006). The triumph of users: Achieving cultural usability goals with user localization. *Technical Communication Quarterly, 15*(4), 457–481.

Sun, Huatong. (2009). Towards a rhetoric of locale: Localizing mobile messaging technology into everyday life. *Journal of Technical Writing and Communication, 39*(3), 245–261.

Sun, Huatong. (2012). *Cross-cultural technology design: Creating culture-sensitive technology for local users*. New York: Oxford University Press.

Sunbury Textile Mills. (2016). History. http://sunburytextiles.com/about/history

Swant, Marty. (2016, November 1). Twitter is now offering brands customer service chatbots for use in direct messages. *Adweek*. http://www.adweek.com/news/technology/twitter-now-offering-brands-customer-service-chatbots-use-direct-messages-174366

Swarts, Jason. (2015). Help is in the helping: An evaluation of help documentation in a networked age. *Technical Communication Quarterly, 24*(2), 164–187.

Taco Bell. (2015). The taco emoji needs to happen. *Change.org petition*. https:// www.change.org/p/unicode-consortium-the-taco-emoji-needs-to-happen-aeb4ebc7-a323-441d-90b9-20b90c83a8c6

Tao, Lin. (2012). A comparative study of perceived politeness in Chinese and Japanese verbal communication. *Intercultural Communication Studies, 21*(2), 185–200.

Tarpening, Ed. (2015, July 28). *The 2015 state of social business: Priorities shift from scaling to integrating*. Best Practices Report, Altimeter Group.

Thomases, Hollis. (2012). McDonald's twitter mess: What went wrong. *Inc.* http://www.inc.com/hollis-thomases/mcdonalds-mcdstories-twitter-mess.html

Torrance, Steve. (2008). Ethics and consciousness in artificial agents. *AI & Society, 22*(4), 495–521.

Tossona, Coreen. (2015, June 3). Should brands choose buzz over integrity? LinkedIn. https://www.linkedin.com/pulse/should-brands-choose-buzz-over-integrity-coreen-tossona

Triandis, Harry C. (2004). The many dimensions of culture. *Academy of Management Executive, 18*(1), 88–93.

Trimbur, John. (2000). Composition and the circulation of writing. *College Composition and Communication, 52*(2), 188–219.

Turing, Alan M. (1950). Computing machinery and intelligence. *Mind, 59*, 433–460.

Van Es, Robert, & Meijlink, Tiemo L. (2000). The dialogical turn of public relations ethics. *Journal of Business Ethics, 27*, 69–77.

Villarica, Hans. (2012). This is why you fall in love with brands. *The Atlantic.* http://www.theatlantic.com/business/archive/2012/04/this-is-why-you-fall-in-love-with-brands/255448/

Vincent, James. (2015, March 26). I used a robot to go to work from 3, 500 miles away. *The Verge.* http://www.theverge.com/2015/3/26/8294855/telepresence-robots-double-robotics-remote-skype-office

Waddell, Kavey. (2015, December 15). We need a new pronoun for artificial intelligence. *Atlantic Monthly.* http://www.theatlantic.com/technology/archive/2015/12/we-need-a-new-pronoun-for-ai/420378/

Wallach, Wendell, & Allen, Colin (Eds.). (2009). *Moral machines: Teaching robots right from wrong.* Oxford: Oxford University Press.

Waller, Randall L., & Conaway, Roger N. (2011). Framing and counterframing the issue of corporate social responsibility. *Journal of Business Communication, 48*(1), 83–106.

Walzer, Arthur E. (2003). Quintilian's *"vir bonus"* and the Stoic wise man. *Rhetoric Society Quarterly, 33*(4), 25–41.

Walzer, Arthur E. (2006). Moral philosophy and rhetoric in the *Institutes*: Quintilian on honor and expediency. *Rhetoric Society Quarterly, 36*(3), 263–280.

Wang, Amy B. (2016, December 28). Can Alexa help solve a murder? Police think so—but Amazon won't give up her data. *The Washington Post.* https://www.washingtonpost.com/news/the-switch/wp/2016/12/28/can-alexa-help-solve-a-murder-police-think-so-but-amazon-wont-give-up-her-data/?utm_term=.93a646e70db1

Wang, Victoria, Tucker, John V., & Rihll, Tracy E. (2011). On phatic technologies for creating and maintaining human relationships. *Technology in Society, 33*, 44–51.

Warwick, Kevin, & Shah, Huma. (2015). Can machines think? A report on the Turing test experiments at the Royal Society. *Journal of Experimental & Theoretical Artificial Intelligence, 28*(6), 989–1007.

Weaver, Richard M. (1953/1985). *The ethics of rhetoric.* Davis, CA: Hermagoras Press.

Weaver, Warren, & Shannon, Claude Elwood. (1963). *The mathematical theory of communication.* Normal: University of Illinois Press.

Welch, Kathleen E. (1999). *Electric rhetoric: Classical rhetoric, oralism, and a new literacy.* Cambridge: The MIT Press.

Wittig, Monique. (1992). *The straight mind and other essays*. Boston: Beacon Press.

Wittke, Volker, & Hanekop, Heidemarie (Eds.). (2011). *New forms of collaborative innovation and production on the internet: An interdisciplinary perspective*. Göttingen: Universitätsverlag Göttingen.

Wolff, William I. (2013). Interactivity and the invisible: What counts as writing in the age of Web 2.0. *Computers and Composition, 30*, 211–225.

Wolvin, Andrew D. (Ed.). (2010). *Listening and human communication in the 21st century*. Chichester, West Sussex, UK: Wiley-Blackwell.

Women's March on Washington. (2017). Sister marches. https://www.womensmarch.com/sisters

Wooley, Samuel C. (2016). Automating power: Social bot interference in global politics. *First Monday, 21*(4). http://firstmonday.org/ojs/index.php/fm/article/view/6161/5300

World Health Organization. (2016). ART coverage table 2000–2015. http://www.who.int/hiv/data/art_table_2000_2015.png?ua=1

World's Finest Chocolate. (2016). Our history. http://www.worldsfinestchocolate.com/about-us/our-history

Wu, Tim. (2002). A proposal for network neutrality. http://www.timwu.org/OriginalNNProposal.pdf

Wu, Tim. (2003). Network neutrality, broadband discrimination. *Journal of Telecommunications and High Technology Law, 2*, 141.

Xu, George Q. (2004). The use of eloquence: The Confucian perspective. In Carol S. Lipson & Roberta A. Binkley (Eds.), *Rhetoric before and beyond the Greeks* (pp. 115–129). Albany, NY: SUNY Press.

Yakovenko, Nikolai. (2016, March 9). Poker and AI: Reporting from the 2016 annual computer poker competition. *PokerNews*. https://www.pokernews.com/strategy/poker-ai-2016-annual-computer-poker-competition-24246.htm

Yang, Wenhui. (2012). Small talk: A strategic interaction in Chinese interpersonal business negotiations. *Discourse & Communication, 6*(1), 101–124.

Yoos, George. (1979). A revision of the concept of ethical appeal. *Philosophy & Rhetoric, 12*(1), 41–58.

Zemliansky, Pavel. (2012). Achieving experiential cross-cultural training through a virtual teams project. *IEEE Transactions on Professional Communication, 55*(3), 275–286.

Zhao, Shanyang. (1991). Rhetoric as praxis: An alternative to the epistemic approach. *Philosophy & Rhetoric, 24*(3), 255–266.

Zhu, Yunxia, & White, Catherine. (2009). Practitioners' views about the use of business email within organizational settings: Implications for developing student generic competence. *Business and Professional Communication Quarterly, 72*(3), 289–303.

Zingle. (2016). Zingle Parking. https://www.zingle.me/industries/parking/

Zuckerberg, Mark. (2016a, December 19). Building Jarvis. https://www.facebook.com/notes/mark-zuckerberg/building-jarvis/10154361492931634/

Zuckerberg, Mark (2016b, December 20). After a year of coding, here's Jarvis. https://www.facebook.com/zuck/videos/10103351034741311/

Author Index

Subject Index

For Product Safety Concerns and Information please contact our EU
representative GPSR@taylorandfrancis.com
Taylor & Francis Verlag GmbH, Kaufingerstraße 24, 80331 München, Germany

www.ingramcontent.com/pod-product-compliance
Ingram Content Group UK Ltd.
Pitfield, Milton Keynes, MK11 3LW, UK
UKHW020941180425
457613UK00019B/489